James Allen is familiar to millions in the UK and around the English-speaking world as the lead commentator for ITV's Formula One coverage. He has worked in the sport as a journalist and broadcaster since 1990, the year before Schumacher's stunning debut with the Jordan team. James replaced Murray Walker as the voice of motorsport in 2001 and, through his extensive work for the *Financial Times*, has established himself as one of the most authoritative writers in Formula One. In 1995 he co-wrote Nigel Mansell's best-selling autobiography *Mansell: The People's Champion*.

Praise for *Michael Schumacher: The Edge of Greatness*

'High octane enjoyment' *Manchester Evening News*

'It is the one book devoted to Schumacher that [Lewis] Hamilton would be advised to read' *Daily Telegraph*

'The book is well researched, has an easy going readability and uncovers a few key points not previously known' Mark Hughes, *Autosport* magazine

'James pulls no punches while revealing the brutal and generous sides to this great champion' *Scottish Sunday Post*

'Allen's look into Schumacher's psyche makes this book a must' *Globe and Mail*, Canada

D1042982

Other titles by James Allen:

The Quest for Redemption
Mansell: The People's Champion

Michael SCHUMACHER

>>>>>>THE EDGE OF>>>>>>
GREATNESS

JAMES ALLEN

headline

Copyright © 2007, 2008 James Allen

The right of James Allen to be identified as the
Author of the Work has been asserted by him in accordance
with the Copyright, Designs and Patents Act 1988.

First published in 2007
by HEADLINE PUBLISHING GROUP

First published in paperback in 2008
by HEADLINE PUBLISHING GROUP

5

Apart from any use permitted under UK copyright law, this publication
may only be reproduced, stored, or transmitted, in any form, or by any
means, with prior permission in writing of the publishers or, in the case of
reprographic production, in accordance with the terms of licences issued
by the Copyright Licensing Agency.

Every effort has been made to fulfil requirements with regard to
reproducing copyright material. The author and publisher will be glad to
rectify any omissions at the earliest opportunity.

Cataloguing in Publication Data is available from the British Library

ISBN 978 0 7553 1650 2

Typeset in Swift Regular by Avon DataSet Ltd,
Bidford-on-Avon, Warwickshire

Printed and bound in Great Britain by Clays Ltd, St Ives plc

Headline's policy is to use papers that are natural, renewable and
recyclable products and made from wood grown in sustainable forests.
The logging and manufacturing processes are expected to conform
to the environmental regulations of the country of origin.

HEADLINE PUBLISHING GROUP
An Hachette Livre UK Company
338 Euston Road
London NW1 3BH

www.headline.co.uk
www.hachettelivre.co.uk

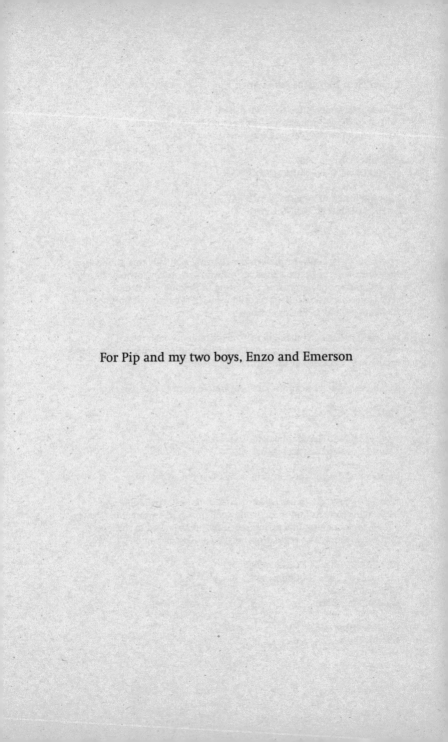

For Pip and my two boys, Enzo and Emerson

Acknowledgements

These things only work if the right people help you. I'm very grateful to many individuals for assistance with this book.

In no particular order I am indebted to Jon Holmes at Jon Holmes Media Ltd, David Wilson and Wendy McCance at Headline, Eddie Irvine, Rubens Barrichello, David Coulthard, Mark Webber, Martin Brundle, Willi Weber, Nick Harris, Frank Dernie, Mika Hakkinen, Max Mosley, Richard Woods, Mark Blundell, Pat Symonds, Flavio Briatore, Ross Brawn, Jean Todt, Norbert Haug, Jock Clear, Luca Colajanni, Claudio Berro, Wolfgang Schattling, Tracy Novak, Katie Tweedle, Ann Neal, Didier Coton, Ian Phillips, Betise Assumpcao, Stephane Samson, Malcolm Clinton, Matt Shires, Tim Whelan, Daniel Williams, Alex Marks, Sheldon Leaman, Michael Schmidt, Kai Ebel, Ed Gorman, Simon Strang, Alex Sabine, Kirsty Ennever and David Glen. And, of course, Michael Schumacher.

Thanks to my father, Bill, and to my wife, Pip, for help with the manuscript.

I am grateful to the following media organisations for source and reference material: *Frankfurter Allgemeine, La Gazzetta dello*

Sport, F1 Racing, Autosport, Die Zeit, Stern, Bunte, L'Equipe, Autojournal, Spiegel, Suddeutsher Zeitung, Die Woche, Sunday Times, Park Lane.

Above all a huge thank you to Pino Allievi, Heiner Buchinger and Sabine Kehm for all their help and support.

Contents

Introduction

Michael Schumacher? I would say that there is a veneer of the ruthless professional racing driver, which is not particularly deep and underneath that is a very decent and honest, well-meaning and quite sentimental individual.

Max Mosley, president of the Fédération Internationale de l'Automobile

Michael Schumacher is a phenomenon created by himself.

He came from a humble background with no money and ended up dominating the world's most glamorous and dangerous sport. When Schumacher clinched his seventh world title in 2004 and then pushed on to a total of 91 Grands Prix victories, he left the greats like Senna, Prost and Fangio way behind and raised the bar to a point that no one had ever imagined possible.

But what people find difficult when contemplating the phenomenon of Michael Schumacher is reaching an understanding of the character of the man himself. It doesn't help that he is quite a reserved person, always wary of allowing the media and the public too close. His sporting ethos was 'never give anything away' and that principle applied as much to his character as to competition on the race track. Many find him an unsympathetic character and for that reason he is not held in such high esteem as Senna, for example. The new generation of Formula 1 stars, like Fernando Alonso and Lewis Hamilton, often cite Senna as their great inspiration: they do not speak of Schumacher. There are a number of reasons for this.

Schumacher had a bit of the devil in him and many people are unwilling to forgive him for that. Combined with this was a meticulous dedication to his craft, the quest for perfection. The French actress Jeanne Moreau once said that 'perfection in a man is easy to admire, but hard to love' and this observation certainly applied to Michael Schumacher the racing driver. He did not have Senna's sense of style, nor his obvious raw passion. Instead, precision, hard work and discipline were his hallmarks; qualities which do not win over hearts and minds. Allied to his latent ruthless streak was the ability to keep a tight control over his emotions. He refused to show his humanity, which those who know him well swear is exceptional, as we shall discover.

Schumacher aroused great jealousy in his rivals because of his success. Within four years of his debut he had already won two world titles and that early success gave him an ingrained confidence which carried him through the remainder of his career. It was a quiet confidence, but it was often mistaken for arrogance by his competitors and enemies, who sought every opportunity to bring him down a peg or two. The young German gave them plenty of opportunities to do so with his uncompromising attitude on the track. And the eager media, with whom Schumacher had an uneasy relationship, were always hungry for stories from disgruntled drivers. Unfortunately he allowed himself to live in a state of denial because he always ascribed any criticisms to jealousy, regardless of how justified those criticisms might have been.

His understanding of what it takes to win was more highly developed than any driver before him. As we shall see, his work extended way beyond the cockpit and he would leave no stone unturned in giving himself the greatest chance of success. He also used his influence behind the scenes in ways few realise. This is an important – and previously untold – side of his story.

In the modern world, with so much money and prestige at stake, how does a sportsman reconcile his burning ambition to succeed with the old-fashioned qualities of sportsmanship and fair play? Beneath the surface with Schumacher was always a disquieting willingness to punch below the belt, to commit a professional foul. But is what Schumacher did any worse than the footballer who takes a dive to win a penalty in a crucial game, or worse than Maradona's famous 'hand of God' goal in the World Cup?

Why was Schumacher prepared to do these things? Why was he willing to go to places in pursuit of victory that his rivals were not even prepared to contemplate? Was it that he was so eager to achieve his goals and so methodical in his planning that when something unforeseen threatened to stop him, in sheer desperation he resorted to a foul rather than lose?

Schumacher was a competitor who stretched the rules to breaking-point on a routine basis and occasionally he went over the limit, especially in a moment of panic, where a split-second decision is called for. But was that something in his nature, or did it develop as his career took off?

His retirement in 2006 and in particular the reaction of the press and public to it, left me feeling that there was a complete disconnect between the real Michael Schumacher and the cartoon baddie he was perceived to be.

Our careers in F1 overlapped and our paths crossed many times. Over the course of 15 years, I was able to see close up how he operated and what made him the champion he became.

This book is an attempt to see behind the tabloid caricature, to get at what drove Michael Schumacher to the edge of greatness.

James Allen
London 2007

CHAPTER ONE

Monaco,
27 May 2006

He had this view that it is a tough business, you have to give everything and give no quarter. He did that and sometimes he overstepped the mark. He knew he had overstepped it, that his competitive spirit had got the better of him.

Ross Brawn, Ferrari technical director 1997–2006

The red car screams down along the waterfront, pitches left into the Tabac corner, missing the barrier on the inside by millimetres. It hurtles towards the Swimming Pool chicane, clattering over the kerbs, a puff of yellow dust kicking out from the skid block as the floor slams down on the tarmac. Hemmed in by barriers on either side, the car is travelling at 120 miles per hour in a space no wider than a tennis court. The impression of speed is incredible. To the people watching from the grandstands and from boats in the harbour it looks stunning, but it's not fast enough. In the duel for pole position a tenth of a second may be impossible to see, but it is easily measured and it defines the winner and the losers.

Out of the swimming pool complex and down towards the Rascasse goes the Ferrari, the digital timer on the steering-wheel telling Michael Schumacher what he did not want to know; he has not improved his time. Behind him on the track, Fernando Alonso, the young man he had identified four years earlier as his likely nemesis, is surely faster. Schumacher's hunch about Alonso has proven correct and Alonso is now his rival for the championship. The older driver recognises many of his own qualities in Alonso and also knows that in many respects the 24-year-old is superior to him now.

Schumacher realises that, at 37 years of age, his powers are waning. The colossal effort he put in during testing before the season started to get his Ferrari car up to speed has not proved enough to ensure his superiority over the Spaniard, who has developed into an exceptional competitor. He trails Alonso in the world championship by 15 points with a third of the season gone. This is a championship he desperately wants to win because, with Alonso in the ascendant and Kimi Raikkonen already signed up as a Ferrari driver for 2007, Schumacher has already decided that this is going to be his final year in Formula 1.

The game is up: only Rascasse corner to go, no chance to make up that amount of time. He's desperate now. Pole position is vital at Monaco and Alonso's going to take it from him. He knows how symbolic this is, the younger driver pushing the older one out, just as he had tried to do to Ayrton Senna 12 years earlier. Not only that, but Mark Webber, Kimi Raikkonen and Giancarlo Fisichella are also threatening his position – he could end up on the second or third row of the grid here, then the race would not be under his control as he wanted it and had planned for it to be.

Instinct takes over.

The brakes lock up, blue smoke swirls outwards from the

tyres. He turns into the right hand Rascasse corner oddly, the car skews left and slows, there is a pause, then very gently the car hiccups forward into a stall. The nose stops a few feet from the barriers. No contact is made, but the marshals are on to it immediately, waving yellow flags to slow the following cars, among them Alonso's, as they approach Rascasse. The drivers have no alternative but to back off. Alonso's lap is ruined, so are Webber's, Fisichella's and Raikkonen's. The qualifying session ends. Schumacher's time is fastest. He has pole position, but what price will he pay for winning at all costs?

* * *

In the Monaco pit lane, Alonso's boss at the Renault team, Flavio Briatore, is raging, seeking out every television crew he can find to cry foul. 'It's a disgrace,' he thunders. 'He is taking everyone for a ride. Someone who is a seven times world champion wants us to believe that he didn't do it on purpose? It's fairyland. It was unsporting and against everything.' Briatore is not finding too many people who disagree with him.

The top three drivers in Formula 1 qualifying are required to appear straight after the session at a press conference organised by the FIA. First they sit down for a short television interview which is beamed live around the world and most of the broadcasters, who have covered the qualifying session, keep their transmissions going to show the interviews. On this particular Saturday, with the storm brewing over Schumacher's actions, the conference would prove to be a must-see event.

In the car taking the drivers to the television interview were Schumacher, Alonso and Webber. Recalls Webber:

I didn't think too much about it at the time when I came into Rascasse and saw the car blocking the track. I just pitted, lap done. I was in the weighing area and Michael said to me, 'I can't believe I'm still on pole' and he was whooping it up and celebrating with Sabine Kehm, his assistant. He was really excited. I started to think, 'That's odd, it's not a great way to get pole, after all.' It wasn't all adding up for me.

We got in the car, Michael, Fernando and I. Fernando was totally pissed off, Michael was happy, putting on this face. The atmosphere was frosty. No one said anything. When we arrived, as Michael sprang out of the car and ran up the stairs, Fernando said to me, 'He stopped on the track deliberately, you know?' and I said, 'Fair enough, mate.' I hadn't seen anything on video at this point, but I was thinking that it was bit odd how this was shaping up.

The interview started and the first question got straight to the point. 'Michael, what happened at Rascasse?'

'I locked up the front wheel and went wide,' answered Schumacher, his face open and untroubled. Beside him sat Alonso, who maintained a quiet dignity throughout the next half hour or so but whose face wore an unmistakeable mask of darkness and anger. On the other side of Schumacher was Webber. Michael continued, 'I wasn't sure what was going on after this because of the positioning of the cars and so on, so I was not aware and in the end I checked with the guys what the situation was, where did we end up, because I didn't expect to be sitting here right now in this position and they said P1, so I was glad considering what had happened.'

This was not the polished English Schumacher was used to delivering at such moments. His mind was clearly running through a lot of conflicting ideas and thoughts at the same time. He lost his fluency. He knew all too well what people would be thinking. Only he knew whether he had parked his car deliberately in the middle of the road to stop Alonso from beating him, but if he had done, he was not about to admit it or to apologise. That is not Schumacher's way.

Did the engine stall, he was asked? 'No, initially not and I tried to engage reverse but it didn't engage and I didn't really want to back up just by myself without knowing what was coming and finally it stalled. I need to check why the engine stalled because there was no reason why it should stall, but I think that after a certain time if the engine is running like that, it switches itself off. I guess that is what happened.'

The three drivers then moved to the main media centre for the general press conference. Before them sat 150 journalists. Schumacher had been in this position countless times in his career, but he never felt comfortable as he later reflected: 'The game with the media was very difficult for me. A half-hour press conference stretched me more than a whole race. That's just not my world. I'm not much of an actor and everyone's always trying to read things into you. I cannot produce emotions on the touch of a button, I don't want to.' And this time he appeared less comfortable than usual.

Now it was a question of who would open hostilities. After ten minutes of phoney war, the first bullet was fired, albeit gently, by Anne Giuntini, the tiny Frenchwoman who has covered F1 for the prestigious French daily sports paper, *L'Equipe*, for many years.

In 1996 she had conducted a long interview with Schumacher in which he had opened up more than in practically any other interview he has done. He had let his guard down for once and spoken openly about many subjects. Ironically Giuntini was also the partner of Denis Chevrier, the man in charge of the engine in the back of Alonso's car.

'I have talked to some drivers who say it is too big, what happened today, to be credible, maybe a bit of a shame if it is true,' she said.

Schumacher looked slightly taken aback, but maintained his calm. 'It would be a shame if it is true, absolutely, but I think it is as usual what you do in certain moments. Your enemies believe one thing and the people who support you believe another thing and that is what our sport is all about.'

'It is not a question of friends or enemies, it is a question of sport,' replied Giuntini coldly.

'I explained to you what really happened and if you want to believe this you believe and some people may not believe this but unfortunately this is the world we live in.'

Schumacher was then asked straight out if he had cheated. His face hardened. 'No, and I don't know why you ask such a bad question. I think it is pretty tough. If you were to drive around here at Monaco you would probably not ask this question.'

Sitting alongside him, Mark Webber noticed a sudden change in Schumacher's demeanour. 'Michael's left hand was shaking. He wasn't comfortable at all. At that point you just knew that the glazed face had come over him. He was putting on a show from then on, he looked across at Sabine a few times. He was in the hot seat. When it's all under control it's slick, but when a few cracks come in then it can go badly wrong with him, then it's not convincing at all.'

Alonso spoke little during the press conference. He was asked at one point if he thought less of Schumacher because of what had happened. 'I have my opinion and I won't say it here,' was the curt reply.

* * *

The atmosphere in the pit lane and paddock was electrified by the drama of what had taken place and the reaction to it. Modern Formula 1 is quite low on drama and the paddock is a largely subdued place most of the time. It feels much more controlled than in the past when big characters like Ayrton Senna, Alain Prost and Nigel Mansell were on the prowl, creating excitement on a regular basis and giving a tremendous buzz to the paddock.

Drivers and team principals today toe the party line, keep everything under control as far as the outside world is concerned, dealing with any potential flashpoints behind closed doors. Blame this on the influence of the major corporations now in F1, the car manufacturers, banks and insurance companies who pour millions into the sport. In their own worlds they like to micro-manage communications, to impose a certain control over everything, and they have imposed those values on the sport. Even though F1 is a sport which thrives on passion, it is rare for that passion and drama to be exhibited publicly.

But on this Saturday in May 2006, the passion was bursting through the veneer of control and the target was Schumacher. Watching the rising indignation it was impossible not to think back to the European Grand Prix at Jerez in 1997, the lowest moment of Schumacher's long career. With the world championship on the line, he had almost driven Jacques Villeneuve off the road during that race, but Villeneuve was able to continue and it was Schumacher who lost the race and with it the championship. He has expressed regret about that incident since, even admitting in 2003 that 'It took me a long time to see what I had done, I probably didn't want to admit it. If there was one thing I could do over again in F1 it would be that race in Jerez.'

A lot of water had passed under the bridge since then. Almost a decade had gone by. In 2000 Schumacher had fulfilled his mission of bringing Ferrari its first world championship for 20 years. He went on to win five titles in succession, something which had never been done before. It brought him greatness and made the new millennium truly 'the Ferrari era'.

But now he was involved in another controversial incident and there was no sign of a shred of regret from Schumacher. Why did he choose this moment, many were asking, so late in his career, with Jerez little more than a distant memory, to dredge up all the old allegations that he was unsporting? He had been involved in plenty of disputes in the intervening years, such as Ferrari team orders which many found unpalatable, and some heavy-handed tactics on the race-track, but nothing which provoked the level of condemnation this had. As in Jerez nine years earlier, there was a smoking gun in Schumacher's hand and a very public trial was about to take place.

On one level Formula 1 thrives on secrecy, but it is hard to conceal certain things. Drivers are scrutinised in intimate detail by computers which ride with them as they speed around the track. More than 2000 sensors placed throughout the vehicle tell the army of engineers in the garage precisely what is happening at every moment. If a driver brakes ten centimetres later than on the previous lap they know about it instantly. If he takes a different line through a corner they are on to it. There is always a debrief after every outing and if a mistake has been made there is nowhere to hide. The computer will always snitch on the driver.

Unfortunately for Michael Schumacher, the stewards of the race meeting can also demand that data, if they feel that a matter deserves closer investigation. With the clamour growing louder by the minute, the Monaco stewards decided to do just that.

* * *

As a racing team, Ferrari under its team principal Jean Todt has been transformed in many ways. The Todt era is by the far the most successful in the marque's 60-year history. There are many reasons for this but chief among them is that the team never gives anything away. Every aspect of the car, its design, how it is raced and how they deal with their competitors and the media is subject to the same overriding principle: give nothing away. This attitude is relentless and stultifying to the opposition, but it has become self-generating within the team.

Naturally it extends to supporting each other in times of trouble. When Jean Todt ordered Rubens Barrichello to move over in the closing stages of the 2002 Austrian Grand Prix, to allow Schumacher to win, the decision was greeted with revulsion by lovers of the sport. It happened in the early stages of a season in which Ferrari were totally dominant and it seemed not only unnecessary, but against the idea of sporting competition. Schumacher did not agree with the decision and he wasn't pleased that he was booed by the crowd on the podium, many of whom believed the move was his initiative. But publicly he backed the decision at the time and never gave anything away regarding any doubts he might have had. This pattern of behaviour had been in place for so long it was now hard-wired into the mentality of the principal players in the team. The process of closing ranks swung into action and Ferrari technical director Ross Brawn supported his driver, however indefensible he may have found what Schumacher had done. 'He lost control of the car in the left-hander (the corner immediately before Rascasse). He locked the brakes and lost the line. We've still got to talk to him and find out exactly what happened. There was a lot of cursing on the radio. We wouldn't do that sort of thing on purpose. Michael had clearly done a very good lap and he was on another lap with low fuel, so it wasn't a deliberate act.'

In a later, private, reflection on this incident, Brawn observed, 'You are a team for better or worse; if we screw up, we screw up together. The kinds of things which can split up a team make us stronger. We looked sensibly at the matter internally, but it bonded us. When you raise a family your kids are not perfect but they are your kids and you look after them whatever happens.'

Jean Todt gave nothing away in his analysis of events. As usual he firmly aligned himself with Schumacher in his moment of difficulty, citing his close personal relationship with the driver and implying that the problem here was not Schumacher's actions but that his enormous success had bred jealousy, which was the real motivator for the critics. 'Michael made a mistake which has been interpreted by most of the people here as deliberate. But he has not been given the benefit of the doubt. Michael has a great character, those who want to understand him will understand. Those who don't will never understand him. I have the privilege of knowing him well, I know who is Michael. I don't think there are many people in F1 who can boast of a heart like his. He's not an extra-terrestrial, he makes mistakes like other human beings. It's just that for him, the mistakes often have serious consequences.'

No one sets out on a qualifying lap planning to block the track and stop the session. Schumacher had the advantage over Alonso in that he was the first car on the track, which is why it hypothetically became an option once he got into trouble, but no one believes that what happened was premeditated.

Nevertheless, in that split second, that instant of panic, knowing that his own sporting performance had come up short, did his instinct kick in and vote for dirty tricks? He had some form in this area. On two previous occasions in races he had blocked the track following an accident at the start in an attempt to get the race stopped, so that he could take the spare car for the restart. On the first occasion, in Austria in 2000, the ploy had failed, but it had succeeded at Hockenheim the following year, although it is debatable whether that race was stopped because of the position of Schumacher's car or because of the amount of damage to other cars, such as Luciano Burti's Prost, which had hit Schumacher and taken off over the top of him.

If you have a competitive car in F1 you go to every race expecting to fight for victory and ultimately to fight for the world championship. So you don't take unnecessary risks, because every point is vital. But maybe if you are staring at retirement at the start of a race, the temptation is strong to get the race stopped so that you can take the restart in the spare car. The instinct to preserve one's position is strongest in this situation and what happened in Monaco, even though it was in qualifying rather than the race itself, was similar to those earlier incidents. But not every driver has such an instinct and even if they have, they are aware that everything is so closely scrutinised. There was no shortage of 'names' around the paddock on that Saturday in Monaco, willing to give their opinions. Most vocal of all was Keke Rosberg, the 1982 world champion, whose son Nico was in his first season of F1. Rosberg was from the flamboyant era of the sport, not in the same league as Schumacher as a driver, but a colourful embodiment of the free spirit which leads men to race cars.

'Does he think we are all fools and idiots?' he fumed. 'It was the cheapest dirtiest thing I have ever seen in Formula 1. He should leave Formula 1 and go home. I hope he is man enough now to get out of the Grand Prix Drivers Association and never mention safety again in his life. He's a cheap cheat.'

Sir Jackie Stewart, three times a world champion, was in Monaco as an ambassador for Royal Bank of Scotland, which sponsors the Williams team. He was more worldly in his appraisal: 'It was a very agile mind management job. But it was too blatant. It reflects on him and Ferrari,' he said.

During the afternoon, there was a great deal of coming and going. Pedro De La Rosa, McLaren's test driver, along with McLaren managing director Martin Whitmarsh, had drafted a petition to FIA president Max Mosley condemning Schumacher and was attempting to get all the drivers to sign it. 'Mr President, we can no longer tolerate this behaviour . . . We are tired of his arrogance, his prevarication . . .' the letter began. Nico Rosberg asked how Schumacher could 'lecture us that you shouldn't block, then he goes and blocks ten cars on the track'?

'Thanks to him I lost four-tenths of a second on my last lap,' moaned Renault's Giancarlo Fisichella. 'Even a five-year-old could understand what he's done. It's really sad. If he'd at least damaged the car, people might have some doubts. But there is no room for doubt with all the inputs he made on the steering-wheel.'

Several drivers denied the existence of the McLaren petition and it is clear that it was an idea born in the heat of the moment, signed by many of the drivers, but which was ultimately never delivered to Mosley. But Schumacher found out about it and that would have repercussions later in the season.

That night Mark Webber was having dinner with his father and girlfriend in the hotel when Alonso approached their table. 'What are we going to do if Michael doesn't get a penalty?' asked the Spaniard. 'He's got to, mate,' replied Webber. 'Looking at the footage, it's ridiculous, they have to do something.'

Alonso wasn't so sure. 'I want to lie down in front of his car,' said Alonso sternly. 'I'm going to pull up on the grid, get out of my car and lie in front of his.'

Knowing Alonso, he would have done exactly that. He felt that he was not just racing against another driver in another team. Like many of the drivers, he felt, rightly or wrongly, that the way the sport appeared to look after Ferrari made the playing field uneven. It was this same feeling which led Alonso to declare at Monza later that year, 'I no longer consider F1 to be a sport', after Ferrari made a protest against him for blocking their driver, Felipe Massa, during qualifying and the stewards gave him a ten-place grid penalty.

But on this occasion in Monaco Alonso's fears turned out to be unfounded.

* * *

It took the stewards eight hours to sift through the evidence and reach a decision, an unprecedented amount of time. Chief steward Tony Scott-Andrews was new to the job. In fact the job itself of chief steward was an innovation for 2006 as the FIA sought to get more consistency in the process of judging at race-tracks. (Later in the year Scott-Andrews would again feature prominently, in the controversy at Monza, which would greatly favour Ferrari.) A lawyer from Banbury in England, the chief steward was aware that this was the first test case of the new system. His fellow stewards that weekend were Joaquin Verdegay, a lawyer from Madrid, and Christian Calmes of the Monaco Automobile Club.

The panel heard evidence from Schumacher, engineer Chris Dyer, technical director Ross Brawn and the team manager, Stefano Domenicali, as well as the FIA's race director, Charlie Whiting, and its software analyst, Alan Prudhomme. They viewed all the available video evidence and studied the all-important computer data from Schumacher's car. They were satisfied that Schumacher had acted deliberately.

The stewards' statement, which was published at 10.42pm, read: 'The stewards can find no justifiable reason for the driver to have braked with such undue, excessive and unusual pressure at this part of the circuit and are left with no alternative but to conclude that the driver deliberately stopped his car on the circuit.'

Verdegay later elaborated on the process by which they had reached this conclusion. He said the following day:

> It was a tough decision because we couldn't get it wrong with a driver's reputation at stake. We don't know if the whole manoeuvre was deliberate but it is certain that at that point he had never done anything of that sort all weekend. He braked fifty per cent harder than he had on the other laps, then he turned the wheel in a counter-steer, which was totally unnecessary and pathetic, which lasted five metres until he could no longer make the corner. He lost control of the car when he was travelling at sixteen kilometres per hour (ten miles per hour). It is totally unjustifiable. And the engine stopped because it was him who wanted it to, by not using the time to engage the clutch. If he had damaged the car (against the barriers) we would probably have put it down as a driver error. But to park the car in this manner, that can only be done deliberately.

Schumacher waited for the stewards' decision in the Ferrari motorhome, which was parked along the waterfront in the marina. A huge media contingent was gathered outside. Throughout the long wait he was relaxed about the outcome, although very angry about some of the criticisms being voiced in the paddock, especially Keke Rosberg's.

He and Jean Todt both felt that Ferrari had put a strong and clear case as to how he had lost control of the car under braking for Rascasse and how the engine came to stall as he hesitated over whether to engage reverse gear. As the hours passed without news, he became concerned that in the dark he would not be able to take the helicopter back to where he was staying, at his manager Willi Weber's villa in Cap d'Antibes, further down the French coast. It would take at least 45 minutes by car from the circuit and with the race tomorrow, Schumacher was anxious not to get to bed too late.

Schumacher could have left at any time as far as the stewards were concerned, as they had no further need for him after his second visit to their room at 6pm. But he wanted to appear in front of the assembled media, to make sure that his reaction would reach the news bulletins and that he would be properly quoted. With him was Sabine Kehm, his assistant for six years.

'He went back to the stewards again at six pm and when he returned he said that the stewards had told him there would be a decision in fifteen minutes,' recalls Sabine. 'At that time we didn't know it would take until eleven pm. At ten o'clock he decided that he had to leave so he said, "Let's talk to the media now" so he did that without a decision being reached. The media blamed him for making them wait but in fact he had only waited around to give them a quote once the decision was out.'

With Jean Todt standing behind him, Schumacher faced the media. His conscience, he said, was clear and he was sure that the stewards would exonerate him.

> I was on the limit and perhaps I pushed too hard. I had already had problems at the chicane and again at the Swimming Pool, the car was nervous. Ferrari has taken its data to the stewards and the FIA has taken its data too. Same answer. Why should I be penalised? Because I was going a bit too fast? My conscience is clear. I know what I did. I also know that in this world when someone has too

much success there are always people around to give him
trouble. I know I have friends and enemies here and that I
cannot convince everyone of my good faith. I don't
understand people who want me to be punished.

By the time the decision was announced that Schumacher had
cheated in the eyes of the stewards and that they had decided
to take away all his qualifying times, thus sending him to the
back of the grid, Schumacher was no longer at the track.

There was a mixed reaction; satisfaction from some and
astonishment from others. Ferrari and Schumacher appeared
to have been given the rub of the green by the stewards and
the FIA on many decisions over the years and it was surprising
that the stewards were so forthright on this occasion. At the
same time, if the driver had deliberately cheated in the most
high profile Grand Prix weekend of the season, was being sent
to the back of the grid sufficient punishment? Later in the
year another driver received the same punishment for missing
a weight check during qualifying – hardly the same calibre of
misdemeanour.

Schumacher's performance the next day in the Grand Prix
was mesmerising. From last place on the grid he made up
seven places on the opening lap. Once he found some clear
track he was able to lap as fast and often faster than the race
leader, Alonso. It was clear that the Ferrari was the fastest car
in the field and that its Bridgestone tyres had an advantage
over the Michelins on Alonso's Renault. As the race unfolded
the same thought passed through the minds of Schumacher,
Brawn, Todt and all their rivals; the Ferrari was unbeatable
that weekend. If Schumacher had just completed that ill-fated
qualifying lap and started the race behind Alonso, he would

still have beaten him easily in the race. Schumacher had not just lost something of his reputation. He had lost a race Ferrari could and should have won. He paid an even greater price later in the season, when he lost the world championship to Alonso. Some might call it poetic justice, but there is little doubt that it was the points dropped at Monaco which cost him that world championship.

'There was tremendous *schadenfreude* in the paddock which I found disagreeable,' says FIA president Max Mosley. 'He didn't handle it very well. If he wanted to park the car he should have brushed the wall and there would have been no discussion. But what I admired about him in that situation is that he never complained about the penalty, he didn't come to me, never spoke to the press about it. He just got in the car and did what everyone will tell you was impossible and (from twenty-second place on the grid) ended up fifth. I thought that was quite something. You often see tennis players when something really bad happens and it must be so annoying. I'd be tempted to just walk off the court. And you get sportsmen who sulk and Michael could easily have sulked but he didn't.'

* * *

In Monaco Schumacher found himself caught in a trap of the kind he had experienced before and which he would normally go to extreme lengths to avoid. The trouble was of his own making, of course, but it was compounded by the fact that he was then made to look as though he neither accepted that he had done anything wrong, nor that he was sorry about it. The timing was disastrous. In the final year of his career, when his legacy was already in place and his list of achievements stretched out far beyond the misdemeanours of the distant past, Schumacher was heading for legendary status. But in Monaco he was cornered and he reacted wrongly at every turn. Sabine Kehm says:

> If you bully Michael he will bully you back, that is his natural reaction. Everyone was speaking badly about him, he reacted in his typical way. Very often he feels bullied by the media. So if people say to him, 'Do you want to say sorry?' he will never say it, he's not able to do it then. He may want to but he would not. It's something he has got from his father. It's his pride.
>
> It's the same with showing his feelings and emotions. If he thinks you demand something of him then he doesn't want to give it to you. Because he thinks, 'Now they will think I'm just giving it to them because they ask for it. That's wrong and I don't want to do that. If I show my feelings it's because I want to not because they ask me.'

Schumacher was left furious by the events of the Monaco weekend. As he left the circuit after the race, he was still unhappy about the way the paddock had judged him. 'We all have some skeletons in our closet, including me,' he said. 'But in 15 years of my career I don't think I've ever had so many critics. I'm used to criticism but these were too hasty. No one except me knows what happened in the cockpit of my Ferrari. Without feeling in your skin the sensations that you get at that moment and the information coming through to you from the car, you cannot judge.'

The 2006 Monaco weekend summed up the enigma which is Michael Schumacher. The Grand Prix itself had shown his sheer genius behind the wheel. His fight-back from last place on the grid to fifth on a track where history says you cannot overtake was awe-inspiring. It revealed all his sumptuous gifts as a racing driver and thrilled and delighted the public. Even his enemies were forced to applaud his exceptional driving and his voracious competitive spirit.

But it had also shown the unsporting side of his character and left a stain on his reputation in what subsequently turned out to be the final stage of his glittering career. He could have made it better for himself and turned around a difficult situation by putting his hands up, but Schumacher the driver was hard-wired into a certain pattern of behaviour in which contrition had no part. Instead he made things worse for himself.

Another aspect of his story, which the Monaco incident vividly illustrated, is the question of legacy. Schumacher never paid much attention to Formula 1 before he got his first drive in 1991 and throughout his time in the sport he did not seem to develop any interest in either its history or his place in it. He was proud to live in ignorance of such things. The consequence of that attitude was that he had no sense of his legacy. Until it was too late.

CHAPTER TWO

The desire to be competitive

The only way to be is to give one hundred and ten per cent for the team. You have to push people . . . You have to have so much balls and confidence to set an example and be ready for the fight. If you want to win you have to be so strong that nothing else matters.

Mika Hakkinen, world champion 1998 and 1999

Formula 1 racing drivers fall into two broad categories; those who are happy just to be there and those who are serious about winning. Many promising talents fall by the wayside and never even reach F1. Of those who do, some do enough to keep themselves employed for a few years and enjoy the financial benefits and the lifestyle. But one of the cruellest things about the sport is that only a very few drivers can actually be competitive at any one time. It is highly unusual to see more than four or five different race winners in any one season and most of the winning is done by the two drivers who end up fighting for the championship.

To be competitive in F1 is the holy grail. Some drivers labour for years to get themselves into a decent car, like Jenson Button for example or Jean Alesi. Others have competitiveness thrust upon them straight away, like Damon Hill, who was given a race seat by Williams after Nigel Mansell's departure in 1992. At the time Williams were dominant and Hill used his opportunity well to win 21 Grands Prix and a world championship. But does that mean that he was a more talented driver than Button or Alesi? It is hard to judge, but probably not. What he represented to Williams at the time was a quick, reliable and, above all, cheap driver who delivered the results of which the car was capable.

But what is F1 competitiveness made of? If a driver is 1.5 seconds slower than the fastest man then he is likely to be a midfield runner at best, unnoticed, making up the numbers. But let's look more closely. Say he is that margin behind at a track like Sepang Malaysia, for example, which has 15 corners. That means he is only a tenth of a second slower around each corner than the fastest car out there. That's not much time at each corner, barely longer than it takes to blink an eye. But when you add it up, it's a huge margin. It will mean that he starts 12 places back on the grid and at the end of the 56-lap Grand Prix he will have been lapped. If he doesn't get himself into a competitive car his career will be no more than a footnote in F1 history. And yet all he's giving away is a tenth of a second per corner.

So the fight to become and to remain competitive is incredibly intense and once you are there it's like balancing on a knife-edge. This is the place Schumacher inhabited for 16 seasons and he deserves huge respect for having had the energy and the motivation to keep himself there. It is a unique achievement.

Schumacher realised early on that when a driver is fighting

for a world championship, it is often the tiniest details which make the difference. A driver does the work the public sees, qualifying and racing his car at the Grands Prix. But he is utterly reliant on his team to do the work the public does not see: designing a fast car and then keeping up the pace of development on the car throughout the year. The driver must also play a role in motivating every member of the team to give the time and effort to improve continuously. It is an exhausting process. Finding and then testing small modifications to the aerodynamics, a few more horsepower, a small adjustment to the suspension, these are the dull but important things, which make a driver competitive and enable him to win world championships.

The drivers themselves know that in terms of pure driving talent, the difference between the fastest and the also-ran is probably three-tenths of a second per lap. That's the bit the driver contributes. So then it comes down to what the driver is able to do with the car he's given and whether he can accept that another driver is more competitive than him. And that is where Schumacher ran into trouble.

What Schumacher did in Monaco in the final year of his career was astonishing. He had already decided before that race that he would retire at the end of the 2006 season, a decision he confirmed to the team a month later at Indianapolis. Despite having this prospect in his mind, when he was striving for pole position in Monaco he was still unable to accept that Alonso was going to beat him and that he would probably end up in fourth place on the grid. His desire to be competitive led him to make the split-second decision deliberately to stall his car on the racing line and hope to get away with it, knowing from bitter experience of the past that if he didn't get away with it, he would face serious criticism. But he was prepared to take that risk.

'I think it was a barely conscious act,' says Max Mosley, who became close to Schumacher later in his career, despite a rocky beginning to their relationship. 'It was just an instinctive last desperate throw in a difficult situation, which hadn't been thought about. Because he is highly intelligent if he had thought about it beforehand he would have handled it better. In that sense it was out of character.'

Paradoxically Michael Schumacher is a very simple and yet complex person. On the one hand there is the man who sees things in black and white – sees the goal and heads straight for it. On the other hand there is the man whose behaviour invites huge question marks. He was prepared to go to extremes in search of victory that none of his rivals would contemplate. Because he was so ambitious and had worked so hard on every conceivable detail before a race to give himself the best chance of winning, he often lost sight of the bigger picture.

Most drivers have found themselves in situations such as Monaco and yet few have behaved as Schumacher did. I once asked his great rival, Mika Hakkinen, why he had never felt moved to behave in a similar way when under pressure and his answer was revealing:

You have to look at the situation long term. You cannot say always, 'I have to win this race, get the trophy.' No, you finish second and then you win the next race. I never wanted to take the risk. I have respect too for the mechanics who work hard on your car, so if you crash and do stupid things they wonder what you are doing. Also if you have incidents you get into discussions with other drivers, pointing the finger about whose fault it is. It's not good for anybody. That is my mentality. We are not here to crash.

In a situation like Suzuka 1998 or 1999 where I had the chance to win the title, would I have just driven into Michael or Eddie Irvine to win the title? No, it wasn't worth it, because you get it back some day.

Look, racing is racing, you have to play little tricks all the time when you are racing, but you have to know the limit of how far you can go. If I'm racing someone, I play some tricks, that's normal, but if they are much faster then there is no point to play tricks. There is no point to be negative. I would do something to make his life difficult but wouldn't take it to that level.

Schumacher was motivated by many things; he was very ambitious, he had come up the hard way and he was more hungry for success than most. He felt he owed the people around him, felt that he *must* deliver the results. He built his determination and his desire to win at all costs into every aspect of his craft and his whole approach to sport. What differentiated him from other drivers who have won races and even championships was that they channelled their determination into occasional moments on the track where it was needed – in other words they lived for the moment, an embodiment of the idea of the racing driver as a carefree daredevil who revelled in the beauty of a life spent on the limit. Schumacher represented a much more methodical and calculated approach to the sport, contradicting the old romantic notions of what a racer should be.

Michael's philosophy was one of which the other drivers were aware, but none could bring themselves to adopt it because they could never be that single-minded. Says Ferrari team-mate Rubens Barrichello:

> He would do anything to win. The day his mother died, the way he fought his brother to win the race [Imola 2003] was incredible. I have to admit that if it had been me with my brother I would have been weak. He didn't care who it was. Maybe he knew how his brother would react and he just went for it. They had travelled together on Saturday night to see her before she died, then they came back. But when they were racing, I don't think he remembered.
>
> People might say, 'But that's what made him so good.' Well fine, I clap my hands for him, but for me some things in life have more importance. I don't know how the hell they went fighting like that. I'm a different person, maybe I'm a more emotional person. Although I have the need to win there are human limits.

Some of his rivals, like Fernando Alonso and Mika Hakkinen, understood that to be a champion you must never give anything away, but they stopped short of taking the ideology to the extremes Schumacher did. Says Hakkinen:

> In one sense you could call it selfish. There is a limit to how selfish you can be before it becomes negative. In a racing car you have to be selfish and you have to go all the way to the limit. Whether you are starting tenth or first you have to push all the way to the end. When you work with people it's the same thing, you have to push them, maximise everything and observe who's doing what and how they work, ask questions. It's very important to develop trust and confidence with the team members. So they can see that all your life is committed to the sport and to the team and then they give you the best shot. I feel that Michael has the same mentality; the only way to be is to give one

hundred and ten percent for the team. You have to push people and even sometimes you piss them off, but it doesn't matter, because if they are not ready to win then they should go somewhere else. You have to have so much balls and confidence to set an example and be ready for the fight. If you want to win you have to be so strong that nothing else matters.

It's very hard to be selfish because a lot of people have distractions; they have families, they travel a lot, they are tired and this and that. You tell them not to think about anything else, only the car, and the only way you can do it is to show your own commitment and get the people to follow. It's very intense. But that's what Michael has done. It's fantastic what he did to continue racing at the level he did for many years, maximum respect.

But of course Schumacher went further and pushed the rules to the limit as well. In the case of incidents like those at Adelaide in 1994, where he collided with Damon Hill, and at Jerez in 1997, where he hit Jacques Villeneuve, he wasn't breaking any rules at the time. It is only since Schumacher and Ferrari took the interpretation of what is fair and what is not fair on the race-track to the absolute limit that rules had to be written to cover it.

Jock Clear, who was Jacques Villeneuve's engineer at Williams during the duel with Schumacher in 1997, claims that Schumacher was also motivated to behave as he did by the knowledge that he had a potentially fatal weakness:

Jacques and I worked out quite early on that Michael would lose if you put him under a huge amount of pressure. He lost the 1998 world championship to Hakkinen by stalling on the grid. I mean, who stalls on the grid for heaven's sake?

It's in that kind of situation where he knows he's not very good and he does everything he possibly can do to avoid ever being in that situation. Jerez was one of those rare occasions when it was down to 'me against you' for the title, on the track. Adelaide was another one, Damon put him under pressure, he lost concentration and hit the wall. In those situations he knows he's not very good and his coping strategy for that situation is 'I know I'm going to fuck it up but I'll still come out the winner.' Adelaide was the right result for him because he won.

Jerez was another occasion, he knew he was asleep and he had made a mistake and he knew that Jacques was going to beat him. And he thought, 'I don't care what people say, I'm still going to walk away from this one the winner and people will say that even when I get it wrong I still win, so I am unbeatable.' Because if he had allowed a reputation to develop for being beaten when you put him under pressure, then he's eroded. But at Jerez it didn't work and Jacques did beat him and that probably irks him more than any other failure he's ever had. And it's astonishing that having had all that time to think about it and come to terms with it, he then did it again in Monaco.

Schumacher once said, 'I never thought I was the best or unbeatable' and one of the few drivers to consistently prove him right was Mika Hakkinen, the rival whom Schumacher respected the most. They had raced against each other ever since they were children in karts and fought many duels on their way to – and at – the very top of the sport. Schumacher never criticised Hakkinen publicly, which was very unusual for him, and that is largely because Hakkinen never criticised him to the press. Hakkinen's attitude was that it wasn't going to change anything so why bother? He would, if necessary, have a quiet word with his rival after a particular incident, but any dispute was kept between themselves. Hakkinen knew when he had the beating of Schumacher.

> Obviously [to beat him] you needed the car to perform. But I think my thing was that I was never emotional in any way; not happy, not sad. We'd sit in a press conference together before the race and we'd joke a little bit, but at the same time I would always observe him. You could see when he was on a peak and when he was not there. He was not much of a poker player like that.
>
> Michael was always aware what level my confidence was at that weekend. He knew it and it was a psychological game, because that was the only time we ever saw each other. Michael tried to say a few things in press conferences to put me off but it never worked and he gave up in the end. There is no point being enemies. Michael is okay, he's a very focused guy.

Aware of his weaknesses, Schumacher put on a front. He wanted his adversaries to see a tough competitor who was ruthless and determined to win. He also wanted them to see a man who had total self-confidence and self-belief, who was never wrong. He wanted them to feel beaten before they had even started and he used every device he could imagine to make things as easy for himself, and as difficult for them, as possible. Of course the danger with this strategy was that the public tuned in to it as well and found him an unsympathetic character.

The real Michael Schumacher, however, the man known and loved by Ferrari team members and insiders, was a warm, sensitive individual, quite different from the stereotype. But he kept a tight rein on his emotions, not wishing to be seen showing any extremes of emotion by his rivals or the public. It seems that he was unsure himself of what might happen if he allowed his emotions free rein. So, as with many other things, he kept himself under tight control. After he won his second world title with Benetton he was drinking pints of apple juice at the team dinner. When one of the team asked why, he replied that it was because he was going to have lots of alcohol later and it would help his body to process it. 'Don't you ever just let yourself go?' he was asked. 'I can't,' he replied.

As he got older Schumacher relaxed a little and would allow himself to go on a good old-fashioned bender with close friends. Some of his parties in the mountains were legendary, with him singing karaoke until his voice had disappeared. But he would atone for it the next day by walking up the mountain to ski, rather than take the cable car.

One incident which illustrates not only what happened when he lost his self-control but which is also a perfect example of the front Schumacher put on for his adversaries, occurred when he crashed into David Coulthard at the wet 1998 Belgian Grand Prix at Spa Francorchamps. Schumacher was leading the race by 37 seconds when he came up behind Coulthard to lap him. Schumacher was fighting Hakkinen for the world championship and as Hakkinen had retired from the race, Schumacher was going to take the lead in the championship for the first time that season.

Coulthard had several opportunities to let Schumacher past, the most simple of which was the 30mph La Source hairpin where Coulthard briefly saw Schumacher's car almost alongside. But Coulthard stayed in front leaving Schumacher wondering what game he was playing. As he exited the left-hander which leads down the hill to the Pouhon corner,

Coulthard did not pick up the throttle as he shifted from second to third gear. In fact he was using just 56 percent of the throttle compared to Schumacher. In a split second the speed differential between them became immense; 100mph compared to Schumacher's 137mph. Although Coulthard was well over to the right of the track, he was still on the racing line. Schumacher didn't read his intention, realising too late that the ball of spray he was driving into had a car right in the middle of it. He hammered into the back of the McLaren, ripping its rear wing off and wrenching the front right wheel off the Ferrari. The wheel flew up into the air and landed in the nearby forest. With the wheel went ten points and the opportunity to take the championship lead to the next race at Monza.

Back at the pits, Schumacher sprang from the cockpit and set off towards the McLaren garage in a rage. He pushed into a crowd of mechanics, trying to get at Coulthard. The mechanics held him back so he shouted across them 'You tried to fucking kill me!' at the Scotsman.

Schumacher has admitted since that this was the only time in his life that he totally lost control and it shocked him. Coulthard has always denied that he acted deliberately, but there is no doubt that the majority of the blame lay with him. What happened next is revealing, as Coulthard explains it:

> The following week there was a test at Monza before the Italian Grand Prix. You could see the depth of passion in the *tifosi* [Ferrari fans]. The crowd booed every time I came out of the garage. That was okay, but when you saw signs painted on bed sheets saying 'Killer Coulthard' I felt threatened by the passion for Schumacher and Ferrari.
>
> It was set up for Michael and me to meet in a neutral

motorhome to talk. It was just the two of us and it was uncomfortable at first. I explained what I was doing and apologised. Then the conversation drifted on to rights and wrongs.

I said, 'You must admit you are wrong as well, it's not all my fault because you ran into the back of me.'

He said, 'No, it's your fault, you were being lapped. It's all your responsibility.'

I said 'You have to understand right and wrong. You must be wrong sometimes.' Then I said to him, 'At home there have to be times when you are wrong and the missus is right.' He said, 'No, I'm never wrong.' He wasn't having it.

You are caught in your tracks, I mean, what do you do in that situation? You don't believe it, that someone is *never* wrong, so you don't debate it because you think they're making a pointless point.

But it left me thinking, 'Is that why he is so good, because he is in a serious state of denial that allows him, even when it's as clear as the balls on a dog that he is wrong, to believe he's right?'

It got me wondering, 'Is that the last little killer bit that I don't have that doesn't see right from wrong, that doesn't see whose mistake it was? Is that what differentiates me from Michael?'

He is unquestionably the most successful driver ever, unquestionably one of the top two or three best, so does it matter? I say yes, it does, it's not just about winning, it's about competing.

Ross Brawn, not surprisingly, has a different view. The English technical director worked perhaps more closely with Schumacher than anyone else during his F1 career, initially at Benetton and then Ferrari. The two were apart only in the 1996 season, Schumacher's first with the *Scuderia*.

When the Coulthard cameo from the Monza test of 1998 is put to Brawn, he laughs and nods his head ruefully.

There are two Michael Schumachers. There's the one who is fighting against other drivers, who is hard and aggressive, tries not to show any weaknesses and doesn't give any quarter because that's what he has to present to the other drivers.

Then there is the Schumacher who is in the team, who loves working with a group of people, loves the team spirit, the empathy, likes to encourage people and discuss things. And it's almost a contradiction because when he steps over that mark and gets on to the track and into that environment he cannot give anything away. Then he steps back into the team environment and he's a really nice guy, a real team player, always concerned about people's lives on a personal level, tries to help with the problems they have. He's always happy to help. It's Jekyll and Hyde because he was determined not to show any soft side to adversaries.

He doesn't have any problem admitting he's wrong within the team. He's a very determined guy and he has to have a very strong character to be successful at what he's doing, but I've always found that if you sit him down and talk things through logically he won't defy logic. Loads of times I've proved him wrong about something.

Schumacher's intransigence towards his competitors is born from the instinct to give nothing away. But it is ironic that in private and with those close to him, he appears to be almost impossibly generous. Sabine Kehm was a journalist with the leading German daily newspaper *Die Welt* in Berlin, before Schumacher approached her to join him as his assistant. She began work in January 2000 and saw at first hand the years of great triumph for Schumacher and Ferrari as well as gaining an understanding of the man. Her perspective on Schumacher's generosity of spirit is enlightening. She says breezily:

> He loves to give presents, loves to make people happy. He cares about people's birthdays and Christmas, everyone gets a present. It's a big job. He would think hard about presents for people, he asked me about it a lot, he would be having a massage in his room after driving and I would be sitting there with a notepad writing down a huge list. He'd ask, 'Do you think this would be a good present for such-and-such?' Sometimes I felt like saying, 'Don't you have anything better to think about?'
>
> He sends flowers to the women in the factory for their birthdays even though he doesn't know them. He wants them to know that they are appreciated. In the end he wants the people around him to be happy because then he can be happy too. They come to him in a happy mood and he doesn't feel he owes them anything. If he notices you have a problem with something he'll ask you about it and try to fix it for you, because he wants you to be happy. That's why the team members like him so much. If someone has a baby he'll ask to see the baby pictures, it gives people a good feeling and it is very important to him. It's the same thing with the football, he played with the mechanics all the time on Thursday at races and then they would sit down and have dinner together, he didn't want to keep himself separate.

The idea of not wanting to feel he owes people anything is important to Schumacher and it comes up many times in his story. Beneath the tabloid stereotype of Michael Schumacher the 'ruthless baddie' is clearly a man of two sides. So what made Schumacher Schumacher? Where were the different facets of his character forged and how did they interact to make the driver both the icon and the hate figure he became?

CHAPTER THREE

The hungry years

Michael is a very shy person, who is always surprised by the enthusiasm he generates in people. He needs to feel comforted by those around him. Like anybody, he doubts. I find him fascinating. He can show an incredible maturity one minute and then ten minutes later behave like a child.

Jean Todt, Ferrari CEO

Michael Schumacher was always fond of tinkering with machines. Of the two Schumacher brothers he is the one who is most like their father, Rolf. Tinkering is in the blood. Rolf was a bricklayer, who would labour for long hours every day on deeply unglamorous projects, like waste incineration plants and chimneys, based in the northern German town of Kerpen, near Cologne.

When Michael was born in January 1969 there was not a great deal of money to go around in the Schumacher household. The turning point in all their lives was to come in 1973, when Michael sat in a kart for the first time at the age of four. Rolf was a member of the Kerpen-Manheim karting club, which rented out an old gravel pit from the landowner.

As a sideline to his building work, Rolf took on a job as the attendant on hire and drive days, renting out the karts, collecting the money and carrying out basic repairs by recycling parts of old machines.

On the edge of the pit was an old house, which came as part of the package. Rolf moved his wife Elisabeth and his son Michael into the house. When Michael was six, his younger brother Ralf was born. The boys' world revolved around gravel slopes, old tyres and the smell of petrol.

Rolf renovated the house and built a café with brown linoleum flooring, which Elisabeth ran. As far as their parents were concerned, the roles for both boys were mapped out well in advance. 'It was planned that Michael would take care of the garage and Ralf the restaurant,' recalls Rolf.

Michael says that both of his parents were disciplinarians, although his mother apparently let him and Ralf grow their hair long, because she said that she had always wanted girls! But there was no competitive or sporting background in the family.

Neither parent was involved in competition, my father was working-class, he had no ambition for racing. He isn't the typical motorsport father, you know, the kind of person who has always loved motorsport, always attended the races and followed it on television, not at all. He was a builder and he simply loved working with tools. One day he had a strange idea to put an engine in my pedal kart, not because he wanted me to become what I am now, but because we were simply having fun. Father and son, doing a hobby together.

Rolf's tale of how he got Michael started on the road to

seven world titles has an almost mythical feel about it; apparently he fished a moped out of a nearby lake, took the engine out and fixed it into Michael's pedal kart, a Kettcar, lashing up a basic throttle mechanism. The kart had no brakes so he attached a rope to it and made Michael drive around him in circles, rather like a trainer breaking in a young horse.

Before long Michael had graduated to driving the rental karts, helping his father out by moving them about and running in new engines. Then he began to compete and to win races.

> I was so enthusiastic about karting, I would be there all the time. I never really thought of anything else. I was competitive straight away and having fun, the two things come together. I never planned to get to Formula 1 for the simple reason that we lacked the means for it at home. When I got the opportunity I was very thankful and I took it, but there was no reason to achieve that. I didn't have a target to fulfil, I never expected anything in particular, so I wouldn't have blamed myself if it hadn't worked out. For sure I'm ambitious, that's my disposition, but if my very best hadn't been good enough, I would have accepted it. It may be that there was also a measure of calculated pessimism which came with it.

The 'calculated pessimism' surely sprang from the sheer impossibility of rising from a gravel bed in northern Germany to become a seven times world champion. But this outlook made him the man and the driver he was. He carried his pessimism with him throughout his career. 'I have never been a dreamer,' Schumacher wrote in 2003. 'Even at the stage where I was working my way through the formula classifications, I always tended to be pessimistic. I was satisfied with what I had. I was always realistic, never wanted to hope for things which might never become reality.'

According to family friends, Rolf maintained a sceptical view of his son's racing activities and was always faintly amazed by what Michael achieved. Thus Schumacher could be said to be a phenomenon entirely of his own making; and it seems that even when he rose to the top level and his immense ambition kicked in, he still carried with him his innate pessimism.

But as a youngster his success was leading him rapidly down a dead-end street. Beyond a certain basic level there was no way that the family could afford to provide Michael with the equipment to compete and, as his talents began to demand competition at national level, the future looked bleak. He entered races with borrowed equipment, or recycled tyres, which had been discarded by visitors to the track, but even in those days it was not uncommon for wealthy parents to spend £30,000 per year on their son's racing. If he could not find some money from somewhere the adventure would soon be over.

Schumacher's difficult rise from the 'have-nots' is not an uncommon tale. Some drivers like Niki Lauda and Nigel Mansell got themselves involved in complicated high risk loans to fund their early racing careers, but Rolf Schumacher would not even consider that. Merely surviving put him into an uncomfortable degree of debt which would take some years and some success for Michael, to clear. As the 1970s drew to a close, there was no obvious way forward. But then Michael got noticed.

'I went there one day and just wanted to drive a rented kart for a bit and I met the Schumacher family,' recalls Gerhard

Noack, who was involved in the local karting scene and who was to become one of Michael's early backers. 'I saw Michael there in a kart he'd built himself and he did a few laps. The lad caught my attention straight away. He was just nine. I got talking to the Schumachers and they said, "We can't do it, we haven't got the money to carry on with Michael's karting." '

Noack offered to help out, acquiring a much faster kart for the boy to drive. But early in the relationship he felt he needed to iron out a few problems with Michael's attitude. He threatened to sell the kart if he didn't take care of it properly.

Looking after the kart wasn't really his thing. He really liked the driving, but a bit of maintenance is required, a bit of preparation. So at one point I decided to say, 'Alright we'll sell the thing.' He came along after school to the track and wanted to have a drive and I said, 'I'm sorry but we haven't got it any more, I've threatened it many times, you haven't kept it clean and well looked after and that's why I sold it.'

Well there were a few tears and his Dad had to console him and then he came back and promised firmly that he'd take real care of his kart in future. Actually we had already bought him a new one anyway and the threat was mainly to show him how things are. From that day onwards he almost overdid it. He cleaned it so much the colour almost came off!

It is tempting to think that this huge shock and the way he began to conduct himself afterwards were somehow the trigger for Schumacher's obsessive attention to detail. All the engineers who worked with the adult Schumacher speak of an astonishing work ethic and an unreasonable degree of thoroughness in every detail, completely at odds with this early picture of the rather slapdash attitude of the boy. What is certain is that it was at this stage of his life that Schumacher's belief was developed that you get out of life what you put into it.

Schumacher is always quick to pay tribute to Noack and his extraordinary generosity at a critical stage in his development. 'He was interested in travelling with me and being my mechanic, tuning my engines. We competed successfully and he then built up his own karting business and soon became the number one kart dealer in Germany. He was supporting me financially and together we achieved something. It would have been impossible for me otherwise.'

In Noack's wake came other local businessmen willing to support the hard-working and earnest boy – carpet salesmen, car salesmen, a slot machine impresario. Frequently brash and coarse-mannered, life on the road with them was not easy to take.

'Often difficult people,' Schumacher recalls. 'They lacked respect for my friends and my family and they were often underhand or unfair and not always straight.'

All this sounds like a Dickensian orphan's rite of passage and it must have been a brutalising experience for an 11-year-old. In many ways he was a child during the week at school and a little adult at the weekends. He had to grow up quite quickly and at the same time he seems to have learned to build a protective shell around himself. He had to stick with his backers, 'because I had no choice if I wanted to make progress'. Unusually for a youngster in his position, his father did not accompany him on the road.

We couldn't afford it. He wasn't around like many other fathers to support and explain and be there for the good

moments and bad. But he was always there when I needed
him, when I went home. When I first started winning I was able
to buy my parents a car and pay the insurance. I was repaying
them. My father was almost crying because we were in
financial difficulties at the time. It wasn't an easy life for my
parents. Most of the time I was away with people who had
nothing to do with my family. From the age of eleven, I always
had a sponsor who came with me on all the trips around
Germany. Was I already a little adult at eleven? Yes, I had to
get used to living with all kinds of people, had to deal with the
various characters.

The most important patron was Jurgen Dilk, whose son Guido
had raced against, and been totally outclassed by, Michael. He
came on the scene just as Schumacher was in need of a new
backer after Noack decided to move on. Schumacher gave
Guido some tips on how to get more out of the machines and
they became friends. It was clear to Guido's father that
Schumacher was a special talent. 'We had become friends,'
recalls Schumacher. 'I had helped his son out and when it
became clear that I had to stop because I had no money he
said. "I'll pay in return for your trophies," which was a good
deal for me. Later on he sponsored me in my first car races. He
put up twenty-five thousand Deutschmarks [ten thousand
pounds] and helped me find sponsors, he was very important
to me.'

Together they rose through the ranks of European karting,
taking on and beating the sons of very wealthy men. At 15
Schumacher won the German national championship, the
following year he was runner-up in the world junior
championship. As agreed, Dilk kept the trophies and Michael
raced the karts. Dilk also played a crucial role in making the

young Schumacher realise the value of fitness. He hired an ex-professional footballer to train with him and from this point onwards, Schumacher would be obsessive about his fitness, always looking for the latest and newest ideas to elevate himself above the rest.

It is not unusual for a top level young driver to make the kind of sacrifices Schumacher was making in his teens. Kimi Raikkonen's family was not well off and he had to leave Finland in his teens, working as a mechanic to help pay for his racing. Robert Kubica was forced to leave Poland as a boy and live in Italy, where the karting scene was cutting edge. These are the crucial years for a young boy who wants to become a racing driver. If you don't get serious until 17 or 18 it is already too late. In more recent times Lewis Hamilton followed Schumacher's path. His father was a railway worker and could not afford to pay for Lewis to go beyond a basic stage, but at the age of 13, Lewis managed to persuade McLaren boss Ron Dennis that he needed immediate help and thus began his own incredible journey to the pinnacle of Formula 1.

But the nature of Michael Schumacher's situation meant that for much of his career he carried the feeling that he owed people. He has since paid them all back, not necessarily with money but with opportunities or roles within his organisation; Dilk was put in charge of managing the fan club, for example. Today, Schumacher feels that he has cleared the debt. He obviously felt acutely uncomfortable being in the debt of others, but in the early days he had no choice.

This feeling of owing people is a fundamental part of Schumacher's make-up and it was particularly strong during his Ferrari years. It had a lot to do with the pressure he put on

himself to deliver Ferrari's first world title for 20 years. The
team had been put in place around him, the resources were
there, everything was in place, he owed it to them to deliver.
The numerous near misses from 1997 to 1999 built an
immense pressure to win in 2000 and when he achieved it, the
overriding feeling was that he had turned a corner in his life,
he no longer owed anybody anything.

Eddie Irvine claims to have a friend who was at school with
Schumacher. According to his story, Michael was the loner,
who stayed at the back of the class, somewhat aloof from the
others. Schumacher himself claims to have been a normal boy
who passed all of his exams at school without excelling at
anything. He left school at 17, and at the time his ambition
was to make a living as a kart racer. If that fell through he
would be a mechanic. 'I had nothing planned. I was not top
class at anything, because the only thing I really concentrated
on was kart racing. I loved it and became good at it because I
did it constantly and I had the talent for it. But I also had a
good opportunity to grow up myself. I took it steady, easy, I
didn't rush things through and I always concentrated on the
project I was working on, never thinking too far ahead, just
trying to be happy with what I achieved.'

Schumacher is grateful for the fact that, despite his
frequent weekends away through his childhood, he was
able to grow up relatively normally, unlike many sportsmen
who have to sacrifice their childhoods in the pursuit of
excellence. Although he was finding his way in life, it seems
that he wasn't a particular hit with the ladies. 'Like any
boy I was interested in girls, but they weren't interested in
me. Karting and motorsport weren't socially acceptable
in those days.'

After school he took a job in a local garage which special-ised in BMW and Volkswagen, run by Willi Bergmeister, who would become a lifelong friend. Schumacher completed his apprenticeship, but his heart wasn't really in it. 'It helped to give me an understanding of the mechanical side, which was useful in racing, but I never wanted to be an engineer. I found it a bit boring to be honest, I preferred driving.'

Schumacher signed off his karting career by winning the European championship in 1987. With the continuing support of Jurgen Dilk, he then switched to cars. He competed in the 1988 Formula Koenig series in Germany, which he won. He also competed in the German Formula Ford series and the European Formula Ford series, in which he finished runner-up to Finnish driver Mika Salo, who was based in England. Schumacher came to the UK at the end of that season to compete in the Formula Ford Festival at Brands Hatch, which is a good early indicator of talent and which has been won by many drivers who went on to F1 and by plenty who didn't. Schumacher crashed.

But just prior to his visit to Britain, he had met a man who was to have a greater influence on his career than anyone to date: Willi Weber.

* * *

Willi Weber was a restaurant and pub owner, based in Stuttgart, who had built up a chain of more than 20 establishments by the late 1980s, but his passion was motorsport. He formed his own Formula 3 team in 1983 with an engineer called Klaus Trella and they called the team Weber Trella Stuttgart, or WTS for short. At the time he met

Weber, Michael Schumacher had no ambition to get to
Formula 1, partly because he had no real interest or knowledge of it and partly because it had always seemed
impossible from where he started out. His only real contact
with the sport was when he had witnessed the great Ayrton
Senna at close range. The Brazilian, then a top F1 driver,
attended one of the international kart meetings in which
Schumacher was competing.

In Weber he found a man who, although he competed in
the junior categories, had his eyes clearly focused on the top
echelon. 'I had been racing for 20 years myself and Formula 1
was always my mission, my ultimate goal but I was too old to
go into it as a driver. So I dreamed of bringing a young
German driver into F1,' Weber recalls. 'That was my clear goal
and Michael gave me the feeling that he was the right
person.'

Germany had always had a reasonable level of interest in
motorsport, touring car racing especially has always been
popular because of the support of the major German car
manufacturers. But at the highest level, Formula 1, Germany
had been poorly represented. The Mercedes Benz team
dominated briefly in Grands Prix either side of the war, but
had not raced since 1955. And success for German drivers has
been very limited. Jochen Mass won a race in the 1970s, but
before that the only stand-out driver was Wolfgang Von Trips,
who came from the same area as Schumacher, but as a
wealthy aristocrat came from the opposite end of the social
and financial scale.

In the late 1980s there was a growing interest in raising the
standard of German motorsport and brokers like Weber were
aware that there was some exciting talent coming through –

drivers like Berndt Schneider, Michael Bartels and Heinz Harald Frentzen.

Schumacher caught Weber's eye at a wet Formula Ford race at the Salzburgring, late in 1988. Weber's team had just won the German F3 championship with Jo Winklehock, their first major success as a team. Weber was on the look-out for his next rising star. 'I'll never forget it,' recalls Weber. 'Michael climbed from seventh to first, showing amazing car control and I knew then he was destined for F1. I watched him in two more races before getting in contact.'

Impressed by what he had seen, Weber offered Schumacher a Formula 3 test at Hockenheim. He recalls:

After four, maybe five laps, Michael had reached his limit and went off the track. He came into the pits. He was quite upset and he said to me, 'That's it then, testing over.' I said, 'No, Michael, it's just the beginning. Now you go and work with the boys and rebuild the car together and then we'll carry on.'

I was amazed by his honesty, his openness. Normally if you give a youngster a chance and he goes off he'll come out with some excuse like, 'wet patch' or 'technical problem', but to say 'I was too fast, it was my fault and now presumably it's all over. . .' As it turned out he was over a second quicker than my current driver. I signed him for 1989 and 1990 and paid him a monthly salary.

Weber also had the good sense to sign Schumacher to a long management contract. Schumacher was stunned. 'He offered me the contract to secure two seasons in F3 which I thought was enormous, I never expected that. I mean one season at that time was very expensive and he simply said, "You drive and don't worry about the financial side." '

In 1989 he won two races and finished third in the championship behind Heinz Harald Frentzen and Karl Wendlinger. There was some rough stuff out on the track and Schumacher learned to give as good as he got, but in one instance early on he was the victim rather than the perpetrator. Some footage broadcast by German satellite station Premiere shows an obviously irritated Schumacher complaining to the interviewer about being cut up by another driver. 'Well I knew we were driving hard,' protests Schumacher, 'but that just wasn't fair and if he does it again then someone should have words with him. There should be consequences.'

According to Weber, Schumacher is 'not the machine which is often presented to us. Instead he is an incredibly thin-skinned individual, with an infinitely big heart and incredible sensitivity.'

This depiction of Schumacher's character from someone who knows him so well is interesting and very much at odds with the way he is seen by his rivals and the public. Jean Todt, who would later become Schumacher's principle mentor, paints a similar picture of a sensitive man in a brutal world: 'Michael is a very shy person, who is always surprised by the enthusiasm he generates in people. He needs to feel comforted by those around him. Like anybody, he doubts. I find him fascinating. He can show an incredible maturity one minute and then ten minutes later behave like a child.'

The idea of Schumacher as a machine is one that has lingered around him throughout his career. Damon Hill would later capitalise on this, calling him a 'robot', an image which has stuck. This impression of Schumacher derives from his extraordinarily consistent driving and his meticulous attention to detail, bordering on the obsessive. Weber tells a revealing story from the Formula 3 days which illustrates this point perfectly.

> He stalled in a race with what appeared a mechanical failure. We took the car apart and found nothing. We put it back together and again it wouldn't move. This was something he found unacceptable. He drove over to the garage and around midnight I got a call from my team manager, Franz Tost, who told me that they had totally dismantled the car, apart from the petrol tank. Franz said that if he opened up the petrol tank then it would be irreparably damaged, we would need a new one, which wasn't cheap and he thought it wasn't necessary. I thought it couldn't have anything to do with the petrol tank.
>
> But then Michael rang and said, 'Mr Weber, we have to get to the cause. We have to take the petrol tank apart.' So I agreed, if it was for his peace of mind. So they cut the tank open and discovered that the inside of the tank was sprayed with something which made the petrol break down and this clogged the petrol pump and that was why it stalled.
>
> If he had not proceeded so analytically, he would have stalled again which would have lost him the next race and that is the Michael Schumacher who wants to know everything. He goes right to the bottom of things. If something hasn't worked as it should you will never hear 'it doesn't work' from him. That phrase doesn't exist to him. Rather it's, 'Let's go through it step by step.'

Third place in the 1989 championship entitled Schumacher to go to the prestigious Macau Grand Prix in November, a Formula 3 race against the world's best up and coming drivers. Although he had competed against top level kart racers, this was the first time that Schumacher had an opportunity to measure himself against the cream of the world's talent and he acquitted himself well.

Macau is a street circuit and it is a very difficult track to master on a first visit as there are two distinct parts to it: the fast, flowing waterfront section, and the tight, windy, technical series of blind corners that runs up the hill. It's a long lap and a long, complicated race, split into two legs. In those days the winner was the driver with the aggregate best time over the two legs, not necessarily the man who crossed the line first. Schumacher won the first leg, but had dropped to fourth in the second leg when he retired with a mechanical failure. The event was won by David Brabham, the British F3 champion, who used his success to springboard straight into Formula 1 the following year. But things didn't work out well for him and a year later he was out of F1 – a cautionary tale for all aspiring racers.

Despite his relative success, Schumacher was still not even dreaming about F1 at this point. However, he had become more aware of it. Earlier that year, aged 20, he had attended his first Grand Prix. Schumacher's WTS team-mate, Frank Shmickler, was due to take part in a support race at Monaco and Schumacher went along to watch. At the time the legendary duel between Ayrton Senna and Alain Prost was at its height. The McLaren pair shared the front row of the grid with Senna on pole. Schumacher watched him go on to dominate the race, beating his rival by an incredible 52 seconds.

It would be nice to report that Schumacher was blown away by the experience and felt that he had found his true calling. Instead he was distinctly underwhelmed. Like his father, Michael is not easily impressed – in fact he goes out of his way to downplay things which are meant to impress. He recalled:

> After a short while I no longer knew who was in what position. Aside from that it was also much too loud for me.
>
> During the pre-qualifying I noticed the difficulties Berndt Schneider was having in a poor car and he is a superb driver. I didn't feel I was on the same level as him. That's why I never thought I might be able to drive a Formula 1 car to the proper standard. I thought to myself, 'That's out of your league.'

Schneider's experience served as a further cautionary tale for Schumacher and Weber. Here was a man, five years older than Schumacher, who had swept all before him in the karting arena, had won the world junior championships and the top European title. He had won the German F3 series two years earlier and then jumped straight into F1 with the Zakspeed team, an ambitious German outfit who were finding themselves out of their depth in F1. He had got that final crucial step on the ladder all wrong and he never recovered from it.

If his career was not managed carefully the same fate could easily befall Schumacher. It is a measure of his realism, and even pessimism, that Schumacher did not feel that he was even in Schneider's league as a driver at this point. It was a character trait that would continue to serve him well as it meant that he kept finding himself being pleasantly surprised.

Schumacher and Weber wisely decided that he should complete a second year in Formula 3 and dominate the series before moving on. He won five races and took the German F3 title. He was just 21. As part of his bonus for winning the title Schumacher got £20,000 and he knew exactly what to do with it. 'My family were really in debt,' he recounts, 'so I gave my father this suitcase full of money! He couldn't believe it. That was something very special.'

Schumacher was now well on his way and within 12 months he would become a Formula 1 driver. But the two most significant aspects of the 1990 season in shaping the Michael Schumacher story were his involvement with the Mercedes Benz sportscar team and his duel at the end of the season with Mika Hakkinen in the Macau Grand Prix.

CHAPTER FOUR

*The road
less travelled*

When I first came into F1 I didn't understand
what it was all about.

Michael Schumacher

At this stage of the story a new cast of characters enters, each
of whom can lay some claim to having played a key role in
getting Michael Schumacher into Formula 1.

As his career began to gather momentum, steered by Willi
Weber, he took the highly unconventional route of signing a
contract to drive in the world sportscar championship for
Mercedes in 1990, alongside his efforts to clinch the German
F3 crown. It was a massive workload to take on and one that
driver managers today would never allow, because there is
plenty of evidence that young drivers can lose their way by
jumping from one type of car to another. These days the top
young drivers are encouraged to focus exclusively on one
series each year.

Journalist Burkhard Nuppenay, who later fought and lost a
court case against Weber for fees he believed he was owed
from a management deal made around this time, claims that
it was he who suggested the Mercedes idea to Weber.

Nuppenay believed that drivers should avoid Formula 3000, the next step on the ladder, because too often good drivers got lost in bad cars. Instead he proposed the Mercedes deal. Gerd Kramer, who was employed by Mercedes and had excellent connections within Formula 1, certainly worked behind the scenes to create the right opportunity for Schumacher. Indeed it was partly on his advice that Eddie Jordan gave the young driver his Grand Prix debut at Spa in 1991. Also Norbert Haug, a former journalist, the newly installed manager of the Mercedes competition department, had a quiet influence on much of what happened next to Schumacher.

Mercedes had made a commitment to develop young German stars. It was generally accepted that the sportscar programme was a prelude to Mercedes entering Formula 1 and the idea was to mix exciting young drivers with experienced drivers like Jochen Mass so that they could learn quickly. Weber says he was never in any doubt that this was a vital step for Schumacher because, coming from a small F3 team, he needed to learn how a big racing organisation operates, as a preparation for when he would ultimately arrive in F1. Thus there was an obvious logic to tying Schumacher's star to Mercedes Benz, if they were bound for F1.

'I believe it was crucial to get such a young man accustomed to such a large team where instead of there being ten people there could be a hundred or more,' recalls Weber. 'There were many critical voices, who were writing him off saying, "Now he's driving in the old man's league, he will never get out of it." '

Despite the offer of £100,000 a year salary and a company Mercedes, it seems that Schumacher himself needed a lot of persuading and his stubborn side came out in the negotiations. He may not have had much of a plan, but he did know that racing a car with a roof was not in any of his dreams. It took Weber five weeks to persuade him.

Schumacher's methodical approach was rather at odds with the conflicting programmes he was being asked to take on simultaneously. A big heavy sportscar, loaded with technology, was a totally different animal from a light nimble F3 car, which had few parameters to be changed when setting it up. But Schumacher learned to adapt, and was able to step out of one and into the other quite effectively. There was the travel aspect too – in between German F3 dates he was jetting off on long-haul flights to places like Mexico City. In four outings with Mercedes he took three podiums including one win, but this record was not without controversy. At Silverstone he was disqualified for not wearing his seat belt at a certain point of the race, although he swore that he was.

But the biggest controversy of his career so far came at the Macau Grand Prix in November. As German F3 champion and a second year veteran at Macau, Schumacher was among the favourites to win. Against him was Mika Hakkinen, who was British F3 champion and sponsored by Marlboro. Hakkinen was on a fast track to Formula 1 and with the PR machine of his sponsors at work behind the scenes, he was far more talked about in international motorsport circles at this stage than Schumacher. But he also backed up the talk by delivering the results on the track and was regarded as one of the fastest drivers for a generation. The pair had raced each other in karts and first locked horns in cars in Germany when Hakkinen had made a one-off appearance at Hockenheim and beaten Schumacher.

The stage was set for a duel, which would continue to

resonate ten years later in Formula 1. The pair were almost the same age, Hakkinen being older by a mere three months. When he retired in 2006 Schumacher admitted that Hakkinen was the adversary whom he had most respected.

But the respect came later. At Macau in 1990, Schumacher tricked Hakkinen into a mistake born out of the Finn's impetuosity, but also out of his naïvety, which cost him what would have been the most important victory of his career so far. It also provided an early indication of Schumacher's vulnerability under pressure and his uncompromising driving in moments of panic.

Hakkinen won the first race by two and a half seconds with Schumacher second. So for the second race, all Hakkinen had to do was finish within two and a half seconds of Schumacher, who passed Hakkinen for the lead early in the race. 'All I needed to do was stay behind him and I would have won. It was a lack of experience on my part,' recalls Hakkinen. 'And maybe I was a bit too ambitious to win. I wasn't ready to take second place.'

At the start of the final lap, Hakkinen was tucked in close behind Schumacher as they negotiated the fast open corners by the waterfront. With a slight speed advantage on the straights, Hakkinen looked as though he wanted to try to win the race outright, even though he didn't need to. The speeds the two drove each other to reach were amazing, faster than the pole position time in qualifying. It was a scenario which was to be repeated ten years later at Suzuka in the showdown for the 2000 F1 world championship, the race Schumacher believes was the most intense and most perfect of his career. Suzuka did not end in an accident; Macau, however, did.

'When he was able to stay with me I knew he was going to

win the race,' recalls Schumacher. 'I was quicker than Mika through the city, but he was quicker on the straights. He was playing with me, could have passed if he wanted.'

Hakkinen was pushing hard as they swept over the line to start their last lap and Schumacher made a mistake. As they steamed down the long straight leading out of Mandarin Bend towards the tight Lisboa corner, Hakkinen decided to go for the lead he did not need to take. He moved suddenly to the right to pass Schumacher. Michael swerved across to cover him and Hakkinen cannoned into the back of Schumacher's car, knocking its rear wing off. Hakkinen's car smashed into the barriers. He jumped out and threw his gloves on the ground in fury. Schumacher drove around the remainder of the lap, the car bucking underneath him as the rear end was quite unstable without the rear wing. Luckily for him there was no damage to the suspension or transmission of the car and it carried him to the finish. Schumacher had won Macau, the biggest event of his career so far. Mika recalls today:

On the very last lap Michael made a big mistake on the fast right-hander and he nearly touched the barrier. He was going so slowly after that and I wanted to get past him. I would have had to change down a gear to stay behind him, he was that slow. So I make a move to pass him and what does he do? Probably not intending me to have an accident but intending to stop me from passing him. I hit him, there was no way I could avoid him and that was it for me. I have thought about it a lot, wondered if he deliberately tried to take me out or was just standing his ground. It was really tough. I never asked Michael what he thought he was doing.

That was the first thing with him, which made me think, 'Mmm . . . this is not good.' There are a lot of things he's done over the years, Adelaide with Damon, Jerez with Jacques, Monaco. Of course we have had some tough races, we've had some close situations but it was okay because I knew what he was like.

Nowadays, with Schumacher's Formula 1 history all too well-known, it is hard to find an objective view on Macau in isolation. 'He beat himself,' insists Schumacher. 'If he had stayed behind me in that second race, he would have won the event. Obviously the get-together we had meant that I was able to win and that was a fortunate moment. I think he was crazy, nobody takes anyone on the last lap, not without a fight. It was good.'

Was this the first seminal dirty trick? Or did Schumacher just read Hakkinen's impetuosity perfectly and force the Finn into a mistake? Either way it was the biggest win of his career to date and when he backed it up the following week by winning another international F3 race at Fuji in Japan, word spread around the industry about Michael Schumacher.

* * *

Schumacher went into 1991 expecting to be a Mercedes sportscar driver, but he ended the year as the hottest new name in Formula 1. Just three seasons into his car racing career he reached the pinnacle of the sport, something he had never imagined possible.

Ironically, though, recognition from the F1 world was slow in coming. Formula 1 team bosses were accustomed to scouting the junior formulae for new talent and the network of driver agents and talent spotters was still relatively tight-knit in those days. One of Schumacher's admirers was Domingos Piedade, the boss of AMG, a high performance department of Mercedes road cars. Piedade allegedly spotted Schumacher in karts and was the man who tipped Weber off to watch the young driver in Formula Ford. He also attended many Grands Prix in the early 1990s and informed McLaren boss Ron Dennis about Schumacher, but Dennis was sceptical about Schumacher's decision to race in long distance sportcar races, because he believed that sportscar racers, with their emphasis on endurance rather than pure performance, were not the thoroughbreds Grand Prix racing requires.

One man who was paying attention to Schumacher's performances in sportscars was Ross Brawn, who was at the time the technical director of Jaguar, Mercedes' main rivals for the championship. Brawn had been in Formula 1 since the 1970s, initially with Williams. In 1988 he designed the Arrows F1 car which finished a highly impressive fourth in the world championship and on the strength of that was hired by Tom Walkinshaw's TWR group to design a world-beating sportscar for Jaguar. The XJR 14 was basically an F1 car with bodywork and the car won the 1991 world sportscar championship, beating the Mercedes. Meanwhile Walkinshaw's company had also been taken on to manage the engineering department of the Benetton Formula 1 team, a development which was to prove highly significant to Schumacher's career. Ross Brawn remembers:

We were racing against Michael, Frentzen and Wendlinger. All of them went on to race in F1. But every time Michael got in the car he was quicker and as it was a fuel economy formula, he also went further on a tank of fuel than the others, so not only was he faster but also used less fuel doing it.

The only time that the Mercedes challenged us was when Michael was driving. They had a policy of rotating drivers whereas we favoured the stronger driver in our team. When we prepared for the race we always had to build in a Michael factor. I didn't know him as a person then, only as a very fast driver. We assumed that he would come through the Mercedes chain into F1, but at that stage Mercedes hadn't made the commitment to F1.

In August Schumacher and Willi Weber were at a race at the Nurburgring when news came though that Bertrand Gachot, a driver with Eddie Jordan's first year Formula 1 team, had been arrested in London for spraying CS gas in the face of a taxi driver. Weber recalls:

Some journalist came up and said, 'Have you heard? They've arrested Gachot, he's in prison.' Jordan didn't have a driver, so I acted immediately, I had to ring Eddie straight away, to see if there was a chance that Michael could get into the car. Easier said than done . . . Eddie was on holiday in Spain at that time. I think I spent about five hundred pounds on phone calls from my hotel at the Nurburgring. I searched for Eddie and then the negotiations began. I said, 'Eddie, please give him a chance.' Eddie said, 'But who is Michael Schumacher?' I had a very good rapport with Eddie at the time. We had been in F3 for many years and I was at that time in the process of buying his Formula 3000 team, which didn't work out – in hindsight, thank God, because I was only buying it for Michael to move him up a level.

Weber had been around the F1 paddock a lot during 1991, trying to garner interest in Schumacher. Here was the opportunity he had been waiting for. Eddie Jordan had instructed his right-hand man, Ian Phillips, to speak to Keke Rosberg, Derek Warwick and Stefan Johansson about filling Gachot's seat and Phillips was close to agreement with Warwick when he received a call from Jordan to say that he had done a great deal with Mercedes and its partner, Sauber. Jordan would receive $200,000 for a test and for Schumacher's participation in the Belgian Grand Prix weekend.

At the time Peter Sauber was acting on the belief that he was building a team in Switzerland which would become the Mercedes Formula 1 team. As it turned out Mercedes did not enter F1 until 1993, because the presiding CEO was not in favour of F1. When they did come in it was only as an engine supplier to the Sauber team. The commitment was to work together, with Peter Sauber responsible for raising money through sponsorship. In the eyes of Mercedes, he failed to do that, which ultimately led Mercedes to join forces with the well-financed McLaren team in 1995. Had Mercedes known what a colossal force Schumacher was to become, perhaps the main board might have played things rather differently. As it was, they were about to lose him for ever.

Eddie Jordan was in a relatively good position as the Jordan 191, powered by a customer Ford engine, had proved a remarkably competitive car in the team's debut season. He asked Weber if Schumacher had ever raced at Spa, the most demanding circuit in the F1 calendar. Weber said that of course he had, after all his home town of Kerpen was only an hour away across the German border. In truth Schumacher had never set foot on the Spa circuit.

'I took Schumacher because of the money,' says Jordan with typical candour. 'Although if I'd known that he'd never raced at Spa it might have been a deal breaker in Stefan's favour. I don't think anyone, even now, would take a driver from sports cars, so I'm not sure that Michael would have got his break into F1 without us.'

The day after the Nurburgring race, Schumacher was already scheduled to travel to England for a meeting with Arrows boss Jackie Oliver. (There had been some contact but no firm offer of a position in Formula 1.) So he made his way to Jordan's base near Northampton for a seat fitting on the Monday and then did a test session on the Silverstone south circuit on the Tuesday. If the test went well, Schumacher would be racing in the Belgian Grand Prix in five days' time.

Eddie Jordan was not present himself at the test, which was overseen by team manager Trevor Foster: 'After six laps he was flicking the car through the chicane and I said to Weber, "This is his race car and it has to be ready tonight at four o'clock, so we have to calm him down a bit." So we brought him in and he said, "I don't understand what the problem is, I am in control." It was just natural speed that he had all the time.'

Schumacher admits he was overwhelmed by the prospect of his first Formula 1 test and both he and Weber were in a state of high anxiety on the day. Writing in 2003, Schumacher recalls it in detail:

> When I got into the car that first day at Silverstone, it was a very special moment. Much more than the race afterwards at Spa, where I just turned up and drove. The test was much tougher because I had no idea what the future held for me at that point and how I would cope. I remember the first three laps clearly. On the first lap I thought, 'Whoops, there goes your F1 career, it's over.'

The car was incredibly impressive, so powerful but at the same time difficult to drive. On the second lap I thought, 'Not so bad' but by the third lap I was really comfortable with the car. It seemed everything was okay.

I just did it, without being told I had to perform well because otherwise I wouldn't be driving in races. I had already achieved things at that time which I had not expected. I went to the Jordan test similarly pessimistic.

I didn't know that day, what effect the test would have on my life. After the event it was very important of course.

After all the time spent watching talented drivers strive to reach F1 only to fail, and worrying if the same fate would befall him, Schumacher was a natural. Fate was extremely kind to him because this was not a back-of-the-grid car he was stepping into. The Jordan in 1991 was very competitive and the deal would springboard him into the upper echelons of the sport immediately. From this point on he would never again drive a bad car. Schumacher did 33 laps that first day at Silverstone and lapped faster than the team's lead driver, Andrea De Cesaris. Two days later, some 18 years after he had first sat in a kart attached to his father by a rope, he arrived at Spa as a Grand Prix driver.

* * *

'When I first came into F1 I didn't understand what it was all about,' Schumacher wrote in 2003. 'I could drive fast, of course, but I had no idea of the complexity of the whole business, which little wheel you had to set in motion in order to get everything going.'

Schumacher's debut that weekend set many wheels in motion. The action on the track was spectacular as he caught everyone's attention with his speed in the green Jordan. On his first day of practice he was a second faster than De Cesaris. He also upset Alain Prost by running into him at the Bus Stop chicane. Schumacher was called to the stewards' office to explain himself. 'What were you doing?' asked veteran steward John Corsmidt. 'He was slow, he got in my way,' said Schumacher baldly.

In qualifying the next day Michael finished seventh. He was the talk of the paddock. It helped that he had made his debut in a well sorted and well balanced car. Had he come in with the Footwork Arrows car, for example, he probably would not have qualified for the race and the furore would not have been so great. But F1 is a hype-driven business and Schumacher had done something truly impressive. De Cesaris was not top class, but he was a known quantity as a yardstick by which to measure Schumacher's performance. De Cesaris was not beaten by a few tenths of a second, but by seconds and was 14th on the grid in an identical car.

After qualifying there was quite a bit going on behind the scenes – the name Michael Schumacher was at the top of the agenda for representatives of the Mercedes, Jordan and Benetton teams. The race lasted only two corners for Schumacher, as he pulled off with clutch failure and retired the car. This even led to a conspiracy theory about the possible reasons for Schumacher's short lived debut, which focused on the advantages for him not competing. He had set the world on fire in qualifying, so why take the risk that the race might not come off so well, so the theory went. Instead the conspiricists speculated that it was in Schumacher's interest to get around the negotiating table as quickly as possible and negotiate a deal to go straight to Benetton.

Indeed for the conspiracy theory to be sustainable, it presupposes a very high degree of composure and calculation on the part of a 22-year-old making his F1 debut. Jordan will not be drawn on this, beyond saying that it was the only clutch failure they had all year. Ian Phillips, however, flatly refutes any conspiracy theory. 'It was our fault,' he says. 'We never did a practice start with him and he was just massively over-enthusiastic. He was so up for it, confidence flying and he thought he could make up five places at the start.'

The great irony of the Spa weekend was that Schumacher could easily have won on his debut. Later in the race De Cesaris was in a position to win, but his engine failed because there was not enough oil in the tank. Starting seven places ahead of him on the grid, the race might have been Schumacher's if he'd just managed to keep going.

Schumacher was actually feeling unwell all weekend and was carried along on adrenaline. He was struggling to sleep due to jet lag from racing in Japan a few days earlier and he had contracted a cold on the plane. His preparation for his debut was terrible and it left him run down at arguably the most important moment of his career to date. Never again would Schumacher be anything other than meticulously prepared for a Grand Prix. To make matters worse, the accommodation at Spa was more suited to his early karting days than a Formula 1 debutant: he shared a room with Weber in a youth hostel. The only way was up.

CHAPTER FIVE

The genius of Michael Schumacher

Schumacher drives like a genuine champion – rounded, balanced, with amazing feel in his backside. His driving style allows him to continually reach the extreme areas without deliberately overshooting them.

Juan Manuel Fangio, five times world champion

By virtue of what it signified for the sport, Schumacher's debut at Spa in 1991 is one of the landmark moments of Formula 1 history. Fittingly for a man who went on to win seven world titles and thus become the most successful driver ever, his was a spectacular entrance. It was clear to everyone that here was a sensational talent and it shook the established F1 team bosses to the core. How had they missed him? Eddie Jordan, more by luck than judgement admittedly, had discovered a prodigy, of whom most of them had been only vaguely aware beforehand.

Over the next few seasons, teams like McLaren and Williams continued to scour the world for exciting new talent, drivers who would come in with fresh motivation and have no fear of taking on the established names like Senna, Mansell, Prost and Piquet. But Schumachers do not grow on trees. McLaren hired Michael Andretti and Mika Hakkinen, the latter turning out to be very successful. Williams gave Damon Hill, then David Coulthard and eventually Jacques Villeneuve a chance and two of them won titles, beating Schumacher. By the turn of the millennium, the team bosses seemed to have settled back into complacency again until Jenson Button, Kimi Raikkonen and Fernando Alonso came along and set off another cult of youth in F1.

Schumacher stood out immediately for his quality and for the thoroughness of his approach. He revolutionised the driver's art. Of course his arrival coincided with the increasing importance of technology and the use of sophisticated tools to analyse a car's behaviour. From the mid-1990s onwards even the laziest driver had to spend many hours in debriefs until late into the evening, whereas his 1980s counterpart would have long ago swanned off to the golf course.

Alain Prost was known as 'the Professor' for his attention to detail and his thoughtful analysis, but Schumacher raised the bar even further, to the point where he was working ten times harder outside the cockpit than in it. Rival teams were forced to criticise their drivers publicly for not putting in the effort like Schumacher.

'Prost was my hero, but Schumacher rocked up and took the story on,' says Mark Webber. 'His attention to detail was just unbelievable; the way he used his power and influence to manipulate situations to suit him. He never let up. He was amazingly hungry. I'm a huge sports fan and I don't think we have ever seen as consistent, determined and focused an individual.'

Schumacher's driving philosophy – which is best summed up as 'maximise everything' – is an extension of his attitude to life, which is that you only get out what you put in. He said in the final year of his career:

> If you don't invest the effort you don't get the performance. To be at the top, whatever the field, you have to give one hundred percent. I have never thought otherwise. The only thing that has changed, the thing I've developed with age and experience, is the quality. I've improved the content of what I do. I'm not just talking as a driver, but as a person. Over time I have understood lots of things I didn't have a clue about before.

Schumacher was always on the look-out for new ways to get an edge over his opponents, to find the winning formula. When he got into partnership with men like Ross Brawn, Rory Byrne and Jean Todt at Ferrari, all of whom had the same attitude, they became an unstoppable force, winning five world titles in a row in the early 2000s. Schumacher left the 'tangibles' like car design and development to men like Brawn and Byrne, while he and Todt worked on the 'intangibles', by stretching the interpretation of the rules and pushing the boundaries of what was acceptable.

However much his character may polarise opinion and his methods may be despised as unsporting by his rivals, there is no denying that for almost all of his career, Michael Schumacher was the best driver in the world. But what was the nature of his genius behind the wheel and how does he himself describe the feeling of life on the limit?

* * *

The starting point for understanding Schumacher's gift is to focus on his speed, according to Eddie Irvine. The Irishman was Schumacher's team-mate at Ferrari from 1996 to 1999 and is as well placed as anyone to analyse what made Schumacher such a great driver. He dismisses all discussion of Schumacher's adaptability, his team-building skills and the many other celebrated attributes as a side issue.

He was quick and everything else came from that. End of story. People see something and then they start to add other attributes. It's like if you see a really beautiful girl and she likes you and then you start to add all these things like, she's really smart, she's really this, she's really that, because you want to believe that she has all these attributes. Then when you break up with her you realise she was just another fucking idiot. People are the same about drivers. I'm not saying that Michael is an idiot, but people want to add all these things. You know what? You add three tenths of a second to Michael's lap times and he's probably worse than a lot of the other guys out there and that's it. Most of the guys in F1, if they were three tenths quicker they'd be legends.

That story about Barcelona 1994 when he finished with only fifth gear in the car? That's an ability to drive a racing car. It's a natural ability to understand a racing car and all the things it takes to get a lap time out of it. He wasn't particularly adaptable or this or that. I've heard people say all sorts of things about Michael and it's all bullshit.

People think that they see all these qualities. But the bottom line is; he was quick and everything else came from that.

Schumacher himself has often echoed Irvine's argument that speed is paramount.

> I'm not a hero, just a guy who can drive quickly. At the beginning of my career, when I first got into an F1 car I thought it was magic. My feet didn't touch the ground and I thought that maybe I was different from others. And I was roundly criticised for having thought that. As I matured I realised that drivers are all made the same. Some are faster than others, but that's all it is. We are not touched by supernatural powers, nothing in what I do gives me the right to think that, as a human being, I am any better than anyone else.

Ross Brawn is perhaps more aware than anyone about what made Schumacher so successful and he too has always identified Schumacher's speed as the overriding factor in pulling off his many audacious race strategies. 'Michael's speed helps a lot. Sometimes it's marginal and everything has to come together to win the race. His sheer speed is often the deciding factor and that is why he always wins the races he should win and often the ones he shouldn't win. And there are not many people who can do that. I recognise a good thing when I see it so I stay close to him.'

Identifying drivers who win the races they shouldn't be able to win, usually because they are against drivers in stronger cars, is an excellent yardstick for measuring the true aces in Formula 1. Without exception, the drivers who can lay claim to being considered 'great' are those who were able to do this consistently, with Schumacher and Senna at the top of the list.

But what made Schumacher so fast? Being quick in a

Formula 1 car is about having a feel for where the limit is and being able to stay on it. That way you extract the maximum from the car and the conditions. A racing car is on the limit in a corner when the g-force pushing the car sideways is almost at the point of being greater than the force of the engine pushing the car forward. It is a very fine line and once you cross it the car spins off the road. If you are well within it, the car goes around the corner with no hint of a spin, but you are slow. The difference between a great driver and one who is barely a footnote in history is the ability to stay on that limit not just for one or two corners, but for whole laps.

The racing driver's art has become extremely technical in modern times and he is required to know a great deal about the engineering of the car, but the fundamental requirement for finding the limit is still the same today as it was in the days of Nuvolari or Fangio; a sensitive backside. The car moves underneath the driver and he has to feel the point at which it is starting to break away.

In the early years at Ferrari and especially in 1996, Schumacher was required to hustle a poor handling car to squeeze a lap time out of it, something which uniquely he was able to do. Sometimes he had to over-drive the car. Ross Brawn recalls his qualifying lap in Budapest in 1998 as a perfect example:

> If you watched the car closely, he was entering every corner looking like he was going to have an accident. I was holding my breath; it would step out at the back before every corner and yet he'd manage to catch it and keep the power on. He was just going for it. There might be a few drivers in F1 who could do that for one or two corners, but

I don't think there's a driver around who could do that at
every corner on a qualifying lap.

Senna was the same. You'd see him on a qualifying lap
and the car would look very uncomfortable, but he'd get
the lap time out of it.

Being on the limit is also about feeling the grip level which
the track is offering and tailoring your braking and cornering
so that you are on the limit at all times but never over it. You
must have an intuitive feel for the level of grip and because
the track is a living thing, with natural oils coming out of it at
varying temperatures, the grip level can change quite
dramatically in a matter of minutes. The driver must have
enormous sensitivity to changes in track conditions. Speed is
not just about doing one fast lap, it is about being able to
sustain laps at close to maximum intensity throughout a race.
As Schumacher reflects:

The most important thing for me is that feeling of being on
the limit, of pushing myself and always pushing the
boundaries. For example, during qualifying at Suzuka in
2001 I did a lap which was eight tenths faster than the
computer said was possible with our car. That was a
feeling of surpassing yourself, which is totally regenerative.
It was such a powerful affirmation for me.

A logical driver always tries to run on the limit. Going
beyond that is actually slower because the car slides in the
corners, which ruins the tyres. And he risks going off. I try
in every corner to find the limit, it's something I just feel and
to find that limit I have to come in faster to the corner than
seems possible. Only by doing that can I find the point I
need to get to and confirm that I wasn't previously at the
limit. Of course I'm interested in my survival. I have no
interest at all in ignoring the limit of the car and risking my

life. What I want is to get the maximum out of the car.

I am a man who reacts to what he comes up against. I generally have a feeling for how fast I can drive, I find the limit quickly, I drive on it and then, at that moment, I decide either 'I can push harder' or 'No, that's as good as it's going to get.' I don't need to feel my way in slowly.

Through the seat of my pants to my shoulders I feel what the car is doing. It also helps that I have a pulse which is forty beats per minute slower than other drivers, therefore I am calmer and can concentrate better.

I make myself as one with the car. Sometimes I feel that it is just as human as I am. Sometimes during a race, I have talked to the car, 'Stay with me, please!' or 'Go on, do it, do it!' I have to build a relationship with it, speak to it.

To me being on the limit is very much the satisfaction of knowing that I have left nothing out which I could have done better. The satisfaction of racing is different, but if you are talking about driving a car on the limit, it's the clock that matters. I always fight against the clock. In the cockpit you can see the numbers and the lower the numbers get the more satisfaction I get. I can feel if I have done a corner well and then I wait until I see the clock for proof.

In his first season at Ferrari, Michael worked with Giorgio Ascanelli, who had been Senna's race engineer at McLaren. Ascanelli has a great insight into how the two drivers compare, at a mature stage of their careers. 'He is a driver who thinks more quickly than the others and who always drives around a problem. Meaning that he limits, or even takes out the discomfort. Michael drives hard whatever you give him, whereas Senna would occasionally refuse the challenge if the car was not up to his standards. Michael puts his wheels where others daren't.'

Taking risks, putting your wheels where others daren't is what people expect from racing drivers. If it was easy we would all be doing it. Early in his F1 career, Schumacher caught the attention of the great Juan Manuel Fangio, who won the world title five times in the 1950s. Shortly before he died in 1995 he was asked by a German magazine for his opinion of Schumacher as a driver and his analysis is enlightening:

There are those who keep out of mischief, and there are the adventurers. We racing drivers are adventurers; the more difficult something is, the greater the attraction that comes from it. Michael Schumacher is one of the most talented among the adventurers. That was already clear to me relatively early on. While others – the Bergers, Mansells, or Alesi too, earlier in his career – drive relatively aggressively, so that they are often over the limit, Schumacher drives like a genuine champion – rounded, balanced, with amazing feel in his backside. His driving style allows him to continually reach the extreme areas without deliberately overshooting them.

It's difficult to say whether he's a real great. He is still so young. True greatness in motorsport only shows after some years. He still has much to learn. I was particularly struck by that after the collision he provoked with Ayrton Senna back then [French GP 1992]. You don't do things like that. Just like a real champion wouldn't carry on when the black flag has gone out, regardless of what his team manager's line on it might be [Schumacher did this at Silverstone in 1994 and was banned for three races].

> Michael Schumacher's character is set up in such a way that he sucks all this into himself, eager as he is to progress. And at some stage he will become even calmer, make even fewer mistakes.

And so it proved. Fangio's idea of racing drivers as adventurers is very attractive and had he lived to see all of Schumacher's career perhaps he would have felt that Schumacher had established himself as the sport's greatest adventurer by dint of the longevity of the challenge he set himself.

Schumacher's instinctive feel for the limit and his ability to drive around problems was a gift, but it could also have a downside for his team as Ross Brawn explains:

> One of the problems with Michael is that he has such great raw talent that he can drive around an imbalance. You have to be careful with that because you can do a change and he will compensate very quickly. He finds the limit straight away. He might be doing similar lap times, but it doesn't throw the changes into focus so you can go the wrong way. If the car is not set up properly he still manages to get a good lap time out of it. There is never the disparity with Michael between a car which is perfect and one which is not so good as you would get with other drivers. This is also a weakness because it makes the difference between a good car and an average car less discernible in testing and you can easily misread how competitive a car really is.
>
> You could go testing with Michael and Eddie Irvine and the gap between them when the car wasn't working properly would be huge, but as you get the car working the gap closes because Eddie benefits more from the car working properly. If you have a car that is not balanced properly, that is stepping out at the back, then Eddie

wouldn't like it, but Michael would still drive it on the limit. You have to understand this and recognize when you have a problem. In fairness to Michael, he'll tell you if the car isn't right. But if your driver is telling you that and yet you are fastest in the test, you don't perhaps take it on board as much as when you are halfway down the field. Eddie was a true barometer of where we were with the car.

Eddie Irvine was thus a vitally important element in the team too. With a driver of exceptional gifts such as Schumacher, it was always important to have a driver in the other car who would accurately reflect what the car was really doing.

The Ulsterman has painful personal experience of the dangers of the team listening only to Schumacher in testing and developing a car.

Sometimes that much natural talent can be a hindrance when you are testing small changes in a car. In 1997 he tested out the biggest aerodynamic step we'd ever had at Ferrari. He didn't like it and they put it back in the truck. I didn't test it then as he said it was awful, but I tested it the following week and went half a second faster.

It's not true about him being a great test driver, that's bullshit, he really isn't. I think you'll find that Rubens and I did a lot on that side. Michael has an amazing natural ability to get a car back to the finish line quicker than anyone. But his testing abilities are very limited. To start with at Ferrari he did all the testing and I did hardly any and it was probably the wrong decision, but who's going to believe Eddie Irvine over a two times world champion? As the years went on they realised it and I did more.

But despite the image he gained later in his career as a

workaholic, it was not always easy to get Schumacher to put the work in at tests in his early days in F1 with the Benetton team. He didn't see the point of it, according to Frank Dernie, a veteran engineer who worked closely with Schumacher at that time.

> I went to Benetton because Ross Brawn said to me, 'We've got this great driver who is so good he can drive around any problem, but he doesn't know how to set a car up,' so I basically trained Michael from 1992 right up to his first world championship in 1994.
>
> To start with all he wanted to know about was how much everyone was earning. I said to him, 'Forget money, this is a business where if you win races you'll earn loads of money but if you win nothing you'll earn nothing so let's concentrate on winning races.' In his first year you couldn't get him to test. Once he was a proper GP driver he thought testing was boring and he used to turn up at Silverstone late having flown out that morning. It took all of 1993 to get him to realise that doing the testing himself would help him in the race, rather than using the test driver's input. Frequently I would arrive at a race meeting in 1993 and we'd mention a new set-up or a development part we were going to use during our pre-briefing and Michael would say, 'I'm not using that, I haven't tried it yet,' and I'd say, 'Well we tested it at Silverstone but you didn't turn up.' He could be exasperating. It didn't come naturally to him to work hard in tests, it had to be beaten into him. But he's a quick learner and once he understood it there was no stopping him.

Alongside Dernie in those early Benetton days was Pat Symonds, who went on to be the engineering boss at Renault when the team won back-to-back world titles in 2005 and 2006. Symonds is the only top engineer who has worked closely with Senna, Schumacher and Alonso. He helped Dernie to mould the young Schumacher into the driver he became, but he admits that he was working with exceptional material.

He has a habit of pushing like mad on the first flying lap; one hundred per cent flat out. Then he'll spend the rest of the session driving at ninety-eight per cent and go around fine tuning the setup of the car until he has it to the point where with him at ninety-eight per cent it is going as quickly as it had earlier when he was at one hundred per cent. Then he knows he's made an improvement in the car. He does this a lot in testing.

Michael is very, very clever and always wants to maximise everything. He was the first driver of the modern era who had this incredible attention to detail, working on every single aspect of his game.

Schumacher himself sees this as a question of discipline. The boy who cried when his patron told him he had sold his kart because he hadn't taken care of it became a methodical perfectionist.

I'm a very disciplined person. I'm conscious of what you have to do to be a professional and as I know it, I do it. I don't leave anything to chance or think, 'Oh that doesn't matter.' Perhaps that is what makes the difference with the others. My belief is to do things properly. I want things to be perfect, one hundred per cent perfect. I have a goal and I am not happy with myself unless I attain it completely. It's what makes me happy. I get great pleasure from accomplishing things.

Although he worked hard to improve every area of his performance, fundamentally Schumacher's gift was that, regardless of how well the car was performing, he was able to drive every lap close to his own personal limit. One of the benefits of that was that he could always adapt to change. If the car started to slide or if it began raining he could cope with it and adapt, still driving on the limit, in a situation where many drivers would ease off.

Jochen Mass observed these qualities in Schumacher closely as his mentor in the Mercedes sportscar team and then as a television commentator for German network RTL in Schumacher's early F1 career. 'He has a tremendous feel for the car, which comes partly from his early days as a go kart racer, because he started very young, but also I think it is instinctive. His immense will power to learn has also helped him. Then there is his confidence. He won two world titles early on and that gives him a lot of additional, quiet confidence. One of his assets is that he knows who he is and if he thinks he can do well, he will.'

Schumacher was always at his happiest when he was on the limit, whether it be in a go kart or a Formula 1 car. Staying on the limit is about feeling when a car is breaking away from under you and making minute corrections of the wheel and the throttle to keep it there. One would imagine that along with balance and feel, lightning-fast reactions would be the other fundamental requirement, but according to Eddie Irvine, Schumacher is deficient in that area, but makes up for it in others.

My reaction time was faster than his. You might think that reactions would be a skill you'd need to be a top F1 driver

but it's a skill Michael doesn't need because he doesn't
have it!

That amazes people, but his real gift was his anticipation
of what was going to happen. I saw it once when they put
some straw bales on the straight at Jerez as a makeshift
chicane. I was standing down there with Gary Anderson
[one-time Jordan chief engineer] and you'd see the cars
coming up, they'd see the gap, then turn. Michael came up
and turned before he saw the gap because he knew that
by the time he got there it would be there. And he didn't
turn in as sharply so he turned earlier and a lot faster and
slid into where he knew the gap was going to be and Gary
and I looked at each other and went, 'The difference is
night and day!'

That is Michael's amazing talent. He didn't rely on his
reactions, because they are not there, I know that.

Irvine also believes that Schumacher's relatively slow reaction
time was responsible for one of the few weaknesses in his
game as a driver, namely his starts. Until Ferrari found the
ideal mechanism to suit him, Schumacher was not famed for
quick starts and he often gave away places in the early Ferrari
years off the start line.

Naturally when one thinks of Schumacher's exceptional
feel for a car one thinks of his performances in the rain, races
like Barcelona in 1996, his first win for Ferrari, where he was
able to stay closer to the limit than anyone. He won that race
by 45 seconds and it was one of his most staggering victories,
but he would argue that it was only when the conditions were
in the process of changing from dry to wet and the grip level
was going away rapidly, that he had an advantage over his
rivals. Once the track was properly wet it was the same for
everyone. 'I am always exceptional when there is a short

moment, in a surprise condition change, then I react obviously much better than others judging from my history. But if it is clear that it is a wet or dry situation the gap is not so big actually.'

He has been criticised on many occasions by Sir Jackie Stewart for going off the road a lot when finding the limit in practice. Stewart believes that the great champions of the past would never have done that, partly because it would have been insanely dangerous to exceed the limits so frequently. Rubens Barrichello, who raced with Schumacher at Ferrari, says the explanation for this was quite simple. 'Why did he spin a lot and go off the race track? Because he only knew how to drive the car on the limit. Which is a good and a bad thing, because you need to look after the car as well. A funny thing happened once at Magny-Cours, the tyres were going off after five laps [in performance terms] there was nothing you could do to manage them. Michael just didn't know how to go slowly, so he was completely destroyed in the race.'

Despite being always on the limit, in general Schumacher displayed great control at the wheel of a Formula 1 car. This is a critical and often overlooked point when assessing drivers. Speed is nothing without control and Schumacher had both. In comparisons with Senna it is often said that Senna was the faster racer, but that overlooks the fact that for the first five or six years of his F1 career he could be wildly out of control. By the time he won his third world championship in 1991 he was at the height of his powers, faster than anyone else and always in control, but Schumacher had that control at an earlier age, probably because he had more self-control generally as a person. Senna would get wound up, take a swing at other drivers, make outbursts in press conferences, whereas Schumacher never raised his voice and only once lost his self-control in public, that time at Spa in 1998 when he was convinced Coulthard had tried to 'kill' him.

Another of Schumacher's great strengths as a driver was his enormous ability to concentrate and through that, to be able to do two things at once. This meant that he was able to use perhaps 75 per cent of his mental capacity to drive the car on the limit while the other 25 per cent was available to think about how the race was unfolding or to take in information from the pits. Ross Brawn observes:

It's the capacity to multi-task which is astonishing. He would be driving a critical part of the race and you'd be having a discussion with him at the same time and you'd never see his lap times drop. I've had drivers who you could only talk to at certain parts of the lap otherwise the lap time would drop. The effort of accepting your input and then replying used to cost lap time. I never saw that with Michael.

I remember once in a critical part of a race he came on the radio and said his lap time on the pit board was wrong. We said it's correct. He said, 'I've just looked on the big screen and I've just done the fastest lap.' We said, 'No you haven't.'

It was his brother Ralf who had, but Michael had seen 'Schumacher' on the screen. He was always coming on the radio telling us about dark clouds and things. I've never driven a Grand Prix car so I don't know what it takes, but I've never had that kind of information from other drivers. That gives him an advantage because he is thinking about the race all the time. He thinks about the car, the tyres, he's the first one to turn the revs down on the engine when he can.

Sometimes though, he had lapses of concentration, like when he fell off in the lead at Indianapolis in 2000. Sometimes it became too easy and I had to get on the radio and say, 'Focus on what you are doing.' He was asking how his brother was doing and things like that.

Many of Schumacher's closest associates talk about his amazing powers of concentration. Schumacher himself says that when he focuses on something he gives it all of his attention and shuts everything else out. He admits that at home he can be reading an article in the paper and if his wife Corinna tries to talk to him he does not hear her, to her irritation.

Schumacher shares this ability to concentrate with many of the truly great drivers, according to Frank Dernie, who has a fascinating theory on the subject.

He has unbelievable concentration, he just does not get distracted. It's about personality types. In World War II they invented a test to find radar operators who could concentrate for long periods of time without taking what are known as 'involuntary rest pauses', or lapses of concentration to you or me. They found that there was a link between introvert and extrovert on that. The more introvert a personality you are, the longer you can concentrate. Many bus companies have found that all the accidents happen with extrovert drivers at the wheel so they do personality tests and choose introverts.

I have observed during my long career in motorsport that all the great drivers and multiple champions were introverts and I think that the greater levels of concentration are critical to that success. For me it all adds up. If you look at the great drivers, Prost, Senna, Fangio, Jim Clark, the two things that stand out are their intelligence and their concentration. You might think that Michael isn't an introvert because he leaps on the podium but as a man he is definitely an introvert, so was Senna, it's just that they are both very professional and worked hard at giving good interviews and playing their part in the show, but it didn't come naturally. People like Hakkinen and Raikkonen haven't bothered to try.

The other thing about him was that he was always looking to learn something new. That is vital because in this business a day when you learn nothing is a day wasted. I remember we had a test at Jerez in 1994 and there is a golf course next door and a lot of great golfers were there at the time and they wandered in to the track to have a look at the F1 cars, people like Jack Nicklaus, Seve Ballesteros and so on. Within two minutes Michael was going up to them and asking, 'Do you have any particular diet which helps with your preparation?' and 'Do you have any technique to help concentration?' and so on. He was sucking information out of them. And all of it was about getting the best out of yourself or your equipment, all the things you need to do. It was very noticeable.

* * *

One area of Schumacher's talent as a racing driver which is not always appreciated is his ability to overtake and, more importantly, his understanding of when not to.

Most of Schumacher's career took place during the era of refuelling stops in Formula 1, which were reintroduced in 1993. This made F1 races essentially a series of individual sprints punctuated by pit stops, so that race strategy became more important than overtaking, which is always risky. Teams work out a strategy, which gives them the best chance of passing the cars they are racing against in the pit stops rather than on the race-track.

Because he sought perfection and wanted to master everything, Schumacher drove to the maximum with this system and won many famous victories without actually having to pass a car on the track. But that doesn't mean that he wasn't brilliant at it. Fittingly in his final Grand Prix, at Interlagos in 2006, he was forced to fight his way through the field after a puncture early on dropped him back. In his final appearance racing a Formula 1 car he put in some truly memorable passes, including one which was loaded with significance, on his replacement at Ferrari, Kimi Raikkonen.

For the first two years of Schumacher's F1 career the rules stipulated no refuelling during pit stops, so the drivers pitted for fresh tyres only. Also the cars were far less reliable than they became in the late 1990s with the advance of quality control in the manufacturing process and so the drivers had to know when to push and when to conserve the car and tyres. Schumacher mastered both systems and got the maximum from them. Ross Brawn explains:

> He was a driver of the modern era. He never overtook anyone if he thought the race was going to evolve so he didn't have to, because overtaking is very risky; you can come off better or worse. In the same way, he would never overstress the car unless he had to. We would keep him informed and say, 'Michael you've got two laps until the pit stops, make sure you stay close to the guy in front, look after your tyres, have everything in place.' Normally because he was at the front of the field you were talking about having to make up one or two places to win a race, not cut through the field. So he was patient.

Sometimes he would make a bad start and I'd say, 'You've got to get past these guys otherwise we are not going to make up the time,' and he would have a go. But you know how hard it is to overtake in Formula 1 because a lot of the cars are so close together on performance. He can overtake when he needs to but he has a very measured approach. He would never overtake if he knew he was going to do it in the pits.

But when a pass needed to be made Schumacher was usually very strong and decisive, although he tended to be more cautious when dealing with certain people he had had an altercation with, like Jacques Villeneuve. He learned to master the art of overtaking in his karting days and he saw it as a blend of instinct, bravery and opportunity, but as with everything in Schumacher's game, there was always a plan behind it.

I prepare myself to attack and I know it's going to work. If you are fair, correct and decisive the others will respect you. I start from a simple principle; if I'm faster I overtake. If I'm slower I don't try.

Kamikaze attacks are not my style, in general I leave an escape route, so that in extremis I can put off the attack if, for example, I see that the other driver hasn't understood what's happening. But when I want to pass I'm clear; it's obvious and there is no risk of incomprehension. Obviously I know my adversaries, some are smart, others not so in control. You have to bear these things in mind.

Of course all overtakes are inherently risky and Schumacher had his fair share of passes that went wrong, with recriminations on both sides afterwards. Eddie Irvine had a very simple theory for dealing with his former team-mate.

He never tried any shit on me. If you look even when I was at Jaguar he stayed behind me once at Spa for seven or eight laps because he knew I wouldn't take any shit. Everyone says 'Michael pulled over on me or pushed me off here.' If you don't move your car he's going to have an accident and he won't do it again. And that's why I never understood these pricks with their complaining. Keep your car there, so he drives into you. If he drives into you he won't do it again, because he's fighting for the championship and you're not.

David Coulthard raced wheel to wheel with Schumacher on many occasions and sees him as a fair competitor in a straight one on one.

I feel safer going wheel to wheel with Michael than with someone like Takuma Sato, but you know that there is going to be some comeback, so you have to make the move stick. He is an instinctive racer. It has to be a decisive one move. You can't do a 'Shall I or shan't I?' slide up the inside.

He was very consistent throughout his career. Of course he was beatable, he couldn't walk on water. I remember Malaysia a few years back in turn two, I nipped down the inside of Michael, I caught him sleeping. We banged wheels. I so much wanted the move to stick, so I gave him the pain. When you pass someone like him you want to give them the pain too, 'Take that, you bastard!'

Schumacher's natural gifts were astonishing and in terms of pure talent there is little doubt that he is one of the fastest drivers ever to have graced Formula 1. But there is much more to winning in F1 than simply driving quickly. As the early Benetton stories reveal he was of course far from the finished article when he began his F1 career. It was only when he began to peel away the layers that he realised how much there was to this sport and therefore how many areas there were, apart from merely driving the car, to be exploited in his quest to become the best racing driver in the world.

CHAPTER SIX

How Schumacher worked

There are two Michael Schumachers. There is the one who is fighting against other drivers, who is hard and aggressive and tries not to show any weakness, then there is the Schumacher who is in the team, the really nice guy, the real team player, who loves the team spirit, likes to encourage people.

Ross Brawn, Ferrari technical director 1997–2006

Michael Schumacher was a born competitor and a born winner, but he could not have achieved his huge success without the help of others. Such is the nature of motorsport, which celebrates the individual but is really more about the quality of the team.

In the early days of his career he relied on various patrons to supply him with competitive equipment, but the results were largely of his own making. The further he climbed up the ladder the more his success depended on having the right people around him and the more he realised how important it was to take great care of them. No driver has ever been able to develop a team around him like Schumacher did and this was what elevated him beyond the level to which his enormous talent would naturally have taken him.

Schumacher also fully appreciated that in a tight competition, tiny details can make all the difference. This is something that so many talented F1 drivers have failed to recognise. By relying too much on the natural talent that has brought them to Formula 1 they fail to grow as Grand Prix drivers, because they do not explore all the avenues that could make them stronger. This is the second layer of what made Schumacher such a great driver – the work he did outside the cockpit to give himself the best possible chance of success.

Juan Manuel Fangio once said, 'You must always believe you will become the best, but you must never believe that you have done so.' Schumacher never stopped learning, never stopped trying to improve his skills, right up to his last day at the wheel of a Formula 1 car. He was a sponge for ideas, information, anything which might give him even the tiniest edge. He combined this with an increasing ruthlessness towards his opponents and a flat refusal to give anything away, a discipline which was to reach its highest expression in the later Ferrari years.

Jean Todt, Schumacher's boss at Ferrari and a close personal friend, believes that in order to be successful in the long term you have to truly understand what makes you successful. Schumacher had perhaps a greater understanding of what it takes to win than any driver before him. And he spelled it out in 2003:

First and foremost you have to respect the performance of even the smallest opponent. I watch a recording of every race that's run, and when I do that I don't just analyse the fight at the front but what's happening at the back of the field as well. A lot of positive things happen there as well as mistakes, and you can always learn from that. Meticulousness and discipline are two more things, because it is in fact in triumph that you have to look more carefully for your own weaknesses than in defeat.

And never think that success is down to your own performance alone. If you start, in a rush of exuberance, listening only to yourself and controlling everything yourself, you take the first step back towards the bottom. The flowers of victory belong in many vases. That's how it is in my case at least, with Jean Todt and Ross Brawn and the whole Ferrari team.

Success, and I have learned this in many areas from people I have met, never comes from one recipe. It's a big combination of many things which have to be together to be successful whatever area of sport or other business you want to be successful in.

And you have to protect yourself from the hype, from words like 'unbeatable'. If I were only to celebrate my own achievements then I wouldn't be self-critical any more and I wouldn't be successful any more. And success is more fun.

Schumacher won 91 Grands Prix, almost as many as Senna and Prost combined, but his objective was always more than just winning. 'I've always been more interested in the way I achieve victories rather than just to achieve them,' he says, and this was a crucial factor in his decision to join Ferrari in 1996, when they were in the doldrums and when he could have had his pick of the winning teams at the time.

That he chose to help rebuild Ferrari is probably

Schumacher's crowning achievement in a sporting sense. None of the drivers who carp at him for being unsporting would probably have taken on what appeared to be a hopeless challenge. Most would have taken the easy route and signed for the Williams team, which was unbeatable in 1996. Schumacher's decision goes a long way towards mitigating the negative effects of the accusations of unsporting behaviour which have always served to undermine his legacy. Initially his objective was to work closely with the team at Ferrari, to lift the team to a higher level and to close the gap on the dominant cars at the time. His willingness to accept this huge challenge when at that time Ferrari was by far the least successful of the top four teams in Formula 1, indicates Schumacher's appetite for hard work. And the more successful he became the harder he worked. He wrote in 2003:

> The more you get involved the more you understand your subject. Where before I was anxious or unsure at the start, now I know how to carry myself through whatever kind of problem it may be. If the driver is confident, it also influences the work of the team, their efficiency, their motivation. It's up to the driver to give the impetus, to be extremely precise and to push everyone in the right direction.
>
> I have the character trait of doing things as well as possible. It would not occur to me to mow threequarters of the lawn.

There are thousands of testimonials to Schumacher's prodigious work ethic from people who have worked with him. Two of the less well known are mechanics from Ferrari who sum up what they found when he began working with the team in 1996. The first is Paolo Scaramelli, who was once chief mechanic for Ferrari legend Gilles Villeneuve. 'He has the same methodical approach to work as Prost and Lauda,' he said in an interview with an Italian magazine in 1996. 'He has a great calmness about him because he is sure of himself, as champions always are.'

The second mechanic, Gianni Petterlini, worked very closely with Schumacher in his early Ferrari years and he tells a similar story. 'He's a complete perfectionist who likes to have everything just right and he lets you know about it. But always courteously, he never gets angry. Unlike the other drivers he takes obsessive care over the cockpit, he puts sponge everywhere to make himself comfortable when he's driving. Also with his pedals he is always looking for the perfect set-up.'

So many times Schumacher could be seen in intense discussion with mechanics and engineers, going through the finest points of detail about his car. Winning two world titles early in his F1 career gave him the confidence to trust his instincts and to push hard in pursuit of what he thought was important. It was vital for establishing his modus operandi. He asked a lot of his team, but he gave them a lot in return and they lined up behind him because it was clear that he represented their best chance of winning.

Although within the team he was always open to discussion and to new ways of doing things, he also had very firm ideas about what he wanted from his car and would never accept that something wasn't possible. He claims that he never raised his voice, but he could be totally immovable if he wanted something badly enough. Sabine Kehm says:

Getting into the car and driving was just the last step. He

needed to have the feeling that he had done everything he could have done in order to compete. He needed to feel that in order to make him calm, to make him able to really concentrate fully. He did not want to step out of the car and feel that there was something else he could have done differently and then exploited it better in the race. The quest for perfection was important to him. He was a sportsman who tried to exploit his technical abilities, but he also loved the competition, the fight. If it all came together he was completely joyful after the race.

The man who worked most closely with Schumacher throughout his career was Ross Brawn. He often uses the word 'weapon' to describe Schumacher and it is intriguing that he views Formula 1 as a type of war game. Certainly it explains the tough, uncompromising way he and the team approached the business of racing.

At Ferrari Jean Todt was clearly in charge of managing the team of people and giving them the resources they needed but Brawn saw himself very much as the general, especially at the race-tracks, deciding the tactics and wheeling out his most potent weapons when required. Some people have always liked to make out that Schumacher was the one really pulling the strings at Ferrari, but on close examination, that was not the case. Clearly without his consistent brilliance in the car the team would not have achieved the success it did, and he definitely worked very hard at building the team around him. But he did not run the team, nor make the day-to-day decisions, despite suggestions from the team's critics that he did.

I had many conversations with Ross about this subject over the years, but for the purposes of this book, I went to see him in Maranello a few weeks after Schumacher's final Grand Prix. I wanted to know what Schumacher did out of the cockpit over and above normal Grand Prix drivers, to learn more about how this shared mentality worked, what Schumacher's role within the management was and exactly where Schumacher's influence over decision making stopped.

Ross's office was very untidy, with boxes everywhere, shelves brimming over with fishing memorabilia. On his desk were piles of old racing magazines and a model of a Ferrari. Lining the walls were old wooden cupboards with boxes stacked on top, Italian wines and lots of books about them. A cricket bat rested against the wall. It was rather like visiting an English version of *MASH*'s Colonel Potter, except that with Ross the fishing flies are not in his hat, but on a board on the wall. Many racing factories are like operating theatres, uncluttered and clinical, but this was reassuringly human.

On the wall was a large photo of the podium from Budapest 1998, which was certainly one of Schumacher's most impressive wins, but as the most prominent of relatively few racing pictures, it was clearly Ross's favourite Schumacher victory too.

We began by talking about never giving anything away. Ross looks slightly away from you when talking, occasionally looking up to see if you are still with him. You are of course, because what he says is so interesting, but also because he has the rare gift for an engineer of being able to express complicated things in a very clear way. He was spelling out the modus operandi of the Ferrari inner sanctum:

Every last detail is critical. It's very rare in modern Formula 1 to come up with a dramatic new concept or idea which will give you a step-change in performance. So you cannot give anything away. You cannot be weak in the 'tangibles', like design of the car, and you cannot be weak in the 'intangibles' like the competitive attitude or interpretation of the rules.

You have to push everything to the limit. Unintentionally sometimes you go over the limit either in reliability or in interpretation of a regulation. You have to force the limits in all the areas and help everyone in the team realise that they have to reach limits. Each department has to be up against the boundaries of what it can achieve all the time. And by doing that you can get a competitive package, but it is not just about performance, it's reliability too, nothing must be too much trouble. Whatever you felt you could achieve you've then got to go out and find another ten per cent.

The good thing with Michael and Rory Byrne and myself and others is that we all knew that we had to do it and we knew the other guys were doing it, so that if you were not doing it you would be letting the side down. It was great to be a part of that mindset; you were part of a group where we were all giving absolutely everything.

It has often been suggested that Schumacher ran the Ferrari team, making key decisions about who his team-mate should be and which engineers to hire. Brawn denies this; in fact Schumacher's influence actually reduced in those areas once some important early appointments had been made, including Brawn and Byrne's own move from Benetton in late 1996. When Schumacher arrived at Ferrari as a double world champion in 1996 he knew that there would be work to do, but he discovered to his horror that the technical department fell some way short of what he was used to at Benetton.

Michael's role evolved a lot over the years. It was a pretty brave decision he took to come to Ferrari in 1996, because he didn't know the structure here. He was a bit frustrated that he couldn't see what steps were going to be taken to put the team on the right track. On the technical side he didn't feel that there was the planning foresight to go into the next years, which he was used to at Benetton. He realised that it needed strengthening.

So in the early stages he was pretty active in making sure that more people joined the team whom he knew and with whom he had empathy and whom he could trust to take care of their part of the business. No one knows whether, if they had continued with the team they had, they would have enjoyed the success they had. He didn't have that confidence, which may have been unfair, but he wanted people around him he knew could do it. He was active in getting myself and Rory to join. He was a very attractive proposition because we knew what a great driver he was. You knew he was never going to let you down.

He always stayed very close to the team in the eleven years he was here, was always very aware of everything the team was trying to do. He is very astute at giving his thoughts and ideas in the correct way through Jean, Rory or myself in a constructive way without destabilising the team.

He never had a management role, but was always involved in the direction of the team and giving an opinion to help take the team forward. But he's always been this fantastic foundation of driving talent that is so galvanising for a team and such a great catalyst for everyone to do their work. You know that this guy is going to take everything you give him and probably find a bit more on the track.

He loves speed, he's a speed junkie. But he also loves

competition, from the depths of winter when you are working hard trying to develop the car and give yourself the best equipment you can. Every aspect of F1 is a competition with other teams. He loved all of that and it's the aspect he'll miss the most.

Schumacher himself radiated leadership qualities, which inspired the men who worked with him, but he never saw himself as the team's leader – that was always Jean Todt. Once he had the people around him that he wanted, Schumacher had a clear notion of his place within that team and there is no suggestion from former colleagues that Schumacher was a disruptive influence. It was interesting in times of failure to note his reaction: he always expressed the view 'we win together, we lose together'. One might imagine that behind closed doors he would read the riot act to a poor mechanic who had put a wheel-nut on wrong but in fact that was never the case. 'It's no good shouting and pointing the finger of blame,' Schumacher maintained, 'it is much more important for someone who has made a mistake to recognise it. It's nothing to worry about, we all make mistakes. But it's vital that we don't make the same mistake twice. I have never been one to raise my voice, shouting is not my style, it never does any good.'

Perhaps the most vivid example of this attitude was at Suzuka in 2006 when Schumacher's engine failed while he was leading the race from championship rival Fernando Alonso. Had he won the race, he would have gone to the final event with a two-point lead over the Spaniard; instead the Suzuka blow-up virtually guaranteed that Schumacher would not retire as world champion and that the team would not win the constructors' championship. He trudged disappointedly back to the pits but when he got there he went around shaking hands with every single member of the team, which spoke volumes about his leadership style. As Williams engineering boss Patrick Head, never one of Schumacher's biggest fans, observed, 'We've had many drivers who have been world champions with our team, but I can't think of one of them who would have done that.'

* * *

Schumacher's career spanned a period of great technological development in Formula 1. One of the key changes affecting drivers was the increasing sophistication of the computing tools available to analyse what the car was doing on the track. This meant that the engineers already had a thorough understanding of a car's behaviour even before they heard from the driver. In many cases this lessened the driver's influence, but Schumacher, despite Eddie Irvine's assertion that his ability as a test driver was overrated, took a keen interest in the new technologies as they emerged and was always looking for ways in which they could be harnessed to give him an extra little advantage over the opposition. Brawn explains:

> The analysis of the car out on track has improved a lot. Technically on a detail level Michael probably had to give more analysis and opinion in 1996 whereas now, the tools we have developed to analyse the behaviour and performance of the car are so good that the drivers want to look at them before they give you an opinion!
> In the old days the driver had to record every detail in his memory of each corner and how the tyres were evolving,

that's a huge amount of information to remember accurately. It's quite a task along with driving the car. Now we've relieved them of that so they can focus on driving the car.

They have a screen which drops down in front of them when they come back to the garage and the engineers can point out to them what's going on. Michael has been extremely competent on that side and has been able to contribute and look at data and understand what is happening.

He has strong opinions but if he can see that you have a firm conviction about something, then he'll go with your view. I think a lot of the time he was strong just to make sure you've thought through your side as well. He didn't want to run the car, he knew that the engineers and myself ran it. He wanted to concentrate on driving it. I've never known him get petulant and say 'Let's do it my way.' In fact he's always been very easy to work with in that respect.

Schumacher was able to process data very efficiently, even under extreme pressure. One of the FIA's senior race officials told me in 2006 about a burst of radio traffic he had listened to during a Grand Prix, where Schumacher was asking questions, like what the time of Alonso's in-lap to the pits had been and how much fuel he had taken on board at a pit stop – he talked all the time, demanding information. But he would also describe what his own car was doing to his engineers, asking for solutions, such as 'It's understeering in turn six, oversteering in turn eight' and so on. A few minutes later his engineer, Chris Dyer, would come on to the radio and say, 'Okay, Michael, for turn six traction control programme 5 setting 2.6, for turn eight programme 3 at 1.5' – things most people would struggle to write down, let alone compute while driving at 200 miles an hour. Schumacher would process the information and then you would see him on the on-board cameras, making the adjustments the engineers had proposed.

This illustrates his unusual ability to concentrate effectively on more than one thing at a time. Brawn was able to use this gift of Schumacher's to great effect, setting out challenging race strategies for him to follow. Sometimes, as in Budapest in 1998, he would feel that a strategy was not working and that a change was needed. Schumacher always rose to the occasion at moments like that.

That Budapest race is one of my favourites among Schumacher's 91 victories. I was in the Ferrari garage throughout the race and once it became clear what Brawn was asking Schumacher to do, it was fascinating to watch the champion rise to the occasion. This was the race where, tucked up behind the McLarens driven by Mika Hakkinen and David Coulthard, Schumacher had no chance to win without a change in tactics. So Ross Brawn switched him from a two- to a three-stop strategy to give him a clear track to drive on and then asked his driver to find 25 seconds in 19 laps. This meant finding the time within himself, maintaining a pace far faster than anything the other drivers could manage. Schumacher pulled it off brilliantly.

The key to the plan's success was Schumacher's ability to run fast laps consistently, which is the holy grail of modern F1 in the refuelling era. Most drivers like to settle into a rhythm and work to a plan, but Schumacher's ability to extend himself for a period of ten or even 15 laps gave Brawn the chance to be adventurous. All he had to do was find Michael some clear track where he would not be held up by other cars.

It helped that in those days McLaren were quite conservative and predictable in their use of race strategy. When Schumacher came in on lap 43 for his second fuel stop and took on a very light load, it was clear to everyone that he was making the switch and would have to stop again. And yet McLaren stuck with their original plan and a lap later sent Coulthard out with enough fuel to finish the 77-lap race. But as the Scotsman was toiling with a heavy car, Schumacher was reeling off laps up to two seconds faster. It was mesmerising to watch as the pendulum swung away from McLaren, who had controlled the first half of the race, and towards Ferrari. Schumacher was in another world, revelling in the thrill of driving at the absolute limit for a period of 25 minutes. It was like a middle distance runner doing a couple of kilometres at sprint pace.

Schumacher was ecstatic afterwards. This was his idea of a perfect race, a team performance of brilliance and ingenuity, with him at the centre of it, being given a tough challenge and rising to it.

Ross looks up from the table to the photograph of Schumacher deliriously celebrating victory in Budapest and smiles.

Michael is intimidating for other people. They were all scared of him. If you gave him the opportunity of a free track then they all started to panic a bit because they had seen it many times before and they didn't know what to do.

When I've done it with other drivers, given them an opportunity, it's not worked. With Michael if the tyres or car aren't up to it, then it might not work, but it won't be because of him. We had a couple of races where he was very fast in qualifying but he was impotent at certain stages of the race because the tyre performance went away. The limit was the tyre performance not the driver or the car. He couldn't do a lot.

If the tyres and car hold up, he'll give you what's possible all the time. Also he liked being given a challenge, he loves to step up to a challenge. Then he wins a race he shouldn't have won and he makes the guys on the pit wall look good!

Schumacher used his power and influence within the team in a constructive way, for the good of the whole team. But there is one area where it has always been suspected that he pulled strings for his own benefit and that is in the matter of team-mate selection. It has often been commented on that Schumacher never had a team-mate who was on his level. Alain Prost, reputedly another arch schemer, had to share his team at various times with Ayrton Senna and Nigel Mansell, whereas Schumacher avoided such competition completely and so took all the glory. Moreover there are many examples of the Ferrari team asking Schumacher's team-mate to move over and let him through, which made it look as though the whole team was working only for him. This requires close analysis because it is another key area in which the accusation that he was unsporting is frequently made.

At both Benetton and Ferrari, Ross Brawn had a say in who the drivers should be, but ultimately it was not his decision and he claims that it was not Schumacher's decision either.

I cannot recall Michael ever saying to me 'I don't want that guy in the car because he's too good.' He had certain people whom he didn't like or who he thought would damage the atmosphere in the team. He loved working

111

with Felipe Massa because Felipe's attitude was very positive and he wanted to work for the good of the team. But he gave Michael a hard time at a number of races. If Michael had concerns with other drivers it was more to do with their attitude rather than whether they were quick or not. He didn't like the idea that this unity he was striving to create within the team could be spoiled by someone coming in and taking the wrong approach. He was worried about having a team-mate who would not fit in.

Jean Todt was quite explicit. 'Michael never asked to have a slower driver than him in the other car. He demanded only that he should have special attention, as it is right that he should. All of us however have to think of the interests of Ferrari. Schumacher and I *are* employees of Ferrari and we *have* to want what is best for Ferrari.'

Todt's attitude was that the team was investing a great deal of money in employing Schumacher, who in turn invested a great deal of effort in trying to beat the opposition, perhaps more than any other driver before or since. Schumacher justified his salary by being consistently faster than his team-mates and by so doing he also proved that he represented Ferrari's best chance of success. So Todt swung the odds in his favour whenever they needed swinging, by making sure that his team-mate gave way to him on the race-track.

Psychologically this is hard for a competitive individual to accept, but beyond that there was no logical reason why Ferrari would want to slow down any of Schumacher's team-mates. Had any of them proved to be consistently faster than Schumacher the team would almost certainly have revised its strategy. But Schumacher's gift was to stack the odds in his favour, as Rubens Barrichello found when he joined Ferrari in 2000. Despite his contract saying nothing about the spare car always being assigned to Schumacher, he found that it was.

Schumacher always disliked being quizzed about the calibre of his team-mates. In an interview with *F1 Racing* in 1999 he said:

I have never had a driver alongside me who didn't initially have the opportunity to beat me and be equal. And it's my philosophy that whoever is the faster driver should be supported by the team, because that's the best way for the championship. And that's what I brought to Ferrari. You saw me helping Eddie Irvine in Malaysia [in 1999] for the championship because that fits with my philosophy. So it's not that I slow my team-mates down by telling the team 'You cannot give him the same fast material' but because I'm faster ninety-five per cent of the time it looks like my team-mates are not treated equally. I remember Johnny Herbert criticising Benetton [in 1995] very heavily for not treating him equally and that was really unfair. I mean he really got the same opportunities with the car, but he didn't use them.

People outside always want to see it as though I slow my team-mates down, but I don't know why they see it that way. Believe me, neither Ferrari nor Benetton have tried to make my team-mates slower. They want to have the two best cars at the end of the day. Naturally there is some difference between human abilities.

Eddie Irvine was Schumacher's team-mate for four seasons at Ferrari during which time he was asked to move over a few times and on several other occasions he moved over before he was called because he knew the call was coming. He claims that although it was made clear to him that he was the number two driver and that Ferrari's priority was to get Schumacher to the championship, that still left him some room for manoeuvre. He recalls:

> I went there to try to beat him, I wasn't there to be his number two. I interpreted it that my job was to hand the race to him and I was happy with that. It was explicit [in his contract], but my attitude was, if I handed him every race they would say, 'Hang on, Eddie should be the number one.' It didn't turn out that way of course.
>
> Why did he need it that way? He went there as number one, he was a two times world champion. It was all set up for Michael to win the championship for them. If I had come in and upset the apple cart I think Todt would have said, 'Shit we have got ourselves a bargain!'
>
> The negative side of the Schumacher effect was that the guy blows everyone away. Michael always made his team-mate's mistakes very visible. Herbert was good in all formulas and was quicker than Hakkinen when they were at Lotus. Martin Brundle did a fantastic job at Jordan, but these guys were nowhere compared with Michael.
>
> One fallacy is that Michael was always given the best equipment and his team-mate got second best. That's rubbish; the guy who's fastest gets the best and it's no different at other teams. There's no use bitching and moaning about it, hats off to Michael. But building a team around a single driver can be counter-productive. I felt people were sometimes reluctant to contradict Michael in case they upset him. There were few people with the balls to argue with him.

Irvine's point about the fastest driver getting the priority treatment is very important. If one considers top drivers in teams other than Ferrari who have been involved in fighting for a championship, inevitably there comes a time in the closing stages of the season, as the pressure builds, when they appeal to the team for its full support. Fernando Alonso certainly did that with Renault in 2006, criticising his team after the Chinese Grand Prix for not putting the needs of team-mate Giancarlo Fisichella second during a crucial part of the race. He behaved similarly when confronted by Lewis Hamilton the following year at McLaren. Many top drivers were critical of the way Ferrari was set up around Schumacher and found it unfair, but they all wanted the same thing, as any serious racing driver would. The difference was that Schumacher got himself into a position to demand – and to get – what he wanted. Schumacher always felt that the criticism he received from his fellow professionals was motivated by jealousy and this is certainly one area where drivers were jealous of his status. Says Rubens Barrichello, his team-mate at Ferrari from 2000 to 2005:

> The only way to beat Michael was to beat him in qualifying because otherwise your weekend was over, unless he had a problem in the race which he never did. But for me he was the most vulnerable team-mate I ever had. If I went well you could see him going down big time. And that was the bad thing. The people around him recognised that because they could pull him up. It made a big impression to see how much he could change from one day to the other. And the importance of those people like Ross and Jean is not to be underestimated.
>
> Michael was the most powerful driver. But speed for speed, I'm not sure he was the best guy, because there were others, including myself. But it was the whole environment, his room was bigger, he had the spare car. With that you understand psychologically that you have

something else. I'm not saying that makes the difference
but when you start adding things . . .

* * *

Another critical part of Schumacher's success was his
scientific approach to fitness. In this he was way ahead of his
benchmark driver, Ayrton Senna. Senna admitted shortly
before he died in 1994 that he struggled with the intensity of
the new system of racing brought about by the reintroduction
of refuelling at pit stops. Suddenly, instead of trundling
around in a car loaded up with 160 kilos of fuel, the drivers
were splitting the race into three sprint races, carrying a
maximum of 50 to 60 kilos at any one time. This alone made
the cars three seconds per lap faster, which put a much greater
physical and mental strain on the drivers. Add to that the
amazing stopping power of carbon brakes and the extra
cornering forces generated by the ever improving aerodynamics and suddenly it became commonplace for a driver to
experience lateral g forces of four or five times his own
bodyweight several times every lap and vertical ones at most
of the major braking zones. This made the business of driving
a Grand Prix car a very stern physical test. And during 90
minutes of racing, fatigue would set in.

Having a very high level of fitness also meant that a driver
could maintain concentration for longer and because he was
not at his own personal limit all the time just to drive the car,
there would be some spare mental capacity to think about the
race. This would often make the difference in a marginal race
when there was little to choose between the performance of
two cars.

Schumacher was the perfect driver for the 'refuelling era' of Formula 1. He had enjoyed a high level of fitness since his karting days, apart from some damage to a knee through overtraining which did become a problem as it would flare up from time to time, restricting his ability to train. Indeed he cited knee problems when he was testing in preparation for his return to the cockpit after breaking his leg in 1999.

Michael worked methodically on his fitness, tailoring it to fulfil all the demands made on him by the races. When he was doing a race simulation in testing, for example, he would get his trainer to take a blood sample from him during a pit stop so that scientists could analyse how his body was coping with the stresses of being on the limit for long periods. He worked closely with the sports clinic at Bad Nauheim in Germany. In 2006 an assessment indicated that despite being 37, he had the fitness level of a 25-year-old.

During his racing career the clinic appointed two physiotherapists to look after Schumacher so that one of them could be with him all the time, whether he was at a race, a test, a promotional day or at home with his family. He made an arrangement with a company called Technogym to provide a mobile gym at all the tests so that when he had finished testing and debriefing he could do a couple of hours of training in the evening.

For anyone interested in trying to emulate him, his fitness programme was to train six times a week, a regime that included several hours a day on a bike, gym work with light weights with lots of repetitions, and some practice on a climbing wall each week, to build up strength and stamina. After all that he would play football either with his local team in Switzerland or with a team of drivers and ex-pros at Grand Prix weekends.

Schumacher always looked spectacularly fit. To see him close up, with his skin drawn tight around his jawbone, he looked more like a racehorse than a racing driver. This had the added advantage that he radiated confidence, which would sap the confidence of his rivals, all of whom were told by their team bosses that they needed to work harder on their fitness, like all areas of their game, to match Michael Schumacher.

CHAPTER SEVEN

The constant little hurdles

Let me tell you something about Michael Schumacher. He is a man who spends every waking hour looking for ways to crush his opponents into the ground.

Norbert Haug, Vice President Mercedes Motorsport

So far it is clear that Schumacher's genius behind the wheel, allied to his prodigious work ethic and team-building skills, made him a tough opponent to beat. But was there more to him even than that? According to his rivals there most certainly was an untold part of Schumacher's game plan. He was accused of using his and Ferrari's power and influence within the sport to stay one step ahead of his rivals.

Schumacher undoubtedly used his role as a director within the Grand Prix Drivers Association to make the sport safer for his fellow drivers. But he also used it as a platform to lobby the governing body. Some people would say that this is merely the prerogative of the dominant beast in the jungle, which Schumacher undoubtedly was from Senna's death in 1994 until his own retirement in 2006. But for the opposition it felt as though they weren't just fighting against another team and driver, but against a system they could not beat.

Renault and Fernando Alonso felt this way, especially during the hard-fought campaign in 2006. At the end of the season, engine boss Denis Chevrier said, 'This battle with Ferrari was not honest,' while Alonso went further.

At the Italian Grand Prix in Monza, Alonso was given a ten-place grid penalty by the stewards for 'blocking' Ferrari's Felipe Massa in qualifying. With the world championship finely balanced, such a big decision, which could affect the outcome of the championship, was intensely scrutinised by the governing body and the media alike.

What had happened was this: in the closing minutes of qualifying, Alonso had suffered bodywork damage in an incident and had had to make a visit to the pits before his final run. Back out on track, he was in a hurry to make it across the line to start his qualifying lap before the chequered flag came out. Massa was on his flying lap and was a few hundred metres behind him as they hurtled down the back straight. Through the final Parabolica corner, Massa complained that his car's handling was affected by the dirty air from Alonso's car, costing him perhaps a couple of tenths of a second. But Alonso was clearly not 'blocking' Massa, he was making every effort to get around to the start line as quickly as possible. But Ferrari sensed an opportunity and put in a protest and the stewards abandoned common sense and upheld the complaint. They moved Alonso back ten places on the grid, wrecking his chances of victory and greatly improving Schumacher's. It was impossible to find anyone, not employed by either the FIA or Ferrari, who backed the decision.

Even Max Mosley, the FIA president, says that he struggled to justify the penalty.

I thought it was wrong. I suppose I can say this now, but I went to the stewards on Saturday evening and said, 'I think that is very hard to justify, will you reconsider it?' and they sat down again on Sunday morning and went through the whole thing. Charlie [Whiting, the FIA race director] took the opposite view. He thought that it was right. It was nothing to do with helping Ferrari. Did he or did he not destabilise the car? Should he or should he not have given Massa precedence? It was a combination of Alonso and Renault's fault that this situation arose. So why should poor little Massa suffer? But still I thought that in the cut-and-thrust of racing and at that stage in the championship, it didn't seem fair to me.

I have to be very careful because I appoint the stewards, but I would never use that and say to them, 'Change this.' I would hope that they wouldn't listen to me anyway. But I did feel entitled to ask them to look at it again.

Alonso was livid. He held a press conference hours before the race at which he famously stated that he could 'no longer consider F1 a sport'. He wanted to fight Schumacher and his team on the track but felt that Ferrari had an advantage due to their supposed 'special relationship' with the FIA, which meant that the competition was unbalanced.

Mark Webber, like most of the other drivers, was dismayed by what had happened to Alonso in Italy and spoke to Schumacher about it during the drivers' parade lap before the race. 'When Fernando got that penalty, I said to Michael, "Why did Ferrari protest? For what's at stake here, Fernando got a puncture, he damaged his bodywork then he was on his out-lap going as quick as he could go, doing his best, even gave Massa a bit of a tow on the straight. Can't you take the whole thing in context, give a half a per cent?" Michael said, "You don't see it from the outside, you just don't see it," and this is what you were up against.'

In the office of race director Charlie Whiting on that Saturday afternoon in Monza, Alonso showed his frustration. He is alleged to have kicked a waste-paper basket across the floor and shouted, 'I know you are trying to take the world championship away from me, but I'm going to fucking well win it anyway.' After the weekend Alonso went on Spanish radio station Marca and said, 'Michael is the man with the most sanctions and the most anti-sporting driver in the history of Formula 1. That doesn't take away from the fact that he has been the best driver and it has been an honour and a pleasure to battle against him.' Then, referring to Schumacher's impending retirement, he added, 'Things will be more equal now.'

Schumacher took the view that Formula 1 is a tough, ruthless business and that to win you have to press home your competitive advantage at every opportunity. Sometimes he would overstep the mark, but who is the arbiter of where the mark is drawn? Is it the FIA, the fans, the media or the other drivers? Some would argue that he was such a good driver that he didn't need to go to such extremes because he would probably have won anyway. But Schumacher was incapable of leaving anything to chance. If there was an opportunity to strike, it must be taken.

In his early years with the Benetton F1 team, he regularly found himself on the wrong side of the FIA, which was intensely uncomfortable for him. But when he joined Ferrari, this relationship was encouraged to flourish. The team has a long history of being at the centre of power in F1 and Schumacher came to understand how valued the views of a multiple world champion were. Mosley got to know Schumacher well when they spent time together on the road working for the FIA's road safety campaign.

Initially Schumacher's participation in this cause was forced on him, as part of the penalty for his collision with Jacques Villeneuve at Jerez in 1997. He was sentenced to seven days 'community service', or voluntary work for the FIA. But when his sentence was served, Schumacher voluntarily continued the work and this cemented a close bond with Mosley, with whom he would travel to various European capital cities. Behind the scenes, Ferrari boss Jean Todt helped to foster the relationship. He had long been on very good terms with Mosley and he skilfully pushed the two men closer together. Mosley says:

> Jean Todt has many talents but his greatest single talent is human relations. When you have someone reticent or shy, as I am, then what Todt does is quite positive. I would be reluctant to call up Michael and say, 'I'm going to be in Geneva, do you want to come and have dinner?' because I feel I'm disturbing people. But Todt said to me, 'If you want to invite him then just call him up; if he doesn't want to go he won't go.' So then we ended up having quiet dinners together. And that was very helpful to me because when I want to talk about things like driver aids [traction control, ABS etc] or what really goes on when they are driving the car, you get a really intelligent answer. I realise that he is a racing driver and he wants to win the championship so he has an axe to grind. But you can learn so much from someone intelligent who is currently driving the cars.

But some rival drivers saw this as a very exclusive club and one from which, rightly or wrongly, they felt excluded. Mark

Webber worked closely with Schumacher on the GPDA and had the opportunity to watch him operate at close quarters. He was dismayed to find the degree to which the great champion was working the system, as he saw it. He felt that it was time that the story was told from the perspective of the other drivers, those trying to compete with Schumacher.

When I first started racing Formula Ford in 1994 he was winning the world championship. In the Webber household Schumacher was the man. My dad loved him, I loved him. He put the cat among the pigeons. All the big guys, Prost, Senna, Mansell, they had a bit on trying to handle him. He was very impressive straight off. There was that real excitement on the podium, which was great to see.

He was golden bollocks in my view. I arrived in Formula 1 in 2002 and finished fifth on my debut in a Minardi in the Australian Grand Prix. Quite quickly I started to realise how clever he is and how clever the whole Ferrari juggernaut is. He had won the race but he knew that the story that day was Minardi and me so he came down and was photographed with me and I thought, 'Bloody hell, I don't know this bloke from Adam,' but then I wondered how cheesy and false it was. Was it genuine or was it really slick?

A couple of races later in Brazil we were in the gym and he came up to me and started asking questions about the first few races from my perspective. When he talks to you he wants to get as many answers out of you as possible with him giving nothing away. If you can keep the ratio to ten to five in his favour you are doing well. You learn that he is very clever in terms of discussions. We struck up quite a sensible relationship during my Jaguar years and then he asked me to be on the Grand Prix Drivers Association.

The closer you get to how he ticks and how the Ferrari

thing is controlled it's amazing, but I guess it also showed some of my own naivety at this early stage of my career at this level. Ferrari had no success for so long then he came along and they ended up dominating the sport to such an extent that he could drive one-handed and win Grands Prix. That was when I started to wonder if the widely held public belief of there being a special relationship between the FIA and Ferrari was true. And if it was, it was hard for the real F1 fan in me, the purist if you like, to take.

I was disappointed that there were lots of consistent small things that just put hurdles in front of the opposition and that pissed me and a lot of other people off quite a lot, things like the ban on Michelin's front tyre in 2003. [At a critical stage of the championship with three races to go the FIA ruled that Michelin's front tyres, which they had been using for over a year, were illegal because when the tread wore down the contact patch of the tyre was wider than the regulations allowed. Michelin argued that if the tyres were checked before running they were legal, but the FIA said that they were illegal once they were running on the track.]

If these views on Ferrari and the FIA were true, they [the hurdles] are brilliantly disturbing bombs. Yes, it's a big business, yes, it's political but come on let's try to make it as fair as we can.

Of course the impression was that Williams and McLaren weren't party to the kind of relationship it is said Ferrari and the FIA enjoyed. It was a message to everyone else and we were left thinking, 'What are we up against here?' So when I saw that side of it, he lost some brownie points for me.

Max Mosley totally refutes the suggestion that there was a 'firm' putting up hurdles to the opposition:

There is a tendency to see something unfair in this business. But no way in the world [is it true]. The penalties [and decisions] are the cut and thrust of life. I think they are jealous of him, it's all nonsense and we would never ever favour someone. Back in 2004 if we could have found a way to slow him down we would have done.

Todt got them [Ferrari] all working together. It is a completely cohesive unit. What he has succeeded in doing there is quite extraordinary. Everywhere he's been he's won and that's because he is an absolutely outstanding manager. I reckon you could have put Todt in the last five years in any of the top five teams and you'd have had the same result.

'Of course the FIA will always deny it but Michael was like "teacher's pet",' says Webber. 'But you couldn't get at it to fight against it. It was nearly unfair, but this is why the drivers felt disappointed with him a lot of the time.'

Max Mosley laughs at the suggestion that Schumacher was 'teacher's pet'.

I can see that, but it's a little bit like some of the teams saying, 'You are too close to Ferrari.' It's because Ferrari talk to me. I never fail to take a call from a driver or return one if I'm busy. Same is true of the team principals. If they don't have contact it's because they don't bother. Jean Todt does bother. I have relationships going back a long way. I've known [Ferrari president Luca di] Montezemolo since the early 1970s. Frank Williams and I go back even further, I did my first deal with him in the 1960s. So I have that kind of relationship with Frank. I don't know Ron Dennis as well, but contrary to popular opinion I get on quite well with him. But he doesn't pick the phone up and I don't feel I have to chase after him. The last thing Alonso wants is me ringing him up and saying, 'Do you want to come for a coffee?' But if Alonso rang me up, or any of them, and said, 'Can I come and see you?' then it's an open door.

Another example Webber cites as having created this climate of suspicion is the track resurfacing at Monza in 2006, which caught all the Michelin teams out as they had not been informed that the surface had been replaced. The surface of the tarmac – its abrasiveness and its levels of grip – is pretty fundamental to the choice of products a tyre company will bring to a race meeting. Bridgestone, who supplied Ferrari, claimed they did not know about the resurfacing either, but Webber is nevertheless suspicious. If they did, it would have given Bridgestone a small head start and meant that the Michelin teams were playing catch-up. 'I'd be astonished if Ferrari didn't know about any adjustments made to the track surface a few weeks before the Italian Grand Prix,' laughs Webber. 'Do you mean to tell me that you can resurface a track in Italy without Ferrari knowing about it? Michelin turned up with their compounds and bang. It's a small thing, but at the same time it's massive. Crafty? Cute? Maybe. But was it fair?'

The subject of favouritism is a very touchy one for the sport and for Ferrari in particular. There is no question that the team has, historically, always sided with the governing body on big decisions. And it has never been afraid to do what it feels is in the best interests of Ferrari, rather than the interests of the sport. To complicate the picture still further, the final few years of Schumacher's Ferrari career coincided with a political and commercial power struggle behind the scenes between the manufacturers on the one side and the governing body and Bernie Ecclestone on the other. The manufacturers wanted to use their collective might to change the way the sport was run, both politically and commercially. They felt that Ecclestone should give the teams a higher percentage of the commercial revenues and that the governing body should be more transparent in the way it governed the sport. Initially Ferrari was on the side of the manufacturers in this dispute.

They formed a body called Grand Prix World Championship and threatened to start their own racing series in competition with F1 if their demands were not satisfied. It was a protracted battle and one of the key stages along the way was when Ferrari broke ranks from the manufacturers and unilaterally signed up with Ecclestone and the FIA in January 2005. The team received $100 million as a golden hello, while Jean Todt explained that Ferrari had to do what was in the best interests of Ferrari. This action polarised the sport, with Ferrari on one side and all the other manufacturers and teams on the other, but it was the tipping point because Ferrari, as the longest serving and most recognisable team in the sport, was the team both sides needed to have a viable racing series. Once Ecclestone and Mosley had Ferrari on board, their grip on the sport was reasserted and it was no longer possible for the manufacturers to consider their own series.

There has long been great suspicion among rival teams of the relationship between Ferrari and the FIA. In the late 1990s, when Ferrari and Schumacher were trying very hard to catch up with the dominant McLaren-Mercedes cars, the Anglo-German team suspected that Ferrari was getting away with using illegal traction control and illegal aerodynamic devices. Nothing was ever proven, but a great deal of speculation was

voiced in the media. Ferrari's rivals believe that many
decisions taken by the FIA during Ferrari's Jean Todt era have
favoured his team, rather than gone against it.

Countering that argument were some major rule changes
which caught Ferrari out in 2003 and 2005 and of course the
heavy penalties meted out for Ferrari's team orders fiasco in
Austria in 2002 and for Schumacher's indiscretion at Monaco
in 2006.

Ross Brawn laughs at the suggestion that the FIA colluded
with Ferrari.

> It was always a joke that FIA stood for 'Ferrari International
> Aid', but all the rule changes that happened over the past
> few years were never to our benefit. The rule change for a
> one-race tyre in 2005 was probably the worst thing that
> could have happened to us. If you look back at 2004 we
> had very aggressive tyres and strategies. We had a four
> stop race at Magny-Cours. The Bridgestones were not
> built to do a whole race distance.
>
> We didn't have a car and tyres that were competitive in
> 2005 and a lot of that was down to the regulation changes.

Webber's respect for Schumacher may have diminished
slightly through a deeper understanding of his methods, but
he is still in awe of his grasp of the sport. He appears
convinced that the Monaco incident was a deliberate act.

> What he created at Ferrari was a motivational marvel, a lot
> of it was down to him. He's an absolute control freak, he
> controls everything, he is so similar to Lance Armstrong.
> They are so clever and they look at every little detail of how
> to get an advantage. The gears spin in his head, like
> Monaco in 2006 qualifying, he stuffed up the second
> sector so he blocks the track in the final corner. A lot of

guys might think of it, but they wouldn't go through with it.

We had done our first runs and he knew we were all going to go quicker again. He knew his pole was very provisional and he could end up fifth on the grid if he didn't find another three tenths of a second. He was on a lap that was not fast enough. In his mind he thought that he hadn't done enough. I was faster, Kimi was quick, Alonso was going to get pole. He knew it was very tight. There is no question about what happened. He took a totally different line, but he fucked it up. Because he is such a team player he didn't want to bend the car because he was thinking of his boys. But we don't practise that kind of thing and it is not easy to do.

When you are in the heat of competition you do things which are sometimes over the edge, I'd be the first to admit it. That's what happens in sport, it's all adrenaline, it's unpredictable. If it was all processional and predictable we wouldn't watch it – look at Zidane in the World Cup finals and so on. There are negative points against many great sportsmen, sometimes they do things which are . . . disappointing. Schumacher did some things which changed my view of him. I probably know of only five per cent of what went on. But that is what they did to get things done.

Don't get me wrong, I'm a huge sports fan and there's no jealousy here. I think he drove some incredible races and to have him racing was amazing. But I was disappointed. And I struggled to stick up for him for as long as I did; people were shooting me down and I stuck up for him for a long time.

I remember once I was giving a talk in a hospitality bus at Silverstone during a test and Michael came round in the Ferrari. The people on the bus were going, 'Ah there's Schumacher, what a wanker,' and all that kind of thing and

I said, 'No, look guys, this guy is doing a hundred laps a day, this is the graft that makes him special. You've got to give him credit.'

He still took huge risks at the end. He had his family, massive security and all that but he had some huge shunts, like when he had a tyre failure at Monza [a 220mph accident during testing in 2004] and for him to be on it like that until the end, that is special, he was a very special driver.

Schumacher built relationships with the other drivers to the degree which suited him and his purposes, but he had few close friends among them, particularly in his later career. Earlier on, Jos Verstappen and Jean Alesi were reasonably close to him, but Schumacher is the first to admit that he is not an easy person to get to know.

I have to admit, it's certainly very difficult to get to know me properly. That takes time. I struggle to open myself up immediately, I can only do that when I really know people, and I'm certainly a rather distant guy. I can't pretend someone is my best friend when that's just not the case. I have a healthy scepticism – that's my general attitude. Admittedly it has been strengthened by certain events in my life. Formula 1 has certainly left its mark on me in this respect, too. The dilemma was: I was alone, and on the other side there were hundreds of journalists writing about me, who were supposed to report about me. Not all of them could know me, of course, particularly since I actually had other things to do at a race weekend and was therefore hardly reachable.

Shortly after his retirement his friend Jean Todt spoke out about Michael's character and the difficulties he faced in an environment like Formula 1. 'Even if Michael has learnt to make himself bullet-proof in order to defend himself against attacks from this high-pressure mini-society, he still remains a sensitive young man who sets store by other's judgements – even if others may believe exactly the opposite . . . He was sent out into the jungle of life at a young age and has learnt not to reveal himself unnecessarily. The so-called arrogance is a self-defence mechanism.'

Mark Webber trod the same path as Schumacher for five seasons and for a while had a warm relationship with him on GPDA related matters, but he always knew where the line was drawn and regrets that Schumacher did not reveal more of himself to his fellow professionals. He feels he owed it to them.

That was never more apparent to me than in Brazil 2006 when we met for our usual GPDA meeting. Of course, we acknowledged that it was Michael's last race and spoke about his achievements and renowned efforts to improve our safety.

There were drivers in that room against whom Michael had raced for fifteen years at the highest level possible, and personally I thought there was a small window of opportunity for him to be open with us about his years in the sport – in his own words to us, and to us only. But instead the whole moment passed without occasion.

I know there was still a world title at stake for him on Sunday (albeit a long shot) but it was a sad moment for me because as professional sportsmen there still remained a frostiness between him and the rest of us – and there had been a small chance to have lifted some of it if he had wanted to.

Was this a lack of respect on Schumacher's part? Respect was a very emotive word to Schumacher. When he started in Formula 1 men like Prost, Mansell and Piquet ruled the roost, but the biggest beast in the jungle was Ayrton Senna, who drove with a ferocious intensity and could not stand the idea of anyone else winning. The Brazilian immediately identified Schumacher as a threat and tried to intimidate him. Schumacher could deal with that, but what he disliked intensely was Senna's lack of respect for him as a youngster finding his feet in Formula 1.

> Respect is important to me. I used to have to fight a running battle with the drivers of the older generation, who played the role of master. If I believe what Gerhard Berger has told me then it was predominantly me who was treated in that way. None of them liked me at first. They wanted to show the young lad the way things are. There were for instance some nice brake tests. You would drive into a full power corner and suddenly the man in front is of the opinion he should take his foot off and block you for a lap. And if you did the same to them, the older drivers couldn't stand it. They claimed I was arrogant if I complained about these incidents. Now that I am an experienced driver I would never act like that with the boys.

According to Sabine Kehm, Schumacher was very affected by the treatment Senna and the others meted out to him and was careful not to repeat it when he became the senior pro.

> He didn't feel he had respect from Senna until the end of 1993 and then at the beginning of 1994 there was a change in their relationship.
>   He suddenly felt respect from Senna, felt he was being treated as an equal, whereas before he had always had to

fight him to get his respect. Michael regrets it a lot that the whole thing came to an end because of Senna's accident, when they were just developing their relationship. He would have liked to have time dealing with him on the same level.

Respect is very important to Michael, to be respected and to give respect to others. He respected all of the drivers, not maybe Villeneuve and maybe also Montoya, but the younger guys in the smaller teams. I remember when the new guys would come in to the GPDA he would always go and see them to welcome them. Because of what happened to him with Senna he was always keen for them to be a part of it.

Mark Webber accepts that when Schumacher became the elder statesman on the grid, he did make a point of speaking to the younger drivers in a non-intimidating way, but he claims that this investment of his time was not for nothing and, when he came to lap them in the race, he could find four or five seconds come Sunday afternoon.

What was clear was that Michael probably had a better relationship with the guys with the smaller, mid-pack teams because they weren't a huge threat to him week in, week out, like the boys who were on the first few rows with him. So, he could afford to be a bit more relaxed with them, and that welcoming demeanour towards them could inevitably on occasion make things a bit smoother for him on the circuit.

I think he was fair to everyone up until he felt they were coming into his area. I experienced that once or twice. In Turkey in 2005 I was coming through the field after a puncture and I was quite quick, trying to get back into the race. Ferrari were slow that day, the Bridgestone tyres

GETTY IMAGES

GETTY IMAGES

Above: Spa Francorchamps, Belgium 1992. Michael at the wheel of the Benetton B192

Left: And celebrating his first Grand Prix win in only 18 races

Below: Schumacher made his Grand Prix debut with Eddie Jordan's team. His race lasted a few hundred metres and then he jumped ship to Benetton

PA PHOTOS

Left: Run-ins with Ayrton Senna were common in the early days. Here Senna tries to intimidate him after a collision at the start of the 1992 French Grand Prix

GETTY IMAGES

ACTIONIMAGES

Above: Things got more heated in a test session at Hockenheim, when Senna took a swing at his new rival

PA PHOTOS

Left: Senna's fatal accident at Imola 1994. Schumacher briefly considered retiring but decided that it was what he did best, what he enjoyed doing the most and that he had worked hard to get to where he was

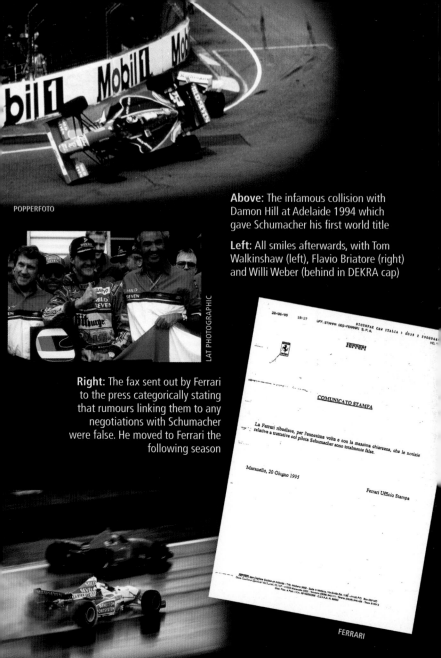

POPPERFOTO

Above: The infamous collision with Damon Hill at Adelaide 1994 which gave Schumacher his first world title

Left: All smiles afterwards, with Tom Walkinshaw (left), Flavio Briatore (right) and Willi Weber (behind in DEKRA cap)

LAT PHOTOGRAPHIC

Right: The fax sent out by Ferrari to the press categorically stating that rumours linking them to any negotiations with Schumacher were false. He moved to Ferrari the following season

FERRARI

LAT PHOTOGRAPHIC

Above: Schumacher's genius was clear in the wet Spanish Grand Prix 1996. Here he sails past Gerhard Berger en route to his first win for Ferrari

The low point of Schumacher's career.
The 1997 championship decider at Jerez, Spain.
Jacques Villeneuve makes his move and Schumacher's second reaction is
to turn in

ALL PA PHOTOS

Left: Schumacher was heavily punished for his actions at Jerez by the governing body, the FIA, but ironically his relationship with FIA president Max Mosley *(below)* flourished as Schumacher accompanied him on many road safety initiatives.

GETTY IMAGES

ACTIONIMAGES

LAT PHOTOGRAPHIC

Left: David Coulthard served alongside Schumacher for many years on the Grand Prix Drivers Association board, but was often disappointed by his on-track behaviour

Below: The shunt at Silverstone 1999. Despite hitting the tyre wall at a relatively low speed, Schumacher broke his leg. Eddie Irvine reckoned the car had 'issues'

PA PHOTOS

SPIELBERG 2002

PAUL-HENRI CAHIER

LAT PHOTOGRAPHIC

POPPERFOTO

Above: Ferrari's team orders fiasco in Austria 2002; Schumacher won the race but sent moral victor Barrichello onto the winner's step. The team was heavily fined for the breach of podium protocol

Left: The rival whom Schumacher respected the most, Mika Hakkinen, takes issue with his tactics after their epic battle at Spa in 2000 which Hakkinen won

Below: Even Barrichello didn't know what Schumacher had in mind when he slowed before the finish line at Indianapolis 2002. Barrichello won by 0.011 seconds

were rubbish. I was much quicker than Michael and Rubens. I came up behind him and I was losing loads of time behind him. I went to pass him, he squeezed me down and we touched. I spoke to him at the next race and he said, 'Well, we were both out of the race, we weren't going anywhere so it's fine.' I said, 'Well, it's fine for you.' Even though we know how much he'd scrap for a point, it was a tough weekend for him.

For Webber, Schumacher was the paragon of everything a racing driver should aspire to be, but there was so much more to it even than that.

He was ahead of the game as a driver and ahead of the game generally. When someone understands the sport that well then it's like Tiger Woods or Michael Jordan, they are just brilliant individuals. He is motivated, well trained, hungry, greedy, all the things you need.

He would have won world championships, but would he have got as many in a sport where you can't 'move things' as much as F1, a sport, say, where you have a swimming pool and you have to just go up and down it?

Sometimes, I don't think he was fair to his fellow competitor. I felt we were being had over. Monaco 2006 was a good example. I said to him a while after that event, 'It shows how hungry and greedy you are to go to that length, to risk that much to achieve your sixtieth pole or something.' It was ridiculous. But he felt that on Sunday afternoon he wasn't going to be able to control everything the way he wanted to, from fourth or fifth on the grid.

But he did a lot of good for the drivers too. We are all safer because of things he did. He worked hard for the GPDA, he worked closely with the FIA on things which were good for us.

But as his professional peers, we wanted him every now

and again to put his hand up and say, 'I messed up,' or accept that he had to come across to our point of view on something. If that had happened two or three times it would have changed a few things.

Schumacher was always ahead of the other drivers in terms of knowing the agenda on circuit changes, safety devices and other innovations. Because he had the relationships and because he always made himself available to travel to important meetings at short notice, he was able to keep himself better informed. Webber says:

> There will never be another Michael, not because we don't have the energy but because there will never be someone who has that much power within and with his team. The rest of the drivers in the GPDA didn't stand up to it because we realised that there was nothing we could do. We accepted defeat. If we lobbed a grenade we would come off worst. We needed him for the great things he did, but the other times he was so frustrating. You wanted to say, 'Just back off a fraction, just sometimes for us as a group.' That's what sometimes pissed us off.
>
> I was disenchanted and I felt I needed to talk to him on my own to regain some respect for the man of whom I had been such a huge fan. I saw Sabine and said I needed to see Michael one on one and we sat down at Silverstone and had a proper chat. He didn't need to give me that time. Most of what we talked about will stay between us but I was pretty happy with how that discussion went and I backed off a bit after that and even encouraged the other guys to try to do the same. I don't know if maybe there is some respect there, but he got some points back from me for talking to me like that.
>
> But at the end of the day I felt the sport had suffered. He

was born the same as the rest of us and he got himself into
such a great position, it was his drive, his talent to focus on
the right areas and get what he wanted, but unfortunately
there were a few things which disappointed us as fans and
competitors. As a sporting nation Australians are some of
the most ferocious competitors you can find. But there is a
line and if it wasn't a fair playing field then that's not cricket
where I come from. It's like Tiger Woods teeing off three
metres down the fairway. I said to Michael, 'In your own
mind I'm amazed that you feel you need to do some of the
things you do. With what you've got, with what you've
done . . .'

Powerful figure, mate, powerful, powerful figure. We'll
never see it again, what he had with his team. Very similar
to Lance Armstrong and I'm lucky enough to have known
both of them.

David Coulthard, like Webber, felt intense frustration at
Schumacher's domination of his sport. He doesn't see
Schumacher as the manipulative character Webber describes,
or at least not to the same degree, but his attitude to
Schumacher's legacy is similar.

I believe true greatness in sport is where you don't need
the referee there. In today's world that is a fantasy. But
fifteen, twenty years ago, maybe further back than that,
you'd say 'Good luck old boy,' and get on with it.

Is greatness about statistics, wins, world titles or is it
results backed up by how you are viewed in your sport and
how you did your winning, the level of respect that you
have?

Was he anti-sporting? Yes, because he's done
unsporting things on the track, which looked premeditated
and he's never allowed a team-mate in the same category

as him in the other car. But I'm uncomfortable to say that. Because I don't understand why he needed to do it, nor how he got away with it.

Eddie Irvine believes that Schumacher was right to use his influence. 'He had a lot of power and he used it. Manoeuvring behind the scenes, everyone does it, if you don't you're not in the game. But when you are the number one driver in the world you can do it a lot.'

CHAPTER EIGHT

Smash and grab

I have been lucky I've been able to show my potential; if instead of a Jordan or a Benetton I had had a Coloni what could I have done?

Michael Schumacher

Even before Schumacher got his Formula 1 break with the Jordan team at Spa in 1991, Mercedes' Jochen Neerpasch had engaged in some discussions with Benetton engineering boss Tom Walkinshaw about the possibility of placing Schumacher at Benetton for 1992, but the sheer impact of his Spa debut made the situation critical and things moved very quickly behind the scenes. Perhaps the most remarkable part of what happened next was Mercedes' part in it. Neerpasch's role in the story is rather like the man from Decca records in the Beatles' story who had them but let them go. As Ross Brawn explains:

> When it looked like Michael was going to appear on the scene in F1 in 1991, by then I'd become involved with Benetton through Tom Walkinshaw. We saw an opportunity. Tom is a very determined person and he set out to get Michael into the Benetton team.

It was a shock to us that Jochen Neerpasch was looking to place Michael in F1 with no strings attached, because even then we assumed that Mercedes would put him in with some clawback. It was too good an opportunity and Tom knew what needed to be done.

Walkinshaw had spoken to Willi Weber during the Spa weekend and tipped him off to the fact that, as Benetton was Ford's works team, he happened to know that Ford would not be supplying Jordan with engines again in 1992 and that the team was likely to go into partnership with Yamaha. Yamaha are a top outfit in the motorcycle world but their brief F1 engine programme was an embarrassment. It was never a full factory effort like the bike project and as a result it fell well short of the standards and budgets required to win in F1.

Yamaha was partnered with the Brabham team in 1991, and it was no great secret at the time of Schumacher's Spa debut that the engines would be moving to Jordan the next year. The engines were not particularly competitive, but they came free, whereas the customer Ford engine was costing Jordan millions. The Irishman had a great debut season, but it had put him close to five million pounds in debt, hence the need for Schumacher's Mercedes money and for a free engine supply from Yamaha. Bernie Ecclestone bailed Jordan out financially and played a role in brokering the deal with Yamaha. He also played a key part in moving Schumacher on to Benetton.

The switch to Yamaha was a sink or swim move for Jordan, it saved his team from bankruptcy, but it also cost him the services of one of the best drivers ever to walk into the F1 paddock. But Yamaha was a deal-breaker in the eyes of Weber and Schumacher. Before everyone left Spa they were moving

rapidly towards a deal with Benetton. 'We knew at the time
that Jordan was going to get Yamaha engines and we felt that
this would be catastrophic,' recalled Schumacher. 'Switching
to Benetton was my big chance. And when that chance came
up we grabbed it. It wasn't pleasant, but that was what I had
to do.'

The whole episode was a classic piece of F1-style
opportunism and was executed in a ruthlessly direct and
expedient manner. The Benetton team was gaining in strength
under its new principal, Flavio Briatore, a long-time associate
of clothing mogul Luciano Benetton. (The team had been
racing since 1986 under the Benetton flag, with five wins to its
credit before Schumacher came along.) Briatore added two top
engineers, Ross Brawn and Rory Byrne, over the summer of
1991 and thus the foundations were laid for what would turn
out to be one of the most successful engineering teams in the
sport's history. Schumacher was the final component needed
to turn the Benetton team into genuine world championship
challengers.

Briatore is one of the most pragmatic team principals in the
sport and he made space for Schumacher by simply turfing
one of his two drivers, Roberto Moreno, out of his seat. The two
leading teams at the time, Williams and McLaren, would not
have been prepared to make room for Schumacher at such
short notice, despite his stunning display at Spa.

Crucially, at this time Schumacher's contract was still with
the Sauber Mercedes sportscar team. The Mercedes board was
considering whether to come into Formula 1 with its own
team, building its own car and engine, as it had in the 1950s.
In fact Mercedes had recruited the British designer, Harvey
Postlethwaite, to work on a chassis design. However, when

they did finally commit to F1, it was only as an engine supplier to the Sauber team. In February 1992 Sauber announced that Schumacher and Wendlinger would be the drivers for their Mercedes-powered entry to F1 in 1993. Sauber insisted that Schumacher's contract was with his team and not with Mercedes. 'Legally, Michael was under contract to Sauber at that time,' says Mercedes motorsport boss Norbert Haug. 'But he didn't want to come. Even if there was legally a possibility, my view was that you cannot make a driver drive your car. He was with a winning team by then and for him to step back . . . it would have been a nice idea for us, but we couldn't force it through. Having said that, we had a great car that year and our first season with Sauber was very strong.'

But five months before that, in the week leading up to the 1991 Italian Grand Prix, Schumacher was still working hard to extricate himself from his initial commitment to Jordan. As the week began Jordan believed that he would be signing a contract with Schumacher on the Monday before Monza, but Neerpasch ensured that the 22-year-old proved elusive. Late on the Monday afternoon Neerpasch arrived at Jordan with a completely different contract from the one Jordan's lawyer had drafted. There were new clauses relating to space on the car and other commercial considerations. It was unacceptable to Jordan who said he would work on it overnight and the parties agreed to reconvene in the morning.

That night Schumacher was signed to Benetton and on the Tuesday morning, shortly before the time of their scheduled meeting, Schumacher faxed Jordan to say that he would not be driving for them any more. Jordan sought an injunction at the High Court in London, claiming a contractual commitment, based on a letter of intent signed by Schumacher at Spa.

Meanwhile Schumacher conducted a secret test with the Benetton team at Silverstone, a few hundred metres from Jordan's factory. The engineer Giorgio Ascanelli was working for the team at the time. 'He was called by us for the secret test. He went like a missile straight away, lapping well inside the times of [Nelson] Piquet. When he stopped we said, "You don't have to push so hard," and he said quite openly, "But I wasn't really trying." ' This was clearly becoming his stock answer to the incredulity his performances inspired.

As well as being scintillatingly fast, he seemed an old head on young shoulders. His path through childhood and especially the endless weekends on the road with adults who were not part of his family had toughened him up. Almost uniquely in my experience of fathers of aspiring racing drivers, Rolf Schumacher deliberately stayed out of the way, let Michael get on with it himself. He was always available to offer advice, but as a simple man that extended to basic values rather than sophisticated strategic thinking. As a result Schumacher evolved into his own person at a young age and with his father not on site he developed his own value system for what was right and wrong in racing. He also developed a protective shell around himself, which few have been able to penetrate. 'When I came in to F1 at twenty-two, I was already quite well advanced for my age as I had experienced a lot in a short period and had occupied myself with lots of things in order to be prepared for the great wide world. I was well ahead of other people the same age,' he says.

That protective shell was called into use as the Monza weekend got under way. Jordan's case was rejected by the High Court on the Thursday, leaving Schumacher clear of that hurdle, but by then a Milan court was sitting to decide

Moreno's claim of wrongful dismissal by Benetton. The Brazilian was trying to make sure that Schumacher could not drive his car in that Sunday's race. He had been told by Briatore that he was being dropped because he was 'neither physically nor mentally' fit to drive the car. Moreno, who had finished fourth at the previous race at Spa and had then worked hard the following week in a test session at Monza, found this totally unacceptable. Said Briatore at the time:

> Last Saturday I spoke with Neerpasch from Mercedes who offered me Schumacher as he had no binding contract. We took him straight away, we were interested in having a German driver and especially one who is so promising. We've signed him until 1995, on condition that from 1993 Mercedes isn't racing in F1.
>
> To Moreno I sent two letters saying that he was not part of our plans for 1992, but as the condition for taking Schumacher was to hire him straight away we dropped him early, paying him up until the end of 1991. A judge in England said that Schumacher has no contract with Jordan, all sorted.

In fact what had happened was that Jordan had insisted on Schumacher signing a contract until the end of 1993 before he drove the car at Spa. Schumacher had spoken to Neerpasch who said that any contract would have to be signed off by Mercedes lawyers, which could not happen before the race, so Jordan got Schumacher to sign a letter of intent. Because everything had been done in such a rush and because of the hurdles put up by Schumacher and his advisers, the letter was all that Jordan had. And Schumacher changed the wording of the letter to say that he would sign 'a' contract after the race, instead of 'the' contract. Allowing that through was the moment at which Jordan lost him for ever.

To be fair, Neerpasch later said that his intention was for Schumacher to drive for Jordan until the end of 1991 and then transfer to Benetton. Schumacher and his backers were not prepared to continue into 1992 with Jordan because they knew that the team would be uncompetitive, but they never intended for Schumacher to jump ship after just one race. Briatore contradicts that version of events, saying that when he met Schumacher and Neerpasch at his London home in the week following Spa, the indication was that he wanted to move immediately.

Jordan clearly believed that he had something which bound Schumacher to him and no doubt privately he hoped that at the very least, even if he was not going to get the driver, he would get some serious compensation. Walkinshaw had offered him a sum of money earlier in the week to back down, but Jordan had refused. 'There was the commitment from Schumacher, from his manager, from Neerpasch of Mercedes, that if we ran Schumacher in the Belgian Grand Prix, it would translate automatically into a contract through to 1994, the details to be defined shortly after Spa,' said Jordan at the time. 'We did that but Neerpasch offered him to Benetton. It's not right.'

Jordan suspected that part of the motivation for Benetton to torpedo him was that his team had done too good a job using a customer version of the same Ford engine that Benetton was also using. The new kids on the block had, in some ways, shown them up.

Arriving in the Monza paddock for his second Grand Prix, Schumacher may have been cleared by the London judge, but the situation was further complicated when the judge in Milan found in favour of Moreno. Schumacher was free to leave Jordan, but Benetton was not free to give him Moreno's car.

With little time left to sort things out before practice began, Bernie Ecclestone convened all the parties at the Villa d'Este hotel in the outskirts of Milan on the Thursday night and brokered a deal. Moreno caved in and accepted $500,000 (£250,000) compensation from Benetton and it was agreed that for this race only he would drive for Jordan, whilst Schumacher woke up on the Friday morning to find himself a Benetton driver. He saw Eddie Jordan and Ian Phillips in the lobby of the Villa d'Este and said simply, 'I'm really sorry, I didn't want it to finish like this.'

Like many race weekends to come in his long F1 career, Schumacher was at the centre of huge controversy in Monza. He was under enormous pressure, but he put it behind him and got on with the job of driving. Because he was so young and new to the business, he was not seen to be the bad guy in this episode, more the pawn. Even Jordan believed that Schumacher was an innocent party in the intrigue.

The situation was being manipulated by those around Schumacher: Willi Weber, Jochen Neerpasch, Mercedes, the IMG sports management group, who were advising Weber, and of course Benetton, rather than by Schumacher himself. But with the benefit of hindsight, reviewing the landscape of his F1 career, it does bear a lot of the hallmarks of what was to come later. The deal was ruthless and not very fair, but it was the right thing for Schumacher at the time. Did the Benetton affair create Michael Schumacher or did he play his part in creating *it*?

Many people condemned the whole affair. Benetton and Mercedes were roundly criticised for their lack of ethics. McLaren boss Ron Dennis coined the term 'piranha club' to describe the environment in which F1 team principals devour each other.

Of the drivers, Ayrton Senna was the only one to be openly critical of Moreno's treatment. But he had sympathetic words for the man who would soon become his greatest rival. 'Often young drivers who are starting out on their careers find themselves in situations which are difficult to control,' he said. 'I'm sure that he didn't want all of this but he probably had to do it because someone was pushing him. We top drivers have to say something about this.'

Senna had gone through something similar in his first year in the sport, when he decided to leave Toleman and join Lotus. The Toleman team dropped him for the Italian Grand Prix at Monza, he resorted to the law, but found that it was on the team's side. It reduced him to tears of frustration, but it also taught him a vital lesson about being meticulous when dealing with Formula 1 contracts, a lesson Schumacher had now most certainly learned, some seven years later. It was ironic, then, the day after the race, when one of the Italian papers ran a story on Schumacher entitled 'The new Senna?'

Once the dust had settled on his transfer, Schumacher buckled down and gave another impressive performance, outqualifying and outracing his new team-mate, three times world champion Nelson Piquet. He qualified seventh and finished the race in fifth place, 11 seconds ahead of Piquet.

'I never realised that F1 was so easy,' he said after the race, sounding a touch arrogant, as he did in those days, before he realised that his plain-speaking English could be misinterpreted. 'I was behind Prost's Ferrari and I thought "If I pass him, it will earn me the affection of the public." But that would have been wanting too much; I am happy to have got to the finish and scored some points. To go as well as I have at Spa and Monza one has to have natural talent, but that is not all. I know a lot of drivers who have that but who didn't have my luck. Without the right car, the right team, you cannot get far. I have been lucky I've been able to show my potential; if instead of a Jordan or a Benetton I had had a Coloni what could I have done?'

Piquet was under a cloud throughout the Monza weekend, incensed by the treatment the team had meted out to his close friend Moreno. He had argued with Briatore, who threatened to drop him from the race, but he also realised that Schumacher represented the future while he was the past. With Moreno as his team-mate Piquet had looked like the reliable old pro, but once Schumacher started putting in the lap times, it was clear that Piquet had come to the end of his career.

Schumacher's immediate dominance over Piquet made him the reference point for the team, despite his lack of experience. Because of this Schumacher never enjoyed a settling in period in Formula 1, sheltered from the pressure by an experienced team-mate who carries the team's expectations. Even for the best drivers it takes several years to learn the ropes in Formula 1. It is one thing to set a fast lap in qualifying, but to do well in races takes experience and time. But Schumacher was under the pressure of expectation from the Monza weekend onwards. Benetton was a young team, pushing hard in all areas to close down the dominant McLaren and Williams teams. Pressure is relative, but just over two weeks after sitting in an F1 car for the first time,

Schumacher was the fastest driver in one of the top teams in the sport. He recalls:

> I was sure of one thing. Nelson would teach me nothing. Because he absolutely didn't want to. I remember the debriefings; I would speak, I would explain everything I had been able to see and feel from the car. He sat there listening without saying a thing. When I went out, then he started discussions with his engineers. It's normal. I was starting out in his team, in place of his friend Moreno; I was new, young and I was sometimes going faster than him, the triple world champion. I hardly expected him to say, 'Welcome, you seem a talented fellow, I'll show you a few things that'll make you even better!'

There were just four races left in the championship and Schumacher settled in quickly to learn about Formula 1. He finished in the points in Portugal and Spain, crashed in practice for the Japanese Grand Prix and retired from the race in Australia. On the Sunday night at the McLaren end-of-season party, Schumacher came up on stage, and joined in singing the Blues Brothers' classic, 'Sweet Home Chicago'. He was very drunk and very happy; a 22-year-old letting his hair down. In the far corner of the room, world champion Ayrton Senna was chatting intimately with supermodel Elle Macpherson. He was a picture of sophisticated glamour, while Schumacher, in his stone washed jeans and mullet haircut, was not. Senna quietly escorted his date out of the room around midnight. It was said that he flew her on his jet to a Pacific Island for a few days. Prost and Mansell were Senna's main rivals at the time, but he already knew that before long Schumacher would be giving him a hard time. Little did he know how hard a time.

* * *

A few days after he got back to Europe from Australia, Schumacher too was to find romance and, in his case, a relationship that would prove permanent. He was at a party in Kerpen, a traditional German *polterabend*, which is a party held the night before a wedding. There he met up with Corinna Betsch, whom he knew well as she had been Heinz Harald Frentzen's girlfriend throughout his time as Schumacher's Mercedes team-mate. He says that he had always seen something special in her. He recalls: 'We talked, more than we had normally and then pow!' He knew he wanted to marry her. They left the party together and have stayed that way ever since.

When he retired from racing at the end of 2006 Schumacher paid tribute to his wife's role in his success.

> Over the past weeks I have once again become particularly aware of how unbelievably great Corinna was over all those years. I had almost seen the intensity and harmony that exists between us as normal. I didn't know it any differently. But it's becoming more and more clear to me how irreplaceable and incredibly clever she always was about it. I mean, I really didn't notice what stability she gave me. She transmitted a great calm to me, and through that I became calm too. That gave me the certainty to see things through with full concentration. She gave me the freedom to have my experiences and my thoughts, and she gave me the feeling that it was right and fine that way. In doing that she steered me on to the right track.
>
> She strengthens me in what I do, she supports me in the way she explains her view of things so calmly. Her opinion is massively important to me because I find again and again

that she has a healthy objectivity about things and keeps the overview. She has a brilliant intuition, but on the other hand she goes about everything she does so methodically and carefully. I admire her. When I look at her I still get butterflies in my stomach.

Corinna is not a high-profile wife. She is at the opposite end of the spectrum from someone like Victoria Beckham. Corinna was always in the background in the public side of Schumacher's career, she only gave a handful of interviews and one of those was using her position to highlight the plight of retired work horses. But she is not a shrinking violet either, and she could often be seen in the paddock on race day, chatting with everyone.

According to a female friend of the family, 'He's a cocoon person. Corinna is his anchor and they complement each other. You could say, he is her brain and she is his heart.' Schumacher was once asked by a journalist from the *Sunday Telegraph* in England whether he had ever been tempted by the groupies in Formula 1. 'I am in love with my wife,' he replied. 'I am satisfied, I am not tempted. When you see what is behind the groupies it is not pleasant. They are only interested in the racing driver, not in the person.' His dignified answer made the journalist ashamed of his question.

Seeing the Schumachers together it is clear that he is madly in love with his wife. He cannot leave her alone, is constantly affectionate with her, to the point where they discussed with advisers whether they should stop acting like that because the media might start a campaign saying that it was staged to cover up a failing marriage. But in the end they decided just to be themselves and be sincere about their love.

They both like to project an image of a perfect marriage,

with everything in equilibrium. He says that there have never been crises in their marriage. The warmth and sincerity that is generated by this image helps to counteract the negatives in his own image which have come from the racing. It's as if he's asking everyone to consider how a man who is so sincere in his love for his wife and his family could be the devil on the race-tracks which he is made out to be. 'When he comes home,' says a family friend, 'it is as if this whole person softens. Then all the precision and speed and the mad rush all disappear.'

Early on Schumacher decided to establish a divide between his public life and his private life and never to let the media through. For this reason there has never been a 'home story' in any of the lifestyle magazines either in Germany or anywhere else in the world. The family constantly receive requests, but always turn them down. Schumacher controls what is known about his wife and his family very closely and there is nothing for even the most investigative journalist to build on. He says:

Otherwise my wife and children would be recognised very often and wouldn't be able to move so freely any more. For us it was clear from the very beginning – Corinna feels uncomfortable being interviewed, so she doesn't give any. That's the main reason. As well as that, I used to observe the wife of Boris Becker and many others. At the beginning they were praised for their openness and then criticised for it later. Something about that didn't fit with one of them and he spoke out about what they were looking for there. At that point my wife and I said 'We absolutely must not lay ourselves open to this situation.' Everyone has now accepted that. And VIP events are not our world – they are too superficial to us. I'm not good at small-talk. I prefer to spend my time at home with family and friends.

Only trusted friends are allowed close to the family. The
Schumachers have never employed a nanny for their two
children. Corinna's mother and her partner are at the house
in Switzerland more often than not and they do the bulk of
the childcare if Corinna is away. During his racing career,
when Schumacher would take two months off in the winter,
the family would move to their house in Norway to spend time
together, with regular visits from friends.

At the end of 2006 Corinna wrote a brief but extremely
affectionate tribute to her husband which was printed in
Germany in a book entitled simply, *Schumacher*.

Sometimes, when I just look at him, an incredibly strong
feeling of deep happiness overcomes me. I look at him and
think 'That's your husband.' Michael is so strong and so
tender, so full of energy and so intimate. He's a good man
and a father from the depths of his soul. I think that we and
the children are a great team.

The nicest thing is that nothing is too much for him. No
matter what, no matter when, no matter where, it's ok. I
have never yet heard him groan or roll his eyes or say 'later,
not now'. Michael is a doer. He just does, and it seems as
if nothing can cause him any problems. That's a great
feeling – it gives you confidence to know that when he
takes something in hand he will get it sorted. Everything
will be okay again in a minute. I love that. And, somehow
or other, you can come to him with anything, ask him
anything. When I'm not sure about certain things
sometimes I just talk them through with him. 'What do you
think about it?' And somehow he always knows what to
do. Somehow he always seems to have everything in his
grasp.

The best thing about it is that we really discuss things

together and that he doesn't withdraw to a supposed position of strength, but really does want to hear my opinion too. And then he lets that opinion count. That's one of Michael's basic characteristics anyway, that he accepts that some people know better than him in certain areas and then seeks this opinion, too.

Michael is also unbelievably honest. That was one of the things that struck me quickly, soon after we got to know each other at around sixteen or seventeen years old. There were a couple of occasions then, like when we played cards, for example, where that was unbelievably noticeable. Cheat? No chance. Michael would never do that – he somehow can't. Something in him resists against it, indeed pretty violently. Therefore I never understood these stories that came up at the beginning 'Schummel Schumi' [Schumi the cheat] and such. Back then I got much more worked up about these stories than Michael. It was an absolute puzzle to me that people could assume such things.

Although Corinna was not Schumacher's first girlfriend, she was the first to form a serious relationship with him. The timing was just right. The penniless bricklayer's son had made it into the jet-set glamour world of the Formula 1 super-rich, but his emotional response to that was to want to settle down with a girl from a similar background to his own. 'I was looking for the life I started to live together with Corinna,' says Schumacher. 'That was my wish, my dream, because I don't like to be alone. I like to share my life and spend my time with someone I love.'

According to Willi Weber the timing for Schumacher of getting into a serious relationship with Corinna was perfect. 'It is important as a young person to have a responsibility, not just for the team or the management, but also a responsibility to a human being whom you love. It was very very important also for Michael to go into a relationship with a woman who he loved above all else and still does today. It changed Michael for the better, he's more positive, more free, even more committed. Everyone wrote, "Now that he's married with kids he'll drive slower." He refuted it all.'

CHAPTER NINE

Battles with Ayrton Senna

Senna was the best driver I ever met.

Michael Schumacher

Michael Schumacher had a great deal of respect for Ayrton Senna. The problem for Schumacher was that he felt Senna didn't respect him. Only in the final months of their rivalry, just before Senna's death at Imola in May 1994, did the Brazilian show Schumacher the respect he craved.

Senna's shadow is cast long across Michael's career. It would be an exaggeration to say that he haunts him, but Senna's death and Schumacher's proximity to it certainly left an indelible mark on a man who, despite appearances, is actually very sensitive. Theirs was the duel that the world was waiting to see, but fate decreed that it was to last for just two and a half seasons – they shared the same starting grid just 41 times. Willi Weber says:

> For all of us what happened to Senna is a great tragic loss and we would have liked to have continued driving with him in Formula 1 and Michael would have liked to have shown him how good he really is. I am sure that Ayrton

> Senna knew that Michael would take over from him. He felt
> it, otherwise it wouldn't have come to these complaints
> between Michael and him. He already knew that there was
> someone quite special in the car who was capable of
> breaking his records and driving faster than he ever could.

In his early Formula 1 career, Schumacher was well aware that
Senna was the biggest beast in the jungle and the young
pretender set out to let him know that he had a new
challenger. The two had many run-ins both on and off the
track, as Schumacher deliberately attempted to get under
Senna's skin. He was aware that the Brazilian was an
emotionally driven man and he provoked him to fury on
several occasions. One thing Schumacher found unacceptable
about Senna was that he would lecture the junior drivers on
safety and respect and then behave on track as if those rules
did not apply to him. When Schumacher spoke out about this
publicly Senna put him down savagely, on one occasion
branding him a 'stupid boy'. Meanwhile their battles on track
were intense and loaded with menace as the two testosterone
driven racers used their 200mph cars to intimidate each other.

Senna was to have a huge influence on Michael's developing character and style. Schumacher was aware that Senna
worked hard to unite the team around him, to get everything
going his way and give him the best chance of victory. He was
outstanding at motivating everyone to improve their own
performance as well as the car they gave him. He would often
visit the Honda engineers in Japan, to the point where they
thought he was a god. At the race-track, in drivers' briefings,
Schumacher observed how Senna talked to the back-markers,
developing a good rapport with them so that they would be
happy to move out of his way in a race. In short, every detail

which he could manipulate to give himself a competitive advantage, Senna would work on. Schumacher was a sponge for new ideas and he noted carefully how the great champion operated. As his own career progressed, Schumacher adopted a similar approach but refined it still further.

Senna also provided Schumacher with his first encounter with what can only be described as the 'win at all costs' mentality in another driver. The Brazilian was totally unable to accept that anyone else could be better than him and was always unwilling to be beaten. When Nigel Mansell won the world title in 1992, Senna whispered these chilling words into his ear on the podium, 'Now you know why I am such a bastard; it's because I never want anyone else to experience what you are feeling now.' Mansell says that his blood froze.

Senna himself had been bloodied by some intense battles on the track with Alain Prost, including the two infamous occasions when the pair collided with each other to win the world championship. Heavy-handed tactics on the race-track were common in those days; these were hard men sorting out their differences at high speed. When he was parachuted into one of the top teams in late 1991, Schumacher found himself mixing with them straight away. In the third round of the 1992 season, just nine races in to his Formula 1 career, he had his first confrontation with Senna.

The occasion was the Brazilian Grand Prix at Interlagos, Senna's home race. The passion for Formula 1 was at its absolute peak among Brazilians at this time, with their beloved Senna the defending world champion and seemingly at the height of his powers. But 1992 proved to be an intensely frustrating year for him as his McLaren-Honda team had fallen badly behind Williams-Renault in the technology race and

Senna couldn't get close to Mansell all year. Senna was not programmed to accept such situations and so he was in a volatile and combative mood in front of his home crowd that weekend.

Schumacher had followed Senna closely during the preceding race in Mexico, observing afterwards, 'It was amazing to follow the world champion, who was my boyhood idol, and realise that I was quicker than him while trying to find a way past.' Senna retired and Schumacher went on to record his first Formula 1 podium finish in third place, albeit some 21 seconds behind Mansell, the winner. But it was the second time in his brief career that he had followed one of the legends on the track and then boasted about how easy the whole thing had been to the media. In the eyes of Senna, Schumacher was a mouthy upstart, who needed taking down a peg or two.

Emboldened by his performance in Mexico, Schumacher found himself again in close company with Senna in Brazil. From one place behind him on the grid, Schumacher made the better start and led Senna initially, but the Brazilian forced his way through in uncompromising fashion. However Senna soon began to have electrical problems and his car lost pace. Schumacher was at the head of a line of cars forming up behind the world champion, all losing time. Disappointed and frustrated by his impotence in front of his adoring fans, Senna was not about to make it easy for Schumacher to pass him. Schumacher got through on lap eight, but Senna slipstreamed him and then outbraked him into the next corner to reclaim third place.

Senna's car let him down after 18 laps and Schumacher went on to record a second consecutive podium, but afterwards he let fly to the media, accusing Senna of playing 'dangerous games' on the race-track. He said that he had been upset by the way Senna had passed him at the start, but even more enraged by his behaviour after that. 'I was quicker than him but there was no way to get past,' he said. 'He began to have problems and was slowing and he prevented me from overtaking him. I said to myself that he was playing with us. I don't know what his game was but it isn't pretty. His behaviour really surprised me. It is not what I expected from a three times world champion.'

Senna had left the circuit by the time Schumacher spoke, but he was livid when he saw the quotes later. It was one thing for a young upstart to question his behaviour, but to do so in the media without speaking to him first was unacceptable. But, true to Schumacher's view that there was one rule for Senna and another for everyone else, on the eve of the French Grand Prix at Magny-Cours in July, Senna held forth about the incident to the media. 'If Michael wishes I can show him the telemetry read-outs from Honda then he could see what really happened with my engine. But I don't give a damn about what he said, he's just a stupid boy.' The world's best driver and his natural successor had got past the stage of marking out territory; now they were on a potentially devastating collision course.

On the first lap of the French Grand Prix a week later, Schumacher was following Senna again when he made a lunge down the inside at the Adelaide Hairpin, the slowest corner on the circuit, presumably thinking of paying him back for the move Senna had pulled on him in Brazil. Senna did not give him room and swung across in front of him. Rather than back off, Schumacher kept coming down the inside and the inevitable collision occurred. Studying the pictures again, with the knowledge of the simmering feud between them, it seems as though Schumacher was looking for trouble. He certainly got it. Senna's car was eliminated on the spot and the race was stopped. Schumacher's car lost its front wing, but was repaired and was able to restart. But on the grid before the restart Senna, who had changed out of his overalls and into a jumper and jeans and who had clearly had time to reflect before acting, confronted Schumacher. An Italian journalist from *La Gazetta dello Sport* got close enough to the pair to record what was said.

'What were you up to?' said Senna, his left hand on Schumacher's shoulder, pressing downwards, his right index finger pointing in his face. 'Who do you think you are? You've made a huge mistake, like in Brazil, even worse. On the first lap with cold tyres and brakes you cannot try certain things. You could have caused a catastrophe.'

Schumacher himself takes up the story.

Senna went on, 'Look what happened, happened, OK, but unlike you I talk to you directly and tell you you've messed up. But I don't go to the media and make it public.'

I told him that I didn't think that this was the right place to have such a discussion. If he wanted something more he should come back after the race.

But he had behaved unfairly to me [in Brazil] and I didn't understand why, so I kicked up a fuss after the race. But he didn't like that especially because I was still the greenhorn in Formula 1. He often came up and spoke [like that]. We didn't get on very well in those days. It wasn't really a lesson he wanted to teach me, but more typical Formula 1 theatre like it was in Senna's days. What was far more important for our relationship was that we got on much better in 1994, when we started to talk to each other like racing drivers should; frank and like colleagues. Senna belonged to a different generation. There was this invisible pecking order and each new driver had to find his place. You had to earn the respect of the other drivers on the track.

It's strange I've always found it hard to talk about him. I never had the need for role models or to follow in people's footsteps, doing as they did. On the other hand he was the best driver that I've ever met. I can remember a karting race in Holland when I was about ten years old. I saw him there on the race-track for the first time; the line that he drove, his style, just wonderful. I didn't follow his career further but one day I got into F1 and met him again.

Jo Ramirez was the team co-ordinator at McLaren at the time and a close confidant of Senna's. According to him, Senna had a plan when he confronted Schumacher in France. 'He said, "Watch me as I give him a bit of the evil eye,"' says Ramirez. 'And then when it was over he said, "Hopefully I've spooked him and it might slow him down a bit." Ayrton always kept a close watch on him, from the very first days. Right from the beginning, he considered Schumacher as the next big threat, way ahead of all the other drivers around at the time.'

Senna told Ramirez that he hoped that the confrontation so soon before the restart would unsettle Schumacher and it did. When the race got under way again, he crashed into Stefano Modena in the Jordan-Yamaha.

With the passage of time, Schumacher tells the story as if he met Senna eyeball to eyeball, but his body language at the time was very much that of the kid being told off by the master and contemporary reports show that he was full of remorse. 'It was a bad day,' he told reporters. 'I messed it all up. The first incident I caused because I came too fast into the corner.'

That said, Schumacher did not take Senna's theatrics on the Magny-Cours grid lightly. In interviews during the following week, leading up to the British Grand Prix at Silverstone, he stuck his head even further above the parapet. 'If it is someone like Senna or Mansell it doesn't matter, if someone is making a mistake in my eyes I have to tell it the way I see it. I don't just shut up because I think I should. They all know what I think of them. They cannot just do what they want with me.'

This was a veteran of a mere 14 races talking about a three times world champion. But more importantly it was another great example of his father's character coming out in the face of bullying tactics. Just as in Monaco 2006, when the media and most of the paddock were trying to bully him into admitting he'd cheated, he refused to play someone else's game and instead bullied them right back. He knew that Senna was a very clever man, but he felt he had also seen enough already to know that he was a match for him on the track. He would not be intimidated.

It is interesting at this point to consider a similar situation in Schumacher's own career when his natural successor, Fernando Alonso, came along. At the British Grand Prix of 2003, Alonso's first season in a competitive Formula 1 car, the pair found themselves disputing the same piece of track on the run down the Hangar Straight at 190mph. Schumacher won the championship that year but it was a major struggle as the Ferrari was not competitive in the early part of the year. Alonso went to pass Schumacher on the right side and

Schumacher drove him on to the grass, in exactly the same way that Senna would have done to him. It was an outrageously aggressive act (which, incidentally, went unpunished by the FIA), but it was strangely evocative of the Senna and Schumacher feud of 1992. Unlike the young Schumacher, Alonso did not sound off publicly about his venerable rival.

When talking about the 1992 season Schumacher still sounds resentful today, referring slightly sarcastically to 'the great Senna' or the 'big Senna era'. It was a baptism of fire for a man with so few races under his belt and it made a massive impression on him. After Jerez 1997, where he tried to drive Jacques Villeneuve off the road, Schumacher referred to this period as having shaped his mentality. Asked if he felt any guilt for his actions he said, 'Not really guilt. I grew up with Senna and remember incidents with Prost and Senna. That's why I don't have the feeling that I am guilty for anything because it was part of the game. I knew it wasn't right, but this is an important moment, anything or nothing, and you go for it.'

Formula 1 is a different sport nowadays, much more controlled and more closely scrutinised. It is a highly dangerous sport, with a dubious profile when it comes to environmental issues, and now finds itself in a world where health and safety and corporate social responsibility are regarded as top priorities. Motor racing fits oddly into such an environment and Max Mosley is working to move the sport towards renewable energy and green fuels to counter unwelcome criticism.

Values change quickly and Schumacher's career spanned both ends of the spectrum. When he started racing in F1, the governing body was run by a Frenchman called Jean Marie

Balestre. Deliberate collisions and intimidation were regarded as part of the game. But by the time Schumacher retired he was considered by many to be a model of anti-sporting behaviour. So how had Senna and Prost been allowed to get away with it?

It is hard for Schumacher to understand this and even harder to accept. He served his apprenticeship amidst some of the hardest and most ruthless drivers in history at a time when the cars were so safe that the drivers could be relatively sure that they would not be hurt if they smashed into an opponent. That could not have happened earlier than the mid 1980s, when the cars began to be made from carbon fibre, because prior to that the cars were so fragile that deliberately driving into an opponent would have been suicide, or murder.

The idea of treating your car as a weapon was at its apogee when Schumacher challenged Senna in the early 1990s. But by the time he himself was the sport's leading man, the rules had changed. He failed to appreciate this and in Jerez in 1997 it caught him out. This anomaly is fundamentally important to understanding why Schumacher is sometimes viewed negatively where Senna is not. The person who may be able to shed some light on this is FIA president Max Mosley.

Mosley was elected president in autumn 1991, shortly after Schumacher's debut at Spa. As a former Formula 2 racer himself, he had always been afraid of contact in open wheel racing cars and says that one of his first goals on assuming the presidency was to change the culture:

I was always worried about wheel-to-wheel contact and cars taking off, because I'd had that happen to me. After

my election in 1991 I met the drivers and said to them,
'This wheel-banging thing has to stop because it's so
dangerous and we'll have a car in the crowd soon.'

After the meeting, Gerhard Berger came to see me and
said that you can't overtake in a modern F1 car without
making contact. But I just tried to change the culture, not
all that successfully, but it did change a bit.

Senna felt outraged about what had happened at the
Japanese Grand Prix in 1989, when Alain Prost had collided
with him at the chicane in their world championship decider.
Senna continued, but the stewards intervened, with the result
that Senna was excluded from the race and lost the world
championship to Prost.

The following year the two drivers found themselves at the
same venue, again disputing the world championship. As
they approached the first corner, Senna simply drove Prost off
the road at around 120mph. Everybody involved in Formula 1
knew what had happened the previous year and sympathised:
the general feeling was that Senna had been robbed in 1989
and that his retaliation was understandable, so nobody did
anything about it. The race director at the time, John
Corsmidt, took no action. Balestre was very unhappy about
this and challenged Corsmidt in the FIA World Council
meeting shortly afterwards, but Mosley defended Corsmidt.
Balestre's efforts to challenge Senna's manoeuvre were foiled
and Mosley carried the day. He takes up the story.

Then in 1991 I became president and Senna won the race
[again at Suzuka and with it took his third world
championship] and he got stuck into the champagne and
then announced on television that he had [deliberately]
taken Prost off the previous year. And I was quite

concerned about that. I feared that Balestre would use this as an excuse to suggest some draconian measure against Senna and I was not yet then politically strong enough to resist it. Ron Dennis was worried as well. He said that he had told Ayrton to apologise, to say he hadn't meant what he'd said, but Ayrton refused.

Ayrton came for a chat and I said to him 'The difference between a professional and an amateur is that an amateur does what he feels like doing, while a professional does what is expedient for his position. What you did was completely the act of an amateur, not something that a professional would ever do.' He was an intelligent man and he saw the logic and his eyes started to well up. Then he said, 'You have to understand that I've been racing since I was six years old and that bastard took a win away from me.'

In the end he saw my point of view and we sat down and drafted a sort of weasel-worded apology, which I thought would give me enough clout if Balestre did try something.

It has to be said that the culture of the time was a bit more robust than now. Everyone just felt that it was completely wrong and someone might have got killed, but they felt that Senna was entitled to do it.

According to Mosley, mitigating circumstances were missing in the case of Schumacher's deliberate collisions with opponents later in his career. Schumacher got away with driving Damon Hill off the road in 1994, but if today's systems had been in place then, Hill would have been awarded the championship. In 1997 at Jerez, Mosley watched the incident between Schumacher and Villeneuve and immediately made up his mind to act.

It was absolutely clear that Villeneuve was going to pass and Michael just turned in on him. At the time he denied that he had turned in to him and the stewards cleared him. But I saw it on television and it was just outrageous. So I dragged it in front of the world council. I got Michael to admit that he had turned in.

Will history judge Schumacher harshly? No. I think that when you do sport at that level under that kind of pressure and you have to think that quickly, you are going to do things like that or you are not going to be successful. And to be a F1 driver never mind a world champion, I think you have to be extremely ruthless and determined. It is a very dangerous, very difficult, very tough job and that degree of ruthlessness has to be there and sometimes it shows itself.

Although now part of the folklore of F1, the Senna and Schumacher collisions were a bad advertisement for the sport and Mosley has taken steps behind the scenes to change the culture, so that it is impossible nowadays for a driver to contemplate taking an opponent off deliberately. The current system, with the FIA race director Charlie Whiting and the two stewards serving under a permanent chief steward, means that a driver would be severely penalised every time.

* * *

Two weeks after their confrontation on the grid in France, Senna and Schumacher cranked their dispute up another notch. Schumacher knew that he had Senna rattled and during a test session at Hockenheim prior to the German Grand Prix he wound Senna up so much that it ended in a fight. Many years after the event, Schumacher recalls:

I was driving a fast lap and Senna was heading for the pits. He was going slowly around a corner, looks in his mirrors, sees me and suddenly goes full throttle on the straight. What am I supposed to do? I brake first and stay behind because I cannot overtake him. The same thing happens at the next corner. Then Senna tootles into the pits, but he's messed up my lap. After a short while the same shit happens again, Senna's looking in his mirrors, he's going slow, then he accelerates on the straight. I kept my cool, but it was irritating and destroyed my testing programme.

Later that day I find myself in Senna's shoes; I am in front, he's behind me. So what do I do . . . ?

Well Senna doesn't like it at all. He breaks off his lap and follows me into the pits where he gets out of the car and attacks me.

The Brazilian swung a punch at Schumacher, who ducked it, and Senna was restrained by some McLaren mechanics who had followed him down the pit lane. Senna was shouting 'You show some respect', absolutely livid and wild in the eye. Schumacher knew for certain that he had the great champion rattled.

What kind of 23-year-old in his first season in the sport can come in and shake up the established order as radically as Schumacher did? What kind of self-assurance, a blind belief in his own rectitude and his own path would allow a young man to stand up to such intimidation by the greatest driver the sport had known to that point? Senna's gift as a racing driver was sublime, but his self-belief was what made him the driver he was. The same was true of Schumacher. Even though he had done comparatively little at this stage, he knew that he belonged in the very highest echelons of the sport. So was it false modesty when he spoke in 1990 about his fears that he might not be good enough for F1? More likely it was his natural pessimism. From the very start of his F1 career, Schumacher did not look like a man who was surprised to be there. He carried himself with a swagger and a confidence which was designed to send a signal to the opposition.

Martin Brundle was Schumacher's team-mate in 1992. He had been Senna's closest rival in the 1983 British Formula 3 championship, matching him for most of the season and narrowly missing out on the title. Martin is a very grounded character, self-critical and full of common sense. He has always believed that what he lacked in comparison with Senna and Schumacher was total confidence in his own ability. 'He [Schumacher] had this confidence about him that mentally can bury you. I don't think it's put on. I think it is just the way he is. He had a lot of arrogance and a bit of immaturity, but he was gifted with speed. He had the ability to question anything that anybody else tried to do. He had little respect for other people's experience and that is actually quite a quality in a driver, if you have that kind of self-confidence.'

Schumacher disputes this theory. 'I don't have the kind of confidence [people] think I have. Not at all. Actually when things don't go well, I always question myself first. I don't believe I have as much self-belief as people think from the outside. But in relation to my rivals, I can't know what their level of self-belief is.'

Brundle, like David Coulthard, believes that Schumacher was hard-wired to believe that he was right and that he could justify any action with his own version of the truth.

He's just like Senna and Prost. He has a natural gift and the incredible self-belief which goes with it. These guys are winners who will push the limits beyond everyone else. They have the most intense, almost *dangerous*, desire and need to win at all costs and somehow they convince themselves that they are not wrong. They'll talk you through the story and they are actually quite convinced that they are not wrong.

Look at Senna and Prost in Japan those two years [1989/90]. Both were convinced that they'd done the right thing. Senna drove Prost off the road, but he could construct a solid reason – even twelve months later – why that wasn't wrong! I think Schumacher did the same in Jerez. He'd be thinking, 'Hang on, I've seen drivers run guys off the road in the past and people thought that they were real racers. Gilles Villeneuve would have been hero-worshipped for something like that.' In other words he believed that those kinds of moves made you a respected gung-ho racer and he was shaken rigid by the reaction he got. Michael's problem was that he was on a pedestal and in today's era of political correctness he learned the hard way that things have changed.

Rubens Barrichello was very close to Ayrton Senna, a fellow Brazilian, and then later became Schumacher's team-mate. He sees them quite differently.

As a team-mate I couldn't always say what I wanted to say. It's funny but Michael always had a different vision. He had so many qualities but if he did something wrong, in his mind it was right. You might think that he couldn't sleep at night, but he did because in his mind he's right. That's how he manages to live his life. I don't see Ayrton like that. Ayrton drove by passion. He would crash into you and then get out and say, 'Sorry, I made a mistake.' I don't think Michael could do that, and that's the difference.

A good illustration of Barrichello's view came a few months after the 1997 Jerez incident. Schumacher had had the book thrown at him for his actions, even been disqualified from the world championship records for that season, a punishment no one has ever received before or since. It was a massive stain on his character. When questioned Schumacher was contrite up to a point, but fundamentally he still felt he was in the right. 'In the past that was the way you did it,' he said. 'If you would not have done it you would have been criticised the other way around. Nevertheless we live in different times and you have to adapt to the situation.'

Of course the conviction that you are always right will only carry you so far: you need to back it up with results. In Schumacher's case he had been a regular on the podium throughout 1992, which was quite an achievement given the dominance of the Williams-Renault package. Nigel Mansell wrapped up the world title at the Hungarian Grand Prix in August, having won 8 of the 11 races to that point. Schumacher had been on the podium five times, but in Spa Francorchamps, exactly a year after his F1 debut, he made his breakthrough, winning his first Grand Prix. 'I felt it coming,' he said at the time. 'This morning in the motorhome, I suddenly felt intuitively that I could win.'

It was a typical Spa race, wet then dry, the track treacherous in places, one of those days when F1 is at its absolute best, because it looks so difficult and dangerous that the man in the street knows there is no way he could ever do it; he is in total awe of the racing drivers' skill. Rain is a great leveller. It takes away many advantages in aerodynamic down-force and horsepower and hands the advantage back to the driver and to his tacticians on the pit wall. Second-guessing the weather and gambling on the perfect moment to change tyres are the keys to winning.

Schumacher's car was well balanced and he felt that it was right under him in the tricky conditions. Ironically it was a mistake and its aftermath which gave him the understanding he needed to win the race. He ran wide at the Stavelot corner, narrowly missing the barriers on the outside. He recovered the car, but was passed by his team-mate, Martin Brundle. The track was drying out and Schumacher looked at the blisters on Brundle's rear tyres as he followed him. He decided it was time to switch to dry weather tyres, so he pitted, one of the first to do so. His speed after the pit stop showed everyone else that he had taken the correct option as he was now running away from them. He finished half a minute ahead of the two Williams drivers to record his first ever F1 victory.

* * *

Schumacher and Senna continued to lock antlers throughout the 1993 season. At the opening race they collided, with Schumacher's car again hitting the back of Senna's and this time being forced to retire. Strangely Senna refused to commit to the McLaren team as the season got under way and proceeded on a race-by-race deal, at one million dollars per event. The reason for his reluctance was that McLaren had lost its works engine supply from Honda, with whom Senna had been very close, and the team was now a customer of Ford, as Jordan had been in 1991. Eventually Senna and McLaren boss Ron Dennis successfully lobbied Ford to give them equal equipment to that used by Benetton, even suggesting at one point that as McLaren represented the company's best chance of winning the title, they should be favoured. Having the same engine, but one development step ahead of Senna's, had been a competitive advantage for Schumacher in the early part of the season and he was well aware when he lost it that Senna had been the prime mover in forcing Ford's decision. All the time he was taking note of Senna's methods.

Senna's vacillation over his commitment to McLaren finally ended in July when a contract was signed. He had won three Grands Prix by that point, but team morale had been undermined by his behaviour and by his refusal to test between races.

It was clear that Senna was unsettled by the continued domination of Williams-Renault and at the Hungarian Grand Prix in August he famously offered to drive for Williams for nothing, ironic given that he had been demanding a million dollars per race from McLaren. But you could understand his reasoning: the Williams was untouchable again in 1993, this time with Alain Prost driving. Sadly for Senna, Williams's advantage was based to a large extent on high tech driver aids, like active suspension, ABS braking and traction control, which they had perfected earlier than their rivals. Senna got his timing wrong though, as these driver aids were duly banned by the FIA at the end of 1993. Not only were they hugely expensive but it was thought that they took away too much from the drivers' skill. So Senna moved to the right place, but at the wrong time.

During Senna's negotiation period with Williams, Benetton boss Flavio Briatore apparently saw an opportunity to raise Benetton's profile a little and spread a rumour that Senna might join the Benetton team. It was the kind of story that the media in F1 loves and the idea of a 'superteam' of Senna and

Schumacher taking on the mighty Williams cars was too good to ignore. The story had legs of its own, but Senna helped it on its way by saying, 'I would have no problems driving for the same team as Michael. He is young, fast and talented. But I am a three times world champion and have won almost forty Grands Prix ... and he only one. For me it would be no problem.'

What Schumacher regarded as Senna's lack of respect for him really irritated him. With Willi Weber working hard in the background to neutralise the story, Schumacher came out and strongly opposed any such idea. 'If Ayrton drove alongside me it would spoil the happy atmosphere that has been built up at Benetton. Senna seems to think he can do things to me on the track which he would not do to others. He has done several things which I am not happy with. F1 is very competitive and you have to deal with these things. Maybe he feels I am the only guy capable of fighting him and getting the best out of him.'

Comparisons between the two drivers were inevitable and continue to this day. At Benetton Schumacher was working with the engineer Pat Symonds, who had also worked with Senna in his early days at Toleman. He made some illuminating comparisons between the two men early in 1994. 'At the same point in their career, in the early days, Ayrton was better,' he said. 'He had a lot more racing experience and the ability to analyse. He was more aware of the car; Michael was a bit impetuous. However on a personal level Ayrton was a bit too intense, Michael is a lot more normal and that stands him in good stead. The complete analytical brain is coming and now he makes fewer mistakes.'

Schumacher took his second F1 victory in the Portuguese

Grand Prix at Estoril, his only win of 1993. From this point onwards in his career there would be only one other year, 2005, in which he would score just one win. The floodgates were about to open which would make Michael Schumacher the most successful driver in the history of the sport.

CHAPTER TEN

The death of Senna

On that terrible weekend in 1994 on which Ayrton Senna and Roland Ratzenberger died, I realised how dangerous our sport can be. It was like a shock for me. In Imola I was faced for the first time with the fact that people really can die in my beloved sport and I seriously considered whether I wanted to accept that and was able to carry on at all.

Michael Schumacher

The 1994 season changed everything for Michael Schumacher. Both his career path and his outlook were altered fundamentally. It was a momentous season, not simply because of Senna's death and because Schumacher ended it as world champion. Much else happened during the year which affected his reputation, his competitiveness, his choice of team for the future and his relationships with the governing body and with other drivers.

It was the year when his anti-sporting instincts were first highlighted, though initially he was largely an innocent victim of his team's behaviour. But he was guilty by association and the mud stuck to him as well. In fact it was really only at the end of the season, in his controversial collision with Damon Hill at Adelaide, that Schumacher was directly culpable. Nevertheless he and his team were branded as cheats on several occasions and as a result, through a combination of bans and suspensions, he was able to score points in only 12 of the 16 Grands Prix. That he managed to win the title under those circumstances is a great credit to him as it was certainly his most hard-fought championship victory. But it was also to set the tone for the dual life he would continue to lead for the rest of his career; Schumacher the great champion and Schumacher the cheat, or 'Schummel Schumi', as the German press nicknamed him.

'I am a different driver now from the one who raced for the first time at Spa,' he said at the start of the season, showing how big a journey he felt he had made already since 1991. He was referring to his position as undisputed number one driver at Benetton, his increased salary and his relative success. Life was so simple at the beginning. Now, after little over two seasons of racing he had two wins and 15 podiums to his credit. For the first time he was entering a season knowing that he would be fighting for the world championship. His quest got off to a dream start, with wins in Brazil and Japan. Then came Imola.

Going into the weekend, Ayrton Senna had yet to score a championship point, while Schumacher had a maximum 20. It was already a big margin for the Brazilian to make up, especially as it was clear that, shorn of its driver aids, the Williams was not the force it had been in the previous two seasons. Benetton's technical department under Ross Brawn and chief designer Rory Byrne had produced a fast, reliable car which in Schumacher's hands would take some beating. There were some murmurings after the first two races about the quality of the Benetton's getaways from the lights at the start of the race. Computerised launch control was one of the driver aids banned by the FIA and all cars were carefully checked to ensure that no remnants of the old electronic systems remained. But Schumacher's starts, which were never his forte, looked particularly sharp in those opening races and for most of the first half of the season.

After retiring early from the second round at Aida in Japan, Senna stood at the trackside to watch the racing and afterwards mentioned to friends his conviction that Benetton was still using traction control. 'Something has to be done,' he told his close confidant, McLaren co-ordinator Jo Ramirez. 'They are cheating. Those cars should be checked.'

Of course it is the easiest thing in the world to arouse suspicion in Formula 1. It is a highly competitive environment and any performance advantage is viewed with suspicion by the opposition and by a media pack hungry for controversy. This is especially true when rule changes are brought in, particularly those which ban a previously widely used technology. From 1994 until May 2001 (when traction control was legalised again, because it proved impossible to police the ban), Schumacher's cars were always the subject of suspicion by his rivals, because he was always so competitive.

The potential for cheating using electronics is a dubious area in F1 politics, rather like drug-taking in cycling, and it is devilishly hard to prove. But for competitors to get away with, for example, illegal traction control undermines the sport, as drugs do in cycling. The problem for Schumacher was that because of other controversies which he and his team had became embroiled in that year, some people were prepared to believe the worst, even if Schumacher was completely innocent.

Traction control works by cutting the power electronically when the sensors tell the computer that there is wheelspin. This allows the rear tyres to recover grip and the car will accelerate better. Rear tyres always struggle to grip out of slow corners, as the driver buries the throttle and delivers over 900 horsepower to the tyres – so controlling that wheelspin can save three or four tenths of a second per lap and also nurses the rear tyres, enough to make a significant difference over a 70-lap race.

Senna was not the only one to voice his suspicions in Aida. The governing body, which had threatened 'draconian' penalties on any team caught cheating, was also suspicious and requested from each team a full explanation of their electronic control systems. Benetton took three weeks to reply, which aroused even more suspicion. But they were not the only ones in the spotlight.

There was a furore when Ferrari driver Nicola Larini made a throwaway comment to the Italian media about the traction control system on his car. The team moved quickly to defuse the row, saying it was merely a 'power reduction' device. After Larini's comments, the FIA looked into the matter and asked Ferrari to remove the system for the rest of the Aida weekend. No action was taken against Ferrari though, prompting rival teams to suggest that it was impossible for the FIA to police traction control effectively.

'My world championship will start at Imola,' said Senna, who had struggled in the opening races with a car which handled poorly in the slow corners compared to the Benetton. Williams had made substantial revisions to the car for the

Imola race. But instead of controlling the championship, Senna was chasing it. It was not supposed to work out this way. With Prost retired, Mansell gone to America and the inexperienced Damon Hill as his team-mate, Senna had expected a clearer run to his fourth world title. Instead Schumacher had the upper hand.

'Schumacher is young, has talent and has a good car and team behind him,' said Senna, who also hinted at a thaw in relations. 'With him I have a calm, professional relationship. I don't want to be his enemy, because he isn't that to me. We should remain rivals.'

The pair had started to talk more about driver-related issues like safety. Ironically they were to have a lengthy discussion about the subject on the morning of the San Marino Grand Prix a few hours before Senna's death.

The shift in Senna's attitude towards Schumacher is confirmed by his friends, among them Jo Ramirez.

Schumacher always had respect for Ayrton, but to start with Ayrton *did* want to put him down as a kid and make him feel like he was never going to beat him. Undoubtedly that started to change at the start of 1994, Ayrton recognised that Schumacher was his rival and they also began talking more between them about the safety side and the respect was definitely there from Ayrton. When Ayrton had no points after two races and Schumacher had twenty points Ayrton was desperate, the pressure was huge.

Anyone who was at Imola that weekend has a permanent imprint of it on their minds. First of all on the Friday afternoon Rubens Barrichello had a spectacular accident in practice and broke his nose. The following day in qualifying Roland Ratzenberger crashed heavily at the high speed Villeneuve corner. The accident looked very bad; the car had broken up and Ratzenberger was motionless in the cockpit. It was an eerily long stoppage, as medical teams tried in vain to resuscitate him. It had been a long time since death had visited a Formula 1 track, eight years, and the sport had come to convince itself that the cars were bulletproof – hence the heavy-handed driving of the Prost/Senna years, the games of chicken, the treating of racing cars as weapons.

Senna was deeply affected by Ratzenberger's death. He had met the Austrian for the first time just the day before in the race control building and they had enjoyed a brief but cordial conversation. Senna had welcomed him to Formula 1 and wished him well. To lose a colleague is shocking and especially poignant as they had met so recently. Senna later visited the scene of the accident with Professor Syd Watkins, the medical delegate, seeking a greater understanding of what had happened.

The next day he seemed happier with his car after finishing the warm-up a second faster than the next car. 'He was determined that he was going to blow Schumacher away,' recalls Williams technical director Patrick Head. The Brazilian is reported to have told his girlfriend by telephone that he had a bad feeling about the race, but he did not express such feelings to any of his friends or colleagues at the track. According to Head, Senna stayed up talking to him and Frank Williams until 11pm the night before the race. 'He was confident about the next day, believing the problem with the car had been overcome, saying we should do this, do that – you know, typical competitive driver.' Nevertheless, he wanted to get back to his farm in Portugal as soon as the race was over and so he asked Ramirez to organise a helicopter to take him to the airport at Forli immediately afterwards.

Senna did however carry one premonition into the Imola weekend. In an interview with an Italian paper he had spoken about how the reintroduction of refuelling stops in 1994 had turned the races into frenzied scrambles. It wasn't so much the risk of fires he was worried about but the fact that the races were now a series of sprints with low fuel levels, placing what he considered an unreasonable strain on both drivers and cars. Whereas before the skill had been in knowing when to push and when to conserve the car, now it was all-out attack. Senna was unhappy that this had been done to spice up the show, without thought to the increased dangers; hence his discussions with Schumacher on the race morning about reforming the Grand Prix Drivers Association to speak out on safety matters, with the two of them as the leading lights.

Senna had taken pole position on the Saturday with a very special lap, faster than the car should have been capable of going. The pressure was really on the Brazilian. In the early laps of the race he was overdriving the car, pushing it beyond its limit. It was obvious to Schumacher as he followed Senna that he could not continue like that for the whole race, the intensity was too great. Schumacher had decided not to try to pass him but to wait, because he knew that Senna could not keep it up. 'Ayrton's car had seemed very nervous through that corner [Tamburello],' recalled Schumacher. 'I could see that it was bottoming quite a lot and he nearly lost it. On the next lap at the same place he did lose it. The car touched the ground, he got a bit sideways and lost it. It looked a dangerous impact but I didn't have the feeling it was anywhere near what happened with Ratzenberger.'

Schumacher never did pass the accident scene. By the time he came around to complete his lap the red flags were out so he stopped on the pit straight. He had seen in a split second Senna's car spear off the track and crash into the wall but he had seen accidents like that before and in every case the driver had walked away unscathed. The worst accident he had witnessed to that point in F1 was Alex Zanardi's huge shunt on the Eau Rouge corner at Spa, where the bodywork of his Lotus had been scattered all the way up the hillside. Zanardi had suffered concussion but nothing worse, and his accident had looked much worse that Senna's. What killed the Brazilian was a piece of his front suspension, which pierced his helmet like a dagger. Apart from that the rest of his body was perfectly intact.

The race was restarted. This did not seem particularly callous at the time because no one knew about Senna's condition, only that he had been airlifted to hospital in nearby Bologna. The drivers climbed back into their cars and went out to race and Schumacher won. Afterwards, he said that as he raced he had imagined that Senna would be fine, his crash had not appeared particularly serious. He told himself that Senna might struggle to race at Monaco at worst. On the podium he was told that Senna was in a coma. It wasn't until several hours after the race that he learned from Willi Weber that Senna was dead. According to his manager he wept like a child.

* * *

Senna once told the journalist Norman Howell that he dealt with his fears by overcoming them one at a time and then building up his courage with each small victory, 'as if they are bricks'. Each year he had more bricks because he had more fear.

Schumacher always downplayed the fear factor and he did it so consistently and so naturally that one is forced to believe that it never troubled him in the cockpit of a racing car. For him the challenge was always to keep the car on the limit whatever the conditions, which carried with it a huge burden of risk. Schumacher was well aware of that, but it did not translate into fear. It made no discernible difference to his outlook as he matured and became a husband and then a father. He spoke about this in 2001, by which time he had two small children. 'In racing conditions it's not really the moment I think, "That's a risk I would take now because I'm single or I'm a married man with a child." You don't think, you just drive to your confidence and your abilities. In testing it's sometimes different, where you know there is a risky moment, the car is not perfectly balanced, you think, "Why should I take this risk now to prove whether it's risky or not?" '

Asked at the start of his final season whether he had become more anxious with the passing years, he replied, 'Anxious is the wrong word. You're more conscious of the danger. If I notice today that there's something not one hundred per cent right about the car, I prefer to take it back to the pits. Before I would probably have driven on.'

Interestingly Jean Todt, the Ferrari team principal who became very close to Schumacher, told German magazine *Park Lane* in 2006, 'Michael has become more anxious and more worried about everything. He always acts so self-confident, but people who are anxious and fragile are inclined to be very protective of themselves.'

As with everything in his life, Schumacher has a controlled methodology for approaching the subject of risk and death. Asked once if he ever thought about being involved in an accident he replied, 'Not really. As a racing driver you don't really approach the subject. Although the weekend in 1994 when Senna and Ratzenberger were killed was certainly one of the worst moments of my life. Before that it wasn't really there that you can actually die in a racing car. I've imagined all strokes of fortune but not this one.'

He briefly considered stopping after Imola, but that was not uncommon. Most of the drivers in F1 gave the idea some thought, especially those like Gerhard Berger who were close to Senna and Ratzenberger. But, like Berger, they decided that it was what they did best, what they enjoyed the most and that they had worked hard to get to where they were. Schumacher spent a few days reflecting and then went to Silverstone in the week following Senna's death for a test session, to see if he still had the passion, the speed and above all the stomach, for Formula 1. Despite being preoccupied beforehand with thoughts of going off the road and crashing, once he sat in the car Schumacher's mind locked into its normal mode and he was able to drive on the limit without any appreciable loss of performance. And he had no fear. 'It has always been like that for me,' he said. 'I just do the job, it's a natural thing.' This was the first time that he had stopped to do some real soul-searching and he found the process disconcerting, but ultimately he got the right answer.

It was so difficult for me, in the aftermath of Imola, to focus my mind properly like a racing driver. I did have some serious problems. I knew too that if I could not do the job the right way, in my own mind, I would have to stop racing. I felt extremely insecure about my racing. I didn't know if I could drive as light-heartedly as I used to. I wondered if the speed was still in me. But all these problems were resolved when I went testing at Silverstone before Monaco.

I was able to get my mind right, to sort things out. But I was still, like everyone, desperately unhappy at the deaths of Roland and Ayrton. I measured myself against Ayrton, he was the fastest driver in Formula 1 and nothing would have meant more to me than to have won my first pole position at Monte Carlo against him.

Whatever his conscience may have been telling him, as a methodical man Schumacher's reaction to the Imola tragedy was to work harder in the field of safety. After the race he was visibly shocked and said 'What has happened this weekend, I've never seen anything like it before. The only thing I can say about this is I hope we can learn from it. We are all of the same opinion and perhaps today the drivers are closer than they were in the past. There are some good ideas, which should be discussed with the right people. The weak point is the driver because we sit with the car around us, but the head is exposed and it cannot take a heavy impact.'

Looking back on this period a few years later, Schumacher reflected on how it had led to the revival of the Grand Prix Drivers Association. 'It struck me how important safety is and how much there is still to do. I think people ought to stay within their limits. These have to be fathomed out and checked. This I see as my task. I have the advantage that I have a certain standing in this profession and also gain a hearing as one of the three directors of the GPDA and as a member of a further safety commission which has regular exchanges with the FIA. In the meantime we have achieved a lot.'

The need for action was intensified when Schumacher's former Mercedes team-mate, Karl Wendlinger, crashed heavily in practice at Monaco. Again the vulnerability of the driver's head was the issue: Wendlinger went into a coma as a result of a serious head injury, and this ended his F1 career. The GPDA was re-formed on the Friday of the Monaco weekend, with Martin Brundle as chairman and Schumacher and Berger as his co-directors. The drivers spent the entire day talking about a variety of issues and challenges which faced them. At the end of the meeting they all slipped quietly away, not wishing to speak to the waiting journalists. Niki Lauda was one of several ex-drivers invited to sit in on the meeting and contribute ideas. He did go and speak to the journalists, creating the impression that he was the figurehead, but the drivers never saw him at one of their meetings again. The weeks which followed saw F1 in panic mode as makeshift chicanes were installed to slow the cars down, rules were rushed through by the FIA to reduce engine power and strengthen the cars' chassis.

Schumacher did not attend Senna's funeral in Brazil. He was advised by the Benetton management that it would not be safe, that in the highly charged emotional atmosphere the German's presence might spark some random attack by someone who thought he was the cause of Senna's death. But he did not attend for his own personal reasons as well; it was the old thing about being asked to show emotions in public, something he has always refused to do. 'I didn't feel I had anything to prove. I did not need to go to the funeral to share my feelings. These obvious gestures are not my style. But I was hit by his death, he meant a lot to me, we weren't especially friendly but he was my idol. I was sitting at home and crying and sharing my feelings with my wife and friends but I didn't feel I needed to do it outside my house.'

It was a highly emotional time for everyone and a time of recriminations and political manoeuvring, one of the gravest crisis moments the sport had faced. No one was quite sure what would happen next. Bernie Ecclestone and FIA president Max Mosley were both told in no uncertain terms by Senna's family that they were not welcome at the funeral. Senna's brother actually blamed them for creating the environment in which Ayrton had died.

Alain Prost, Senna's bitterest rival, went to the funeral and was criticised for alleged hypocrisy. Schumacher did not go and was criticised for not paying his respects. There was no right answer. 'On the one hand I regret not having flown to Brazil,' recalls Schumacher. 'But on the other, I'm not someone who has to sit in a church to believe. I can feel grief without attending a burial.'

Two years later he visited Senna's grave, which sits beneath a solitary tree on a rolling green hillside in the Morumbi district of Sao Paolo. He went privately with Corinna, shortly before the 1996 Brazilian Grand Prix.

> I actually wanted to do that beforehand, but in peace. For me and for him and not for anyone else. I couldn't have the hype. That's why I didn't go to his funeral and that's why I didn't go to his grave straight away, although it was expected of me. I had to sort it out in my own mind. It was important to go to him, but in tranquillity. That's how I wanted to pay my last respects to him.

I just wept. I remembered the moments in which we were together, the good and the bad. And then I thought that he really meant a lot to me, that he was a role model for me.

Senna was my idol. Even today, I find the fact that he is gone completely unreal. Senna was the best. Period. To drive alongside him, to fight with him, to beat him – it was a feeling beyond description. I still can't understand why he of all drivers had to die. He who seemed so unearthly, so invincible, so unequalled.

Senna's influence on Schumacher runs very deep. There is little doubt, sifting through the evidence of Schumacher's career, that he was heavily influenced by Senna's behaviour as a racer. He admitted after driving into Villeneuve at Jerez that 'in the past that was the way you did it' referring to Senna's behaviour in similar situations. In other words, he had perhaps weighed up the situation and decided that was what Senna would have done, and would have got away with it, so he should do the same. It is this emotional bond to Senna the racer which got Schumacher into trouble. What he could never understand is why Senna was allowed to get away with it by the media and the public, whereas he came in for an avalanche of criticism. One observer, the veteran photographer Paul Henri Cahier, suggested that the difference was that Senna's attack on Prost at Suzuka was a grand and passionate gesture, quite magnificent in its ambition, whereas Schumacher's collision with Damon Hill in Adelaide and with Jacques Villeneuve at Jerez were brought on by desperation and a desire not to lose. Max Mosley takes a similar view, albeit expressed rather differently. For him, Senna's act was understandable because of the way he had been treated the year before whereas with Schumacher's, 'that was to win the championship, there was no great emotional reason for doing it.'

Schumacher carried himself in a very different way from Senna, because he did not have Senna's natural charisma. But he most certainly recognised a rare quality that the two men shared: the belief that they had a god-given right to do whatever they thought was right in pursuit of victory.

Sabine Kehm, who worked alongside Schumacher for seven seasons, makes an interesting observation on Schumacher's feelings about Senna. 'He admired Senna a lot. I spoke with him several times about it, but it always comes to a certain point. He doesn't want to open up. In the end he is a very sensitive guy, he's very sure of himself if he knows what's going on, but he knows that he has certain soft spots. And he knows that if he opens up he's not sure what will come out, so he doesn't ever open up.'

This rings very true and it is undoubtedly the reason why Schumacher did not attend Senna's funeral and why he has stopped short on other difficult occasions in his career, when a simple expression of contrition would have saved the day. Schumacher knew his own limitations; he is a man whose self-control is extraordinarily refined, but he also knows that he has emotional faultlines. He is unwilling to visit that side of himself and even less so to let the public see it, so he retreats into his protective shell and hides the real Schumacher from the public, preventing them from properly understanding him. As he got older he hid behind the shell more readily because he was tired of being asked to be a performing monkey, to show his emotions on demand for public scrutiny.

When defending his position on this subject, Schumacher

often cites the example of Mika Hakkinen, who threw away victory in the Italian Grand Prix of 1999 with an unforced error, when he was under pressure in the championship and badly needed the ten points. Hakkinen found what he thought was a quiet place among the trees, sat down on his crash helmet and cried his eyes out. He was spotted by a television camera in a helicopter and his distress played out live in front of the world. Schumacher reflects:

> Mika showed some humanity, some emotion and what did the journalists do? They screwed him for it. So what should you do? Well, you should try to keep a balance and that way you don't show everything you are feeling to the outside world, because if you do it's used against you in a bad way. So you do a professional job and that sometimes means you're not really doing what is human, what is natural. You protect yourself and all of us are doing that, I think, to some degree.

Schumacher did this so successfully that he was often described as 'a robot'. But one occasion on which he spectacularly lost his composure was when he won the Italian Grand Prix of 2000 and burst into tears in the press conference afterwards, when told that he had equalled Senna's total of 41 Grands Prix victories. Looking back on that moment years later, he said that his tears were embarrassing to him. 'I don't know why, but Ayrton's story is a story that has always followed me. Every time I am confronted with it I get very emotional. Of course you don't want to admit it at the time, you make a conscious effort to hide your emotions so as not to reveal a weakness to others.'

In fact, although it was the mention of Senna which tipped

him over the edge, his reaction was as much due to the release of the pressure which had built up steadily all summer after the 2000 championship had appeared to be slipping away from him. On top of that, he had been told that morning that Willi Bergmeister, one of his close allies from his early days and his first employer, had suffered a massive heart attack. It was too strong a cocktail of emotions for him to keep a lid on.

*   *   *

With his first victory at Monaco under his belt, Schumacher had opened up a commanding lead in the 1994 world championship over his new rival, Senna's Williams team-mate Damon Hill. Schumacher had four wins from four and was cruising. Even a gearbox fault during the Spanish Grand Prix, which left him stuck in fifth gear for most of the race, could not slow him down. In a tale which has become part of Schumacher folklore he adapted his driving style and brought the car home in second place behind Hill.

Further wins followed in Canada and France. With almost half the season gone Schumacher had 66 points to Hill's 29 and was virtually within sight of his first world title. But then the trouble started.

CHAPTER ELEVEN

Schummel, Schumi

This is my third season with Benetton.
Why didn't we do any cheating last year?
We don't suddenly start cheating particularly with
the performance advantage we've got and
the driver we've got.

Ross Brawn

In the summer of 1994 several things happened in quick succession which undermined Schumacher's grasp on the world championship but, more damagingly, undermined his reputation. First he got into trouble with the FIA for ignoring a black flag, which means a mid-race disqualification. Then his team was caught cheating when investigations into a pit lane fire revealed that they had been removing filters from the fuel line to speed up delivery. Finally in Spa, Schumacher drove an outstanding race to win, only to find that his car was disqualified for an illegal floor. But worse than all of those things was the FIA's discovery that Benetton had maintained a programme in the car's computer which the driver could use to activate an illegal launch control system. Thus Schumacher's integrity was thrown into doubt and he had one brickbat after another thrown at him. He found the experience profoundly unsettling.

Though the mud stuck to Schumacher, much of the blame must fall on the team. Many seasoned F1 observers felt that there was a vendetta by the FIA against Benetton and it has often been suggested that it may have suited them to spice up the championship by cutting Schumacher's huge points lead. But there was more to it than that.

Following Senna's death the FIA rammed through a series of drastic rule changes intended to slow the cars down and make them safer. Of greatest concern to the teams was the introduction of a stepped floor on the cars, to ensure that they did not run too low to the ground, as Senna's car had done in Imola. But floor height has a profound effect on aerodynamics and the teams felt that to rush into making alterations would make the cars less, not more, stable. Many teams felt that the FIA's package of changes was too hasty and ill thought out and demanded more consultation.

Shortly before the Spanish Grand Prix in late May, Benetton boss Flavio Briatore wrote an open letter to FIA president Max Mosley, questioning his ability to police the new rules and to enforce safety. His final paragraph was incendiary. 'You continue to insist on these ill-conceived measures. It is our opinion that the ability of yourself and your advisers to judge technical and safety issues in Formula 1 must be questioned.'

Briatore, although very close to F1's other major powerbroker, Bernie Ecclestone, was still relatively new to the sport, having started in 1989. He was at the helm of a brash new team which was closing in on its first world title, threatening the cosiness of the elite, represented by McLaren, Williams and Ferrari. This letter was effectively a vote of no confidence in the FIA president. The Italian was asking for trouble if the team subsequently transgressed and Benetton duly got it in spades.

The Silverstone black flag incident, a notorious story in Schumacher folklore, started out as an innocent little piece of gamesmanship, which escalated into a scandal and finally to a three-race suspension. That threw the title race wide open. Schumacher had been outqualified by Damon Hill, who was starting from pole position. But as they drove off on the formation lap, Schumacher sprinted ahead. The rules say you should hold formation on the parade lap or start from the back of the grid. The start was aborted for other reasons and Schumacher did the same again on the second parade lap. Clearly he was trying to unsettle Hill. The stewards should have made him start from the back of the grid but instead the race got under way normally. The stewards deliberated for a long time and eventually imposed a five-second penalty on Schumacher for his infringement, but they did not spell out that it was a 'stop and go' penalty where the driver is obliged to make a visit to the pits thereby losing him time and position.

The Benetton management spotted this omission, and realised that some errors had been made in race control so decided to play it crafty, expecting to argue afterwards that they believed that the time would be added to their driver's overall race time at the end. The clerk of the course, however, was expecting the team to bring Schumacher in within three laps, to serve the penalty.

Failure to observe a stop and go penalty is a disqualifiable offence and a black flag was shown with the number five, indicating that Schumacher should come in and get out of the car. He carried on racing, ignoring the black flag for three laps. At this point, and after discussion with the stewards, the black flag was withdrawn, and the team brought Michael in, but he proceeded to the end of the pit lane, served his five-second stop and go penalty and then rejoined the race. The team had made mistakes but so had the clerk of the course, who had failed to notify the team of the original offence within the required 15 minutes and had not followed the correct procedure. The stewards let Schumacher keep his second place but fined him and the team £15,000. However FIA president Max Mosley picked up the baton and the situation quickly spiralled out of Benetton's control. 'We always got along well, I liked Michael, there was no animosity on my side,' says Mosley. 'As the mafia say, "It's nothing personal, just business." What happened was that Flavio went to Bernie and tried to get him to sort it out, but it was nothing to do with Bernie.'

Mosley summoned Schumacher to a special hearing in late July, two weeks after the incident. Schumacher rather unwisely commented on his summons to the media. 'It is all a lot of hot air,' he said to some German journalists. 'I don't think it is right to interfere with the championship like this. All the theatre is rather stupid. Okay, I passed Damon and I wasn't supposed to. The thing is, I wasn't alone, I got a penalty and the misunderstanding was a mistake of the team. That was solved after a discussion with the stewards. I don't expect any more action than has already happened.'

But this was not hot air, it was deadly serious and when Schumacher and Briatore walked into the court room in Paris they realised that the Silverstone incident was only a part of the rap sheet. The FIA had taken the on-board computers out of every car after the San Marino Grand Prix and sent them away for detailed analysis. They now accused Benetton of having 'a computer system containing a facility capable of breaching the regulations'. Although the FIA could not prove that the launch control system had been used in Imola, the fact that the software was clearly there and that it took only a simple sequence of controls by the driver to activate it, was considered by some to be damning enough. In their eyes it raised questions about the team's and, by extension, Schumacher's integrity.

As for the Silverstone incident, Benetton was fined $500,000 and censured for not knowing the rules properly, while Schumacher was suspended for two races. As he got up to leave, Mosley said, 'Oh and by the way, we're taking away the six points for Silverstone.'

Schumacher, as Mosley recalls, 'was not happy'.

The decision turned the world championship on its head. In statements to the press at the time, Mosley further questioned Schumacher's integrity by saying, 'The version of events supplied by Schumacher, that he had not seen the black flag, is unacceptable. The black flag is like the red card in football. The player shown a red card should leave the field immediately and that's what Schumacher should have done.' Briatore aggravated the situation still further by saying in the Italian press, 'I told Schumacher, via radio, to stay out on the track.'

It seemed a very harsh penalty at the time, even to Schumacher's rivals. A few years earlier Nigel Mansell had ignored a black flag during a race and then crashed into another car, but received only a one-race ban.

Schumacher is still angry about the Silverstone incident and the way it reflects on him to this day.

I didn't ignore the black flag, I hadn't seen it. I'm not saying that I hadn't made a mistake, but so did the FIA.

My impression at the time was that it was a set-up and I was the scapegoat. We had a big lead in the championship and a lot of people were happy about us getting this penalty. It turned into a real trend against us. The way Flavio Briatore dealt with it didn't really help either. You swim against a current that is so powerful that despite being really strong yourself you can say what you want and no one is interested.

With some distance now I can also say that you tend to look at those events from a different angle, you don't just see your own side of it. Maybe that's going to happen to Alonso too, if you think of the situation at Monza in 2006, when he thought he was punished unjustly by the FIA. He thought there was a conspiracy against him. I had a lot of sympathy for him and I understood his reaction because it reminded me of 1994. I told him that after the Monza race, when we met at the airport in Geneva.

It is interesting that Schumacher makes the comparison with Monza 2006, because many felt the same way, that Alonso was unfairly penalised. But Schumacher had learned from his experiences in 1994, realising that it is important to be on good terms with the FIA. He would also have been aware that Ferrari had escaped unpenalised over the 'power management' story in Aida while his team had come unstuck.

With the FIA having thrown the book at Benetton at the Paris hearing, the scene was set for an extraordinarily dramatic German Grand Prix weekend. With the race being a 120,000 sell-out, with most of the fans there solely to see Germany's first title contender for over 30 years, it was not the ideal time for him to serve a two-race suspension. Benetton appealed the punishment which allowed Schumacher to race in front of his home crowd.

But worse trouble lay in store. The FIA issued a briefing document that weekend, which explained the details of the dormant launch control system concealed within the Benetton software. The explosive revelation was that the FIA's software analysts in Liverpool had worked out how easily the system could be activated.

The statement said: 'To arm the system the driver must hold down the downchange paddle and then flick the upchange paddle once. The downchange paddle must then be released. The driver then applies full throttle when appropriate and a flick of the upchange paddle will set the car in motion.'

So had Schumacher been cheating like this all season? The FIA concluded that the best evidence was that the device had not been used in the San Marino Grand Prix, the race after which the computer from Schumacher's car had been analysed. But their statement still left a gigantic question-mark hanging over his performances throughout the year. Certainly his start at the French Grand Prix had aroused great suspicion, but Benetton technical director Ross Brawn categorically denied any wrongdoing.

Michael was useless at starts last year, he has [now] developed a technique of using the clutch and throttle in a way that eliminates wheelspin.

The risk involved with being caught and eliminated from the championship is tremendous. If we were foolish enough to use such a system willingly and be caught we would be putting two hundred people and their families' futures at risk. Our success has been gained by hard work and the talents of Michael Schumacher. Unfortunately it is a cross we have to bear that people seem to look for easy reasons why we are successful.

He would not necessarily have been aware of the deleted system this year, because it was irrelevant. I know Michael. He would not have used a system that was illegal with all the consequences it would have brought. I am categoric on that point.

More recently, in an interview published in *Motor Sport* magazine, Brawn revealed more details of what happened behind the scenes that year.

In 1994 we were simply accused of cheating. It was all ensnared in a giant political row going on between Max Mosley and Flavio, who had written a letter to the FIA saying Max wasn't fit to be president. Flavio came to Rory and me and said, 'We're going to concede this one, because all Max is going to do is take away our points from Imola.' And I said, 'If you do that deal then I will walk out of the door and so will Rory because we haven't done anything wrong. You won't have a technical director or a chief designer.'

That was the tragedy of traction control. Whichever team did well there was always innuendo. But when they made it legal again the same teams were winning so either everyone had it before or nobody had it before.

But the allegations of cheating kept on piling up. During the German race the team suffered a spectacular fire during a pit stop for Schumacher's team-mate, Jos Verstappen. When an investigation was carried out on Benetton's fuel rig it was found that they had removed a filter, which would have the effect of speeding up the flow of petrol at a pit stop, thus reducing the time the car would be stationary in the pits.

The team pleaded guilty to the charge, but said that the modification had been carried out by a junior mechanic without consulting the team management. The hearing took place a week after Schumacher was disqualified from the Belgian Grand Prix for having a floor which did not comply with the regulations. It was the team's fourth brush with the FIA over the summer and the FIA noted in its judgement that Benetton 'undertook to make substantial management changes so as to ensure that a similar event could never happen again', which was its justification for letting them off without punishment for the fuel filter issue. Briatore denied having given such assurances.

Technical director Ross Brawn made a strenuous defence of his team, denying all allegations of cheating. 'This is my third season with Benetton,' he said, 'Why didn't we do any cheating last year? We don't suddenly start cheating particularly with the performance advantage we've got and the driver we've got.'

A very frustrated Schumacher sat out the Italian and Portuguese Grands Prix, watching them on television in a café near his apartment in Monaco. He wanted it to be known that he was upset at the way that his name had been dragged through the mud and that his dominant performances had been undermined by the allegations of cheating. Rumours began to circulate that he was considering leaving Benetton, possibly joining forces with Mercedes at the McLaren team in 1995. The stories were emanating from journalists close to Schumacher and Willi Weber. It was clear that he needed to distance himself from the Benetton team and the steadily mounting allegations.

The German media had given Schumacher a hard time over

the summer, coining the phrase 'Schummel Schumi', which is halfway between 'crafty' and 'cheat'. But, not for the last time, Schumacher and Weber used the media to get what they wanted out of the situation, putting pressure on the team. Schumacher let it be known that he was unhappy that the team was not capable of looking after his image. 'I could leave Benetton,' he said at one point, 'if it were proven that the team had cheated.'

In a survey conducted at the time by one of the leading German newpapers, 65 per cent of fans thought that Schumacher should leave Benetton, that the team was harming him. Schumacher did little to discount the Mercedes stories by saying, 'I am a free agent at the end of 1995 and I will choose the best option available to me at that time.'

Although it was a lot less public than the switch from Jordan to Benetton in 1991, what was going on behind the scenes was another battle for Schumacher's services. And whereas the 1991 saga was all over in a fortnight, this one dragged on for another year. Willi Weber confirmed that, 'We have written to Benetton to say that we wish to discuss our contract, we will not continue driving under the current conditions.' But Briatore dismissed this as normal posturing to achieve an improved financial package.

In fact Weber used the situation masterfully to play hardball with Benetton. He held talks with Williams, McLaren and Ferrari and used these discussions to leverage a deal with Benetton for 1995, which doubled Schumacher's retainer to around $1 million per race while at the same time removing their previously held option for 1996. Schumacher would therefore be free to accept the best offer from elsewhere for the 1996 season. Financially this worked out very well for him as he almost doubled his salary again when he signed for Ferrari.

In late summer 1994, McLaren announced that it was joining forces with Mercedes Benz, whose stated aim was to get Schumacher in their car. Weber was quoted as saying, 'From 1996 we would regard Mercedes-McLaren as our number one partner, it would be our dream team. He has never really broken off his contacts with Mercedes. There has always been a wish to work with them again.'

With his two-race suspension, Schumacher was out of the cockpit for a month and, in his absence, Damon Hill closed to within one point of him in the world championship. The German's first world title, which had seemed a foregone conclusion two months earlier, was now in serious jeopardy.

In his frustration and bewilderment at this giant political game which was going on around him and in which he felt merely a pawn, Schumacher made some ill-advised media statements. He was moved to lash out in the German magazine *Auto Bild*. He claimed that the top three finishers in the German Grand Prix, won by Ferrari's Gerhard Berger, had all had the same worn down floor problem as he had suffered in Belgium and yet they went unpunished. He then further attacked Ferrari, saying that the FIA had been 'very kind' to Ferrari by letting them off without punishment for their 'power reduction' system at Aida. Ferrari's Jean Todt, later to become Schumacher's closest racing ally, reacted furiously: 'In relation to the rash statements of Schumacher, Ferrari has nothing to say except that the car of Berger, after the victory in Germany, was checked by the FIA scrutineers and found in conformity.'

Schumacher was on the offensive though, and at a test

session in Portugal immediately after his ban ended, he made a verbal attack on Damon Hill in a meeting with the British press. It was pretty clear what he was trying to do; to unsettle Hill and take away some of the momentum the Englishman had managed to build up during Schumacher's enforced absence. But it was clumsy and rather contrived as there had not been any obvious animosity between the pair thus far that season. But now that Hill had encroached on Schumacher's territory, the gloves came off. It was a classic piece of macho F1 behaviour – when you suffer pain, you give some out. Schumacher had felt bullied by the FIA all summer and now he was going to pass on some of that suffering to his title rival.

'There were a lot of stories from Hill's direction about the "cheating car" and that sort of thing,' Schumacher said. 'Every time we proved that we never cheated, they twisted it around and said there was something else to answer. He always seemed the English gentleman but when you are in trouble you get to know people.'

He added, 'Hill has not beaten me this season in any race without interference from outside.' Hill, he said, was a 'little man' who was 'never a number one driver and had been thrown into the job'. This was a particularly off-colour remark given the circumstances of Hill's promotion after the tragedy of Imola. Schumacher's ill-judged remarks added a charge of meanness and poor sportsmanship to the official charges he had accumulated through the season. Schumacher learned from it, however. Although he continued to play mind games on his rivals for the remainder of his career, he never again descended to such nastiness in the delivery of his statements. Those close to him advised him that this episode had been a bad own goal.

After clinching the championship title in Adelaide, Schumacher retracted his remarks. It was that rarest of species; a full, contrite Schumacher apology. 'Earlier in the year I said that I didn't have the same respect for Damon as I do for some of the others,' he said. 'I have to admit that I was wrong. What he has done over the past two races [Japan and Australia] has been a fantastic job. He has been a great rival and I must apologise for what I said.'

Hill had beaten Schumacher at the penultimate round of the championship in Japan, thanks to Benetton being caught out with the wrong race strategy for a rain-interrupted race. But at the season finale in Adelaide, Hill had pressured him for 36 laps, so much so that Schumacher made a mistake and ran off the circuit, damaging his car against a wall. As he swerved back on to the track, Hill tried to pass him down the inside, but Schumacher cut across him, crashing into the Williams in an impact which sent his own car up into the air and put the front suspension of Hill's car beyond use. It was his second mistake of the weekend, as he had destroyed his original race car in a big accident during qualifying.

At the end of a season full of controversy, most of it involving him, Schumacher had his first world title and he dedicated it to Senna. 'For me it was always clear that I wasn't going to win the championship and Ayrton was. I'd like to give it to him because he is the driver who should have earned it. He had the best car, he was the best driver.'

It was a gallant attempt at a charm offensive, designed to offset the darker side of his championship year and restore an impression of good sportsmanship. But the damage had been done and he was perceived very differently now by the F1 community and the world at large.

He had of course thoroughly deserved the title, no one would deny that, having been banned from two races and disqualified from two more. But if there was some sympathy for the way he had had his championship lead taken away from him, there was also a feeling that he shared some of the guilt. His reputation had taken a battering and although he had put in some sensational performances in difficult moments, he had also shown in Adelaide that he was liable to crack under extreme pressure and punch below the belt. This perception is something that he never shook off, despite all the brilliance of what was to follow in the next 12 seasons.

The major question mark at the end of the 1994 season was how complicit he had been in the team's misdemeanours. Schumacher believed that this was the wrong question, that minor things had been blown up to make the team look bad. 'If I finish a race like Spa with a wooden plank [on the floor] which is one millimetre too thin, one should not talk about fraud,' he said. But he also aligned himself with his team and took his share of the responsibility. Revealingly, in an interview at the end of the season, he said that he still believed that the way to win is to sail close to the wind: 'I'm there to co-decide how riskily the team behaves,' he told Swiss journalist Mattias Brunner. 'And as for the FIA, I have to admit that one millimetre too little is one millimetre too little, but there seems to be room to move as there were other decisions in similar situations. But the car was not in order and I will not accuse anyone for it. It's like the warm-up lap at Silverstone. Others did the same, but I was caught. I have to live with that.'

What is most striking about the 1994 season is how Schumacher and his team were made an example of and that is not uncommon in F1, it happens to this day. Essentially he was a victim of a greater political game, which was arguably started by his own boss. Had Schumacher not collided with Hill at the end of the season and then a few years later driven into Jacques Villeneuve at Jerez, the 'Schummel Schumi' tag would probably have remained a mere souvenir of 1994 and would more than likely have got lost in the mists of memory behind the more painful recollections of Senna's and Ratzenberger's deaths.

Unfortunately, though, the 1994 season set the tone for the rest of Schumacher's F1 career: here was a man perceived by many to be prepared to go to places in search of victory which his rivals would not even contemplate. The seal was also set on his departure from Benetton. They were now an established top team, which as Renault they remain to this day, but Schumacher's heart was set on a move away, partly to escape the controversy surrounding his name.

In the aftermath of Adelaide many people took the view that he had deliberately taken Hill out to clinch the title and Max Mosley has indicated that if the incident had happened today, 'There would be a major inquiry and whether Michael would have got away with it is open to doubt.'

Hill was dignified in defeat and made no suggestion that he felt hard done by, saying 'I've nothing against him. When a championship is decided at the last race, things can happen.'

Schumacher had grabbed the title with brutal force, but he would argue that the FIA had played its own savage game by trying to take it away from him. It was strangely appropriate that a season of such twists and turns should end with an incident like this, but it wasn't over yet; in the days following the race, the FIA decided to take another look at the incident. Bernie Ecclestone, then an FIA vice president, said that there was new amateur video footage which cast doubt on Schumacher's behaviour. 'Obviously the FIA wants to look into this because you can't have drivers deliberately running into each other, can you? The FIA is at liberty to deduct existing points, even take someone out of the world championship.'

His words were just a little reminder to the team and to Schumacher to keep their noses clean in future.

CHAPTER TWELVE

Made in Italy

We were in the shit in 1996. I remember
when the car came out I said, 'That looks worryingly
different from everyone else's car.' It turned out
that everyone else was right and we were wrong.

Eddie Irvine, ex-Ferrari driver

Schumacher breezed past the opposition in 1995 to clinch
his second world championship for Benetton. He dominated the season, put in some performances which crushed
the confidence of his main rival, Damon Hill, and arrived
at a controversy-free title with two races to spare. He was
26 years old, the youngest ever double world champion at
the time and the world's undisputed number one driver.
But he was also on the move and could more or less name
his price.

It had become clear during the summer of 1994 that a move
was the right thing for his career and there were three
potential candidates; Williams, McLaren, and Ferrari. Of the
three, only Williams was in a position to offer him a
championship-winning car. McLaren had suffered a patchy
run of form since losing Honda and Ayrton Senna in the

early 1990s and its first season with Mercedes was disastrous, the team finishing a distant fourth in the world championship with less than 25 per cent of the points tally of Benetton. Ferrari meanwhile had been steadily improving under Jean Todt, who had been in charge for three seasons. But the team was still a long way from the performance levels of Williams and Benetton. Willi Weber recalls:

> I had difficulty in getting the idea across, persuading him that Ferrari could be a good partner for us. He saw things a bit differently and said, 'Willi, do you know that when I drive up behind them, they're easer to overtake than almost anybody else? Are you sure this is the right move for us?'
>
> It would have been easy to go to McLaren, naturally that was a strong car and a driver looks for the potential in order to win the most races. But after much work convincing him, also for Michael to convince himself, after he'd thought it over he saw simply that there was an incredible amount of potential lying dormant in this Ferrari team.
>
> We had the opportunity to get out of our contract one year early and naturally we wanted to change and for me, needless to say, Ferrari was a legend. Ferrari was something which had always fascinated me. I myself have driven Ferraris for many years and knew that all the drivers who were under contract with Ferrari in Formula 1 had quite a different status than Benetton, so Ferrari is the aim and the great dream of Formula 1 drivers. For Michael, Ferrari was just a competitor at the time and he hadn't taken the time to look at them.

There were sporting reasons for going to Ferrari as well as commercial ones. One of the key considerations in Schumacher's mind was that he didn't necessarily have to go for the fastest car, as Senna, Prost, Fangio and many of the greats had always done. Looking around the F1 paddock it was clear to him that there was no one on his own level to beat. Unlike Senna and Prost who had to beat each other, Schumacher was in a league of his own at the time and he liked the idea of building something up together with a dedicated group of people, rather than simply slotting into the best team on the grid.

When people criticise Schumacher for his anti-sporting instincts they often forget this decision, which was probably the single greatest sporting gesture he made in his career. It ranks alongside anything that any other driver has done. To accept the challenge of returning the sport's most celebrated brand back to its former glory was not something that many people would have done in Schumacher's position and it is to his enormous credit that he did so.

On Ferrari's side, too, there was some concern, as its president Luca di Montezemolo explained a year later: 'When Todt started talking to him, I said, "But are you truly convinced that Ferrari is in a position to guarantee him a winning car, either straight away or even soon?" '

Commercial considerations made the deal particularly attractive to Weber. He had a production line of Schumacher merchandise, which grew to almost 100 items over the years which followed. Chief among them was the baseball cap, which sold in its millions. Part of the deal Weber negotiated was that Schumacher had the right to use the Ferrari logo, the famous Prancing Horse, on Schumacher merchandise. This was a hugely valuable asset to the brand. The canny Weber also negotiated a clause whereby Schumacher was able to have personal sponsors over and above his responsibility to Ferrari's main sponsors. He signed Michael up with Nike and with Canon, both of whom offered multimillion-dollar annual contracts and enjoyed long partnerships with him. The cap sponsorship was worth in the region of five million dollars per year as Schumacher was virtually never seen without his trademark cap. It all added up to an additional income which roughly doubled the basic Ferrari retainer.

As far as McLaren Mercedes was concerned this was one of the main deal-breakers. Ron Dennis does not allow his drivers to have personal sponsorship deals, preferring to pay an additional fee to the driver to focus solely on the team's sponsor requirements. And the personalised baseball cap would not have sat well with him either. Although McLaren was prepared to offer a higher basic retainer than Ferrari, it was nowhere near what Schumacher and Weber stood to make from the additional income under the Ferrari deal and also greatly restricted their commercial freedom.

As for Williams, Frank Williams had briefly been drawn in to paying large salaries for Alain Prost in 1993 and Ayrton Senna in 1994, but it was never his style to offer a driver more than ten million dollars per year and Ferrari was offering more than twice that amount. 'I would have loved to have had Michael in my team,' says Sir Frank Williams. 'I did try once. We had a couple of conversations with Willi Weber at the end of 1995. The desire was serious, but we had never paid a driver the kind of sums they were asking. It's nice to dream. Michael is an absolutely fantastic driver, up there with the best.'

Looking back on the summer of 1995, Schumacher admits

that he didn't fully understand what he was getting himself into by joining Ferrari.

When I joined Ferrari I had the conviction that it was the right moment to go there. I had to choose between two teams, the other being Williams. We talked a lot and I thought hard about it. Let's just say that I didn't want to just jump into the best car. People would expect me to win everything. But I like to fight, I like racing.

I did not know what Ferrari was when I joined. And I had to learn that. It was a challenge to go there because they had been so unsuccessful. But now I feel like I know the brand and I know what it feels like to drive for them. It is amazing to see how Italian people are involved with their team. For them it's like a parent or the Pope. The whole country is behind us, not just a city, like a football club.

But it took Schumacher a long time to understand what Ferrari was all about. Part of the reason for that, according to his assistant Sabine Kehm, was that he was not prepared to embrace the emotional side of Ferrari:

It was really in the last three or four years of his career that he understood the whole Ferrari thing. He didn't understand it for a long time. It has to do with him opening up more.

The first world title with Ferrari in 2000 was a big turning point for a lot of things, because he did what was expected of him. He didn't open up before that because he hadn't fulfilled his duty. He wouldn't have been able to forgive himself if he hadn't achieved it and maybe had the feeling that if he'd concentrated more he might have done. But from 2000 onwards and with every world title he added, he felt more secure and he opened himself up inside the team and let the emotions of Enzo Ferrari and all the Ferrari myth infuse him. Before that he didn't allow himself to get sucked into it because he hadn't delivered yet.

Once again the picture is of a man with extreme self-control, perhaps afraid of the emotional side of himself and regarding it as a potentially damaging element. Despite his innate self-confidence and the boost that it must have received from winning two world titles relatively early in his career, Schumacher nevertheless felt insecure at the heart of Ferrari because he had not yet delivered on their enormous expectation of him.

In this context, it is illuminating to consider the pressure the driver put himself under and the despair he felt when, for year after year, that first Ferrari title refused to come. Schumacher went home empty-handed from his first four seasons with the team, despite being a title contender for all but the first year. It was reasonable for him to expect that, having imposed himself so clearly in 1994 and 1995, he would do so again with Ferrari within two to three years. This lack of success gives some insight into the desperation which drove him to crash into Villeneuve at Jerez during the 1997 title decider.

Before they made the decision to join Ferrari, Schumacher and Weber had been watching the team's progress under Jean Todt and it was clear that he had taken away a lot of the politics which had previously held the team back and caused it to underachieve for almost 20 years. That Ferrari had gone so long without winning the world championship despite its huge budgets, great resources and influence within the sport, was a scandal. But a succession of high profile engineers had been through the revolving doors, seeming to view a lucrative spell there as good retirement planning. Todt was the strong man the team needed at the helm, but he couldn't achieve success for the team on his own. Schumacher was a vital part of the jigsaw, whilst the final crucial piece was the Benetton engineering double act of Ross Brawn and Rory Byrne, who joined Ferrari at the end of 1996.

Schumacher realised that it would be virtually impossible to retain his world title in 1996, knowing what he did about the technical level of Ferrari. Speaking at the end of 1995, shortly before his triumphant arrival at Maranello he said, 'They have reached a level that doesn't need much more to become a top team. This [last missing] bit I hope, with me together with the people already in the team, [means] we are going to do it.' But little did he know what a shambles he was walking into.

Schumacher marched into Maranello for the first time on Thursday 16 November 1995. The local police estimated that a crowd of 50,000 was there to welcome him. It truly was a stage-managed pageant, a hugely symbolic one too, as the great hero rode into town to rescue the Ferrari legend. Never before had the arrival of a new Ferrari driver sparked such passion among the fans. Schumacher was the champion of champions, with him in the team it would surely be only a matter of time before the world championship returned to Maranello, putting an end to 16 years of hurt and lost pride.

Ironically it was not a Ferrari tradition to hire great champions. Enzo Ferrari did not believe in doing that – he preferred to hire potential champions. The exceptions were Fangio, who was a necessity at the time, and Prost, who was hired after Enzo Ferrari's death.

Schumacher arrived at around 11am, wearing a blazer and a crisp white shirt. He met Ferrari president Luca di Montezemolo and the team principal, Jean Todt, and for the benefit of the photographers and camera crews from all over the world he then went for a drive along a perimeter road of the factory with his new team-mate Eddie Irvine in a road-going Ferrari 456 GT. He drove as far as the front gates of the factory, outside which the huge crowd strained for a view.

He was then taken to the Fiorano test track, which is next door to the race team factory. There he made his first visit to Enzo Ferrari's office, which sits in the middle of the track next to the pit garage, and which was to become his home away from home for the next 11 years when he was testing. The building is a stone-built house of three storeys, with red shutters on the windows. Inside Enzo's study is full of black and white photos from the old days, and models of cars in glass cases.

Schumacher and Irvine were given a lunch of tortellini, followed by an escalope of veal with truffles. While they ate, the crowd made its way to the few vantage points around the Fiorano test track and waited. Shortly before 3pm Schumacher did a couple of reconnaissance laps in his Lancia road car, then the V10 Formula 1 engine burst into life. After one lap he had to stop because a gearbox seal had broken – not an auspicious start. It took until 4.30pm to fix it and in the meantime Schumacher and Irvine did a few laps in the Ferrari 456GT. Back in the racing car he managed only 17 laps before darkness fell but the great Ferrari adventure had begun. Schumacher told the Italian media that evening that there was a lot of work to be done but he promised to be in a position to challenge for the 1997 world title.

A glance at Ferrari's history showed the scale of the challenge facing Schumacher: no world title since 1979 and in Ferrari's whole history only six drivers had ever won the title, with four of them doing that only once. Ferrari may have been the spine of continuity in Formula 1 since its invention in 1950, but it had never been particularly successful.

At the time Schumacher joined, Ferrari's technical department was split between Maranello and England, something which Montezemolo had put in place on the advice of Niki Lauda, but which Todt and Schumacher considered not sustainable. The team's technical director was John Barnard, who wanted to be based near his home in Surrey, England. (Because his stock was so high at the time he signed with Ferrari he had been more or less able to name his terms.) Without his day-to-day supervision, however, the team's competence suffered in many key areas, like research and development and gearbox design, and it took Ross Brawn several years to build these areas up to his required standard. Schumacher was expecting great things when he joined Ferrari, but he was quickly disappointed and as the season went on he began demanding changes.

Eddie Irvine recalls the sinking feeling that the drivers had when they got their first look at their car for 1996.

We were in the shit in 1996. I remember when the car came out I said, 'That looks worryingly different from everyone else's car.' It turned out that everyone else was right and we were wrong. It was the second worst car [after the Jaguar R2] that ever sat on a race-track. It was madness, the exact opposite of what Ross brought to the team. It was all inspiration and no measurement.

How Michael drove that car, I'll never know, it really impressed me. I was scared to turn the steering wheel because you didn't know if it was going to turn immediately, in half a second or in a second, you had no idea what it would do. He drove it on every millimetre of the road. I couldn't stand getting into it. He won three races, which is one of the greatest achievements in motor racing history. He had four pole positions with it and I stood there in awe of his performances that year. That was the year that Michael really earned his money.

I'm totally averse to aerodynamic sensitivity, I don't like a car where the aerodynamic package moves. The first Ferrari was a massively pitch sensitive car and roll sensitive. I think that is where Michael's genius came out, because he could drive around that, I couldn't. But then as Ferrari got better over the next few years I got closer to his pace. I don't think I was trying harder or anything like that, it's just that the car came to me, the understanding of what the driver needed from the car got better.

In the 1996 Ferrari Schumacher was powerless to take on the Williams of Damon Hill and his new team-mate, Jacques Villeneuve. He put in some superhuman performances to win at Barcelona, Spa and Monza, but at his suggestion Todt contacted Ross Brawn and Rory Byrne and persuaded them to leave Benetton and join Ferrari. Byrne had been planning to retire and set up a scuba diving centre in Thailand, but he was talked out of it. The two men were not allowed to leave Benetton until the end of the season so they were not able to have much input into the 1997 car, nor to get started on rebuilding the technical competence at Maranello.

Morale was low at Ferrari in 1996. The engineer responsible for Schumacher's engines, Enzo Castorini, recalls the mood: 'We were pessimistic. When would we be winners again? Never.'

Ignazio Lunetta, Schumacher's race engineer, had worked with the team's previous drivers; Jean Alesi and Gerhard Berger, and found Schumacher a breath of fresh air.

> The relationship with Michael is calm, normal. Despite all the affection I have for Alesi I have to admit that there is a huge difference. Michael gives a lead, as every driver should. Not like Berger who wants to be listened to like a technical director even though he isn't one, either in rank or competence. The presence of Schumacher translates to us in the absence of excuses and of pressure on the team. There were some bad moments in 1996, the worst probably Canada when the clutch broke. We had done a bad pit stop and then the driveshaft broke. When he came back to the pits we looked each other in the eye and burst out laughing.

It was a laughing matter for others in Formula 1 too. Swiss journalist Roger Benoit organised a sweep, which Bernie Ecclestone and others paid $50 to enter at each event during 1996, betting on which lap Schumacher would retire from the race. At the French Grand Prix things hit a real low point when Schumacher retired on the parade lap, failing even to make the start line. His car was lifted on to a lorry and he was driven back to the paddock, still sitting in his car, a picture of impotence. When Ross Brawn got the reliability under control in the years which followed, to the point where Schumacher went an entire season without any technical problems, that particular book was quietly abandoned.

Brawn's arrival in late 1996 couldn't come soon enough for Schumacher. 'It was a pretty brave decision he took to go to Ferrari because he didn't know the structure there,' says Ross Brawn. 'He was a bit frustrated that he couldn't see what steps were going to be taken to put the team on the right track. On the technical side he didn't feel that there was the planning or foresight to go into the next years, which he was used to at Benetton. He realised that it needed strengthening.'

There are two races from 1996 which serve as contrasting examples of the kind of season it was and which provide enlightening testimony of the kind of behaviour in a crisis which Schumacher could have done with displaying more often.

As the winner of the two previous Monaco Grands Prix, Schumacher knew that the race around the streets of the principality offered a rare chance of success for the Ferrari team. The differences between a good car and a bad car are minimised there and the driver can make more of a difference to the outcome. He duly took pole position with a scintillating, high risk lap, flirting with the barriers lining the track.

Race day was wet and given his unmatched prowess in the rain, all the indications were that Schumacher's first win for Ferrari would be a mere formality. Instead he crashed on the first lap of the race. He made a poor start, allowing Damon Hill to pass him and then he slid straight into the barrier at Portier corner. It was entirely his own fault. He walked disconsolately back to the paddock, locked himself in the Ferrari motorhome and was alone with his thoughts for half an hour before facing the media. When he came out he played it perfectly:

I am extremely upset. Upset and angry with myself,
because I alone am responsible for this mistake. It's an
incredible mistake. I hit the kerb, couldn't control the car;
it's all my fault. The track was slippery but that's the same
for everyone. I alone have made this huge mistake. I'm
human and I make mistakes, but I'm particularly upset for
Ferrari because this was the first real opportunity we've
had to win together. Now I have an even greater duty to put
things right, to repay the team and its fans.

There was no question of him ducking the blame or of making
excuses. It was a full blown *mea culpa* of the kind his critics
would like to have seen more often. It served him well; the
media gave him credit for his contrition and the public
sympathised with him.

There would be other highly controversial occasions in the
future after which those close to him thought he would act as
he had at Monaco that year, but it was a very rare occurrence.
Despite all the evidence of the benefits of putting your hands
up and admitting you've got it wrong, he came to believe that
the media demanded apologies, especially the Italian media
which loves a good Catholic confession of sin to clear the air.
And increasingly as the years went on Schumacher wasn't
prepared to give them what they wanted. Of course there is
the obvious difference that this was a simple mistake, which
did not involve anyone else, whereas many of the other
incidents were at another driver's expense.

By an extreme irony, when he climbed aboard his Ducati
Monster motorbike to ride back to his apartment, he got a few
hundred metres before the engine died! Truly it was not his
day.

Following the Monaco soul-baring, Jean Todt observed that

'Schumacher accepts other people's mistakes, but not his own.' This is very true and is a hallmark of many great drivers. In this instance, there simply was no other explanation for the accident: he had lost control of his car and it troubled him deeply.

Two weeks later Schumacher had the opportunity to 'put things right' at the Spanish Grand Prix in Barcelona. It was another wet day and this time he didn't put a foot wrong. It was one of the greatest exhibitions of driving the sport has ever seen. Such was his dominance and speed, it was as if the track was dry for him and wet for everyone else. In atrocious conditions, at times he was four seconds per lap faster than the nearest competitor. Again he drew comparisons with Senna, one of very few people who have ever been able to show that level of superiority. In normal conditions on a technical track like Barcelona the Ferrari would not have had a prayer against the aerodynamically superior Williams cars, which had been almost a second per lap faster in qualifying.

The Ferrari had a persistent clutch problem that season and Schumacher made another poor start, dropping to ninth place. He passed three cars on the opening lap but was almost seven seconds behind the leader, Jacques Villeneuve. Eddie Irvine went off the road trying to control his Ferrari, as did Hill in the Williams. Schumacher soon passed Alesi, Berger and Villeneuve and then simply drove off into the distance. By lap 39 he was one minute and 12 seconds ahead. He made the other drivers look like novices. The Ferrari engine then began to misbehave, an electrical fault causing cylinders to cut out intermittently and prompting fears that another retirement beckoned. Schumacher slowed down and nursed the car home, nevertheless winning by more than 40 seconds. In the final laps he broke the tension in the Ferrari pits with a joke over the radio. 'Do you think we could fit a heater into this car, it's freezing!'

Schumacher appeared to revel in the conditions, but he was motivated as much as anything by the fact that he felt he owed a debt to the team and its supporters after Monaco. Their trust in him, which he clearly felt was under threat, was more than restored and his joke over the radio showed that he wanted them to feel good.

Watching the race closely, you can see Schumacher changing his lines through the corners, searching out the grip. While the other drivers are merely content to hang on and stay on the road, Schumacher is seeking perfection in the most difficult of circumstances. He was able to stay on the limit for large parts of the race, where others were unwilling even to explore where the limit might be on such a day. 'I tried different lines because in three or four places on the circuit, the grip was really critical and you risked losing control of the car,' he recalled. 'Before making a few passes I also made sure to run in the wheeltracks of the car in front. I didn't take any risks, I was always alert and had the car under control.'

After Barcelona a very difficult summer followed, with retirements and little indication of progress. The pressure mounted from outside and voices were calling for Jean Todt to be sacked. 'It was awful,' recalls Schumacher. 'The pressure of expectation from other quarters was getting greater all the time. Everyone was demanding Jean's exit. I said that I would go too if that happened. I believe since then we were completely able to rely on each other.' But then Schumacher won at Spa and the relief was immense for both men. He followed that with an emotional win in Italy, which really lifted the pressure off the team. The Monza victory ended a Ferrari drought there which had lasted for eight years. Afterwards the scenes beneath the podium were over-whelming as tens of thousands of people stormed the track as a giant Ferrari flag was unfurled. It was a demonstration to the world of the power and magic of Ferrari and Schumacher had been the one to give the fans their pride back.

Schumacher's parents were there to witness the spectacle and his mother Elisabeth spoke to the *Gazzetta dello Sport* newspaper in the paddock after the race. 'We only come to the races a couple of times a year. For sure you feel a greater joy being here, but you also suffer more. We watched from the grandstand and it was fantastic. Monza is lovely with all these people who love Ferrari and well done to my Michael. I haven't managed to hug him yet, he's busy and we have to leave. I'll congratulate him on the phone, which is always a mother's lot.'

Schumacher, too, was caught up in the emotion of the occasion, announcing that he and Corinna were expecting their first child. It was a huge high, one of the best of his career:

I was thinking about the baby as I went from corner to corner. It is a beautiful thing. Certainly my life will change. I will have to give up my spare time and my sleep. It will mean that I come to Grands Prix to rest! A child is the most beautiful gift that anyone could desire.

The *tifosi* have waited for this moment for a long time. They deserve this win. I'm happy for them and for the whole team. It's impossible to express the way I feel about

winning at Monza in a Ferrari. Looking down from the
podium I got goose bumps with the emotion of it.

It was a great day all round for the Schumacher family. Behind
the scenes Willi Weber had concluded another deal, one
which was yet to be made public. Michael's younger brother,
Ralf, would be on the Formula 1 grid the following season. He
had been signed, with just a hint of irony, to the Jordan team.

CHAPTER THIRTEEN

The other Schumacher

The constant comparisons with him annoy me.
I'm sick of hearing that. I have never felt I am in
the shadow of Michael. I am his little brother.
Michael goes his way, and I go mine.

Ralf Schumacher

Ralf Schumacher is a very different commodity from his brother. Six years younger, he had an easier time growing up because the financial hardship in the family was not so severe as in Michael's early years. On the surface, their characters appear to have been formed by their experiences; in simplistic terms, Michael has the edgy drive of the self-made man, whilst Ralf has the more confident approach of the second child who has had it all laid on. This translates to the way they race, with Michael always putting in maximum effort, trying to make things happen, whereas Ralf would dominate if the car was working perfectly, but fade from view if it wasn't. Michael was very ambitious, Ralf more inclined to wait for things to come to him; Michael had very few off days, Ralf rather more.

When Ralf came into Formula 1 in 1997 Michael suddenly had an important ally in the paddock. He had never found it easy to get along with the other drivers, having upset quite a few of them over the years and so had few friends on the grid. Ralf didn't care for most of his peers either and they provided a refuge for each other. The pair would often be seen together in the early days, visiting each other's team motorhomes, relaxing together in their rival uniforms. In the evenings away from the track they would often eat together. They made a pact early on that they would not discuss the inner workings of their teams. This was especially important when Ralf moved up the grid in the early 2000s. In more recent years, after Ralf got married, they were seen together less often at the circuit and their relationship cooled, largely as a result of a clash of cultures between their wives, according to close associates.

Friends of the Schumacher family say that Michael is closer to their father, Rolf, many of whose characteristics he has inherited, while Ralf was closer to their mother, Elisabeth, who died in 2003. Michael says:

> Ralf came along when I was six and a half, but I don't remember him disrupting my world. Later the age difference became a problem, though. When he was about five he wanted to be doing the same things I was doing, but without the responsibilities. I had to sweep up the go-kart circuit, but Ralf always managed to disappear when there was work to be done. We'd fight over that. When we were alone at home I looked after him, but he wouldn't always listen to me.
>
> Our parents treated us differently. But they were fair – it was just that we had a different life by the time Ralf came along. There was more money, there were more possibilities. It didn't make me jealous. There were just moments when I thought he had it easier. He had more toys and did less for them.

Ralf followed in Michael's wake. He raced karts from a very young age and it was a shared passion for the brothers. As the senior, Michael always tried to pass on advice and experience, but Ralf wanted to do things his own way. There is some amusing video footage shot by German television station RTL of a karting event when Ralf is around 12 years old, which gives a cameo of what their relationship was like. Ralf is quite fat and has a scowl on his face the whole time. Michael is lecturing him on what lines to take and where to brake, and then gets annoyed when his brother goes out and ignores all his advice. 'Michael has always tried to help me by sharing his experiences,' recalls Ralf, 'but I never listened. Looking back you realise that maybe you should have listened, but at the time you don't want to.'

Ralf followed most of Michael's steps up the racing ladder, moving from karts to cars and competing for Willi Weber's team in Formula 3, winning the Macau Grand Prix. Weber brought him into Formula 1 with the Jordan team, aged 21. But from there on their career paths diverged. Michael went on to dominate Formula 1 with Ferrari, winning 91 Grands Prix, while Ralf won six races for the Williams team and then his career stalled at Toyota. Like his brother, however, he has earned a huge amount of money out of the sport, largely thanks to the deal-making genius of Willi Weber, with whom Ralf split in 2005. I once asked Ralf if he would like one day to be Michael's team-mate and his first response was, 'Who could afford it?'

The two are quite different to deal with. Michael is very professional and patient with the media and the public. He sees traps and trick questions coming a mile off and manages all conversations to suit himself. Ralf can be quite dismissive and often turns questions around or picks an argument. But he is intelligent, like his brother, and has quite a lively sense of humour, which he developed from working with British teams for nine years. Perhaps also because of this his English is better and more natural than Michael's.

Michael was often accused of arrogance in his youth, somewhat unfairly. Ralf, when he was emerging from Formula 3, was genuinely arrogant, but without the credentials to back it up. It seemed on first meeting him that he considered himself to be on the same level as his brother, despite having achieved very little of substance to justify this. But to his credit he matured quickly and established a positive reputation with the Jordan team, where he was paired with Giancarlo Fisichella in 1997 and with Damon Hill the following year. In 1999 Weber moved him on to Williams and when BMW came on board in 2000 it seemed to be only a matter of time before he and his brother would be fighting it out at the front of Grands Prix.

In the end they never disputed a world championship between them, which is more of a reflection on Ralf than anything else. Their battles in races were relatively few, the best being at the 2001 Canadian Grand Prix, where Ralf beat his brother fair and square after a duel lasting the entire race. They made history that day, becoming the first siblings to finish first and second in a Grand Prix. 'Thank God there aren't three of them,' joked Mika Hakkinen, who finished third.

Michael was concerned for his brother's safety when he started racing in Formula 1. Having seen what he had seen over the years, he did not want to imagine his brother suffering a bad accident. At the 1997 Brazilian Grand Prix,

Ralf's second F1 race, Michael was worried. 'The track is very bumpy and difficult and watching him drive made me quite afraid,' he said. 'You see the car on the edge, moving around a lot and you know it's possible for him to have a major accident.'

As time passed Michael became more relaxed about it. But then at Indianapolis in 2004 his worst nightmare came true as Ralf suffered a major accident during the race, hitting the concrete wall hard at 180mph. Bits of the car were strewn across the track. Ralf's body had taken a huge impact, calculated at over 70g. He was unconscious, slumped in the cockpit. The race director sent out the safety car to control the pace of the field and Michael, who was leading the race, was forced to drive slowly past his stricken brother for several laps before Ralf was extricated and taken to the medical centre. The experience must have brought back memories of Senna's fatal accident and Michael admitted as much in his comments after the race. 'The worst thing was seeing him there for so long,' he said. 'They kept telling me that things weren't too bad. But I have heard this many times in the past and it turned out differently.'

It was noticeable in the weeks following Indianapolis that Michael was highly sensitive to anyone suggesting that he had acted callously in carrying on racing whilst his brother was in distress. Some mischievous soul had told him that I had said something along those lines in my television commentary on the race, which could not have been further from the truth. I found myself in the curious position of telling Michael he shouldn't believe all the rumours he hears!

The two brothers certainly had their run-ins on the track. A collision at the Nurburgring in Ralf's first season cost his brother valuable points in his title battle with Jacques Villeneuve. Michael was prepared to use the same intimidating tactics on Ralf as he did with his other rivals. It always seemed a bit odd that he was prepared to put the squeeze on his brother, but to be fair what else could he do? If his brother stood between him and victory then he had no alternative.

The most extreme example of this occurred at the Spanish Grand Prix of 2000. Michael was running third and pushing hard to make up lost ground, having suffered a few setbacks during the race. He was ahead of Ralf when he got a slow puncture. As Ralf came up to pass him, he blocked him, then pushed him out so wide through the corner that Barrichello, Michael's team-mate, was able to dive past Ralf and steal his position. At the end of that lap, Michael came into the pits for new tyres. Ralf was furious. The German media seized on it and ran 'sibling rivalry' stories for several days. 'Ralf was unhappy,' recalls Sabine Kehm, 'but they just discussed it between themselves and it was fine again. Both of them are very good at putting things to one side, they always manage to keep it to themselves.'

The next race after Spain was in Germany and on the opening day of the race meeting, Michael sought to defuse the row during a joint press conference. 'It was a clean fight in Spain. We had a chat, but not as people wrote. We are brothers and know what to do. We have to fight on the limit. We drive for different teams and never give presents. But we can be more on the limit because we can rely on each other not to play dirty games.'

Ralf agreed, 'We like fighting,' he said. 'There were black marks on my car but it was a clean manoeuvre by Michael. I hope it stays that way.'

A few months later Ralf reflected, 'I was very angry after Barcelona, but that was because I thought Michael was about to call into the pits and therefore he should have made it easy for me. But Michael will always race and he will always race me. That is how we are.'

Another famous flare-up occurred at the Monaco Grand Prix in 2005. Michael was desperate for results that year because his car was uncompetitive. In the closing stages of the race he came up on his team-mate, Rubens Barrichello, and Ralf and put aggressive moves on both to try to pass them. Ralf was furious. 'He's crazy,' he told the German television station RTL. 'He should have switched on his brain before he tried a move like that. Another millimetre and one of us could be dead.'

These were pretty inflammatory words, but by this time the brothers' relationship had deteriorated, perhaps exacerbated by the distance which developed between their wives from around 2003 onwards. The two wives are very different women. Corinna Schumacher stays largely out of the media spotlight and works hard with Michael to create the image of the 'perfect couple', with two happy children and a paddock full of animals. Cora, on the other hand, revels in her celebrity status as Ralf's wife. She is very accessible to the newspapers and celebrity magazines and often turns up at the race-track wearing something eye-catching. Some have wondered whether she has perfected the long, slow walk down the paddock for the benefit of photographers using long lenses.

'Their [Michael and Ralf's] relationship got worse in the last two or three years,' says Sabine Kehm. 'They've grown apart. It's a very natural thing. Ralf has his family in Austria, Michael has his family in Switzerland. They used to meet at the track but now there is the whole wives situation and, of course, Michael defends Corinna and Ralf defends Cora, so they have their differences there.'

The game was fuelled by the German media, who always maintained a fascination with the 'battling brothers' storyline. For example, in 2005 Cora gave an interview to a German celebrity magazine:

Corinna and I have little contact. We holiday in different places, we hardly phone, we live somewhere else. A pity really, as we both have children. But Corinna's nature and mine are totally different. I am a sincere, cosmopolitan woman. Not the sort who puts on an act or parades the fact that she is Mother Teresa.

My sister-in-law is stuck with the label of being the 'perfect' wife in the 'perfect' world and that sort of thing. This is an image which Michael and Corinna have built up their whole life, the ranch, the family. And then there's me who's put in a different category. It's written that 'Cora's thong is sticking out of her trousers', so I have to take care not to be photographed from behind.

It is a fantastically catty piece and typical of the way that Cora has few qualms about acting contrary to the expectations foisted upon her as the sister-in-law of Germany's most famous sportsman. As Michael's adviser, Sabine Kehm was on the other side of the story and she had a clear strategy for dealing with the situation.

The German media have Cora's mobile number and Ralf's mobile too so they are easy to get. The media wanted a response from us, but we always said nothing. I told Michael and Corinna, 'If you react now, they will use that again and again.' He stayed strong and we always stuck with that. The tabloids went crazy because we did not play their game.

But privacy was very important to Michael. If he felt that the media was in his home as well he would not be able to deal with it. He needs his home as a refuge. Now he is retired he will try to stay out of the public eye for the rest of his life.

Ralf's burden throughout his career has been the expectation which comes with being Michael Schumacher's brother. He has his own career and his own way of going racing, but he is always measured against his immensely successful brother. Although he had nothing like the struggle that Michael had to get into Formula 1, he has had a harder job in many ways because he has never been allowed to be entirely his own man. Even during the first race meeting of 2007, after Michael's retirement, he was asked many times what it was like not to have Michael around.

Michael always recognised the pressure on Ralf and was protective of his brother. 'When I became successful in Formula 1 there were new opportunities for him as well,' says Michael. 'But that doesn't mean he had it easier as a driver. Ralf had to overcome different hurdles, for example people's expectations. He couldn't be quite so relaxed. I'm sure it was more difficult for him than it was for me. You can argue that Willi Weber and I paved his way and supported him. But at the end of the day he had to prove himself and face his critics alone.'

Ralf certainly had to accept the comparisons with his brother in the early days but as time has gone on and he has enjoyed his own relative success, he has become less tolerant of people who deny him his own identity as a racer.

The constant comparisons with him annoy me. I'm sick of hearing that. I have never felt I am in the shadow of Michael. I am his little brother. Michael goes his way, and I go mine. There are people who think I only got into F1 because of who my brother is, but they are jealous people who don't like me. And those people will always try to explain away my success. But that's normal, it's best not to care about those things. It was hard when I first came into F1. But once you are in it you don't care what people think.

We've never had any rivalry or jealousy between us. I never compare myself to him. World championship title or not, I've achieved what no one would have expected, getting into Formula 1 second, as the little brother.

The two brothers were united in their grief during the San Marino Grand Prix of 2003, when their mother Elisabeth died the night before the race. She was only 53 years old, but had been ill for a long time and was in a coma for her final days. Michael and Ralf were at her bedside before the weekend and actually travelled to Imola from there, but Michael was desperate that the German newspapers should not find out that he was in Germany. He wanted to keep the public exposure of this sad moment to a minimum. Unfortunately he was not able to achieve this as her condition worsened over the weekend and with news of her death on Saturday evening, his grief would have to be played out in public on race day.

After qualifying on the Saturday afternoon Michael and Ralf immediately flew back to Cologne. They returned the next morning and Michael put his emotions behind him and went out and won the race. On the podium he could not conceal his tears and he looked up to the heavens as the German national anthem was played. This was very public grief of the kind he was always very unwilling to show, the kind he felt would have been expected at Senna's funeral. As they had spent quite some time with their mother in the week before her death it was not such an abrupt or shocking experience for the brothers as it appeared to the public that weekend. They had said their goodbyes *before* flying to Imola. Nevertheless, to those who knew Michael well and worked closely with him, he was obviously highly emotional that weekend. Sabine Kehm says:

> He was very limited, very cut out that weekend. He was doing what he needed to do and nothing else. Before Saturday he was on the phone to people in the hospital when he wasn't driving or in briefings. When he came back on Sunday it was really heavy. But there was never a question that he wasn't going to drive.
>
> She raised the kids on the kart track and she was such a part of it that it would have been strange not to drive that race. They felt it was the best thing that they could do because life had to go on. And for Michael it was clearly the only place he could imagine himself, because he wanted to be alone with himself. Because this is where he really feels natural, it's his environment. He really wanted to get in the car and drive. The problem was leaving the motorhome. He just didn't want to go out and he definitely didn't want to cry in front of all those people. He just stayed in his room with Corinna.

Schumacher's room in the Ferrari motorhome was a small space, no more than ten feet square. Inside there was a massage table, a backless stool and a small side table. On the wall were two flatscreen televisions. It was his home away from home, a place to hide from the glare.

After his victory, there was no way to duck the podium ceremony, so he simply had to go out there and allow the viewing public around the world in on his private grief. It was one of the most difficult moments of his career.

Elisabeth had been separated from Rolf since 1997. He had a new partner, Barbara, who accompanied him to one or two races a year. Elisabeth lived alone in the Schumacher family house at the old kart track in Kerpen. The house may be the same one she raised her family in, but there were obvious signs of the changed circumstances of the family as there were now security gates in place, closed-circuit television cameras and guard dogs. She was rarely seen in public and hardly ever spoke, but she granted an interview to the popular German magazine *Bunte* in June 2001, two days after Ralf and Michael made history by finishing first and second in the Canadian Grand Prix. She revealed that she did not see her grandchildren very often as she did not like flying, but that 'Michael regularly sends photos'. She had not actually spoken to them since the weekend.

I watch all the races. I was alone. A girlfriend rang me up who complained because she had a bet on Michael and Ralf won. I never bet on either of them. When the race started I could see that he was quicker than Michael. But he doesn't let anyone past in a hurry.

I never worry about them racing. Both of them know what they are doing. I am quite certain, they would never drive in such a way as to endanger each other. Sometimes I cry with joy after a victory – but only when I am alone. I always hope that they stay healthy. Both of them don't want to give up for a long time, especially Michael, he's so ambitious.

At the time of the interview, the German press was excited about Ralf's impending marriage to Cora at a register office in Salzburg, near where he lives. His mother's comment on this is perhaps the most revealing part of the interview. 'No one has talked to me about the marriage. I only know about it from the papers and from the telly. I watch all the programmes, hear what Ralf and Michael have to say. Ralf will no doubt tell me in good time for it.'

Asked whether she was sad that she saw the boys so infrequently she said, 'Both of them have a lot to do. The races, the preparation, the many appointments. We talk on the phone.'

CHAPTER FOURTEEN

Jerez and the fall from grace

I think that when you do sport at that level under that
kind of pressure and you have to think that quickly,
you are going to do things like that or you are not
going to be successful. And to be a Formula 1 driver
never mind a world champion, I think you have to be
extremely ruthless and determined. It is a very
dangerous, very difficult, very tough job and that
degree of ruthlessness has to be there and sometimes
it shows itself.

Max Mosley

At the start of 1997 the expectations of the Ferrari team were
not high. Schumacher's target was to 'win more races than we
did last year', while Ferrari president Luca di Montezemolo
declared that it would be 1998 before the team was ready to
mount a title challenge. As it turned out they vastly exceeded
their expectations and Schumacher went into the final race at
Jerez ahead on points of his rival, Williams Renault driver
Jacques Villeneuve.

The car Schumacher raced that year had been designed by
John Barnard and his team in England, but over the winter

they were replaced by Ross Brawn and Rory Byrne who had moved to Italy to head up the technical operation. Brawn's plan was to bring everything back under one roof in Maranello and he began the laborious process of finding talented engineers for every department. Initially he had to import a lot of expertise from England, as the standard of the technical base in Italy had dropped. The gearbox department, for example, was virtually non-existent. But part of the strategy was to train up young Italian engineers for the future, to reinforce the idea that 'made in Italy' was something of which to be proud.

The design group in England and the engine group in Italy had become so disconnected that fundamental mistakes were made in putting the car together. Brawn brought the two sides back together and imposed his master plan on them; the result was Ferrari's total dominance of the sport from 2000 until 2005. In that time the team developed almost perfect reliability and at times pushed the boundaries of performance way beyond the reach of rival teams. All the time the key engineering roles were understudied by Italians and this process culminated in Brawn and chief designer Rory Byrne handing over the reins at the start of 2007 to three Italian engineers, Aldo Costa, Luca Baldisserri and Mario Almondo. After a ten-year period of Brawn's rule, the team was put back into the hands of the Italians, enabling them to control their own destiny.

Brawn installed real discipline into the team, making them take every aspect of racing seriously. I have watched them many times, practising pit stops as the sun sets on the eve of a Grand Prix, Brawn standing there with a stopwatch in his hand, not moving on until everything has been done to his complete satisfaction. This discipline was essential to Schumacher, but was clearly missing from Ferrari when he arrived as he observed wrily at the time: 'With Benetton if practice began at nine o'clock, someone would come and get me at five to. At Ferrari it was time for another cappuccino.'

As the 1997 season began, Brawn examined Barnard's car and scratched his head. 'John's car is fairly different from what I'm used to; different weight distribution, different geometry and I don't know how he arrived at those things. So we have a lot of unknowns and question-marks hanging over certain aspects of the car.' Luckily for Ferrari many of the rival teams underperformed that season; McLaren and Benetton were not consistently able to challenge at the front and Williams, the team to beat, made many mistakes, which Schumacher and his team capitalised on. Williams had a big speed advantage as the season started in Australia, but Ferrari's relentless development programme quickly brought them up to the same level. But the fact that Schumacher was even in the hunt for the world title was largely down to the driver himself, who was outstanding on many occasions. He won in the wet in Monaco and at Spa, he won in Canada and France and at the penultimate race in Japan. Thus he went to Jerez a single point ahead of Villeneuve.

* * *

The 1997 European Grand Prix at Jerez in Southern Spain was a surreal experience. I remember the sheer ridiculousness of qualifying on the Saturday afternoon, when Villeneuve, Schumacher and Heinz Harald Frentzen all set identical lap times to within a thousandth of a second – something which had never happened before. People were saying that it must be a fix, but how could the timekeepers fix that? And why would they want to? In any case the teams have computer telemetry systems, which chart the progress of the car around the track very precisely. If a car had not done what the timekeepers said it had done they would know instantly. Villeneuve was on pole by virtue of having set the time first, then Schumacher, then Frentzen.

There was some bad feeling about Schumacher's qualifying lap as he had set the time while marshals were clearing away his brother's Jordan, which was stranded at the side of the track. A tractor was pulling the car away from the race-track and normally one would expect the marshals to wave yellow flags, warning the drivers to slow down. But despite the obvious danger, amazingly there were no waved flags for Schumacher, who did not lift off the throttle as he passed the scene.

This went down badly with the Williams team, as yellow flags were a sore subject with them that season. Jacques Villeneuve had ignored them three times during the year and at Monza had been handed a suspended one race ban. When he did it again in practice in Japan he was thrown out of the meeting and had to race under appeal. The team were pretty angry with him for that, as it was not as if he hadn't had enough warnings.

Villeneuve had given too much away to Schumacher by making this basic error. It is no exaggeration to say that the incident was directly responsible for setting up Jerez as the nail-biting title decider it became. Going into the Suzuka weekend, the penultimate round of the championship, Villeneuve was nine points ahead, so even if Schumacher won both the final races, two second places would have been enough to give Villeneuve the title. Instead a situation was created by the result at Suzuka whereby Schumacher had 78 points to Villeneuve's 77. In other words, Schumacher would be champion if neither car finished at the final race in Jerez, an exact repeat of the scenario from Adelaide in 1994.

Villeneuve and his Williams team cleverly talked up this situation on the Saturday evening in Jerez, throwing the spotlight on to Schumacher and reminding everyone of what had happened in 1994. The duel between the two men had become personal and Villeneuve was as much focused on beating Schumacher as he was on winning the world title. His race engineer Jock Clear explains:

Gradually, Jacques' competitive respect for Michael increased and his personal respect for him decreased as Michael did more and more Michael-esque things. We all know Jacques has very strong opinions and it was clear that he was going to swing against Michael as a driver and as a person, as a result of some of the things he'd experienced.

Jacques always said that Michael's demeanour on the track was far too arrogant. He carried himself on the circuit as though he had a God-given right to be there, rather than being just another competitor trying to do his best alongside the rest. This is undoubtedly one of his strengths and one of the reasons why he was such a force for so long and, let's face it, Senna was exactly the same.

Because Jacques was Michael's most direct competitor in 1997 it became personal. But if you look at the wider picture Michael was like that with everybody. He didn't pick Jacques out, but Jacques took it very personally. Jacques believes that everything you do with respect to those around you, you either do it as a machine, which doesn't care who the victim is, or you know the victim and you are making a judgment about your respect for them and that is always the way Jacques sees it.

In the press conference after qualifying Schumacher was asked whether he would try to take Villeneuve off at the first corner, like Senna had done to Prost. Schumacher took this badly. 'I absolutely refute this kind of talk,' he scowled. 'In sport you must be, above all, fair. I want to win in a legal way, like a gentleman, with good sportsmanship. For sure in motor racing you shouldn't give presents and you should fight hard from start to finish. But we are fighting for a world championship and I want to think that we will be correct and legal.'

Schumacher had seemed the more nervous of the two drivers all weekend. Most top athletes dismiss talk of feeling pressure at high-stakes moments. They always say that the pressure does not come from outside, but from within. It is obviously a coping mechanism for crunch moments, but in Schumacher's case there is no doubt that he felt a huge responsibility to deliver the world title to Ferrari. That was what he had been hired for and, although he had not expected to be in a position to challenge for it as soon as 1997, mistakes by Williams and some inspired performances by him had created the opportunity.

The disconcerting thing for him about Villeneuve was that he was a tough character, mentally very strong. Schumacher had always sought to unsettle his rivals by playing mind games on them, using the press to send out messages to undermine his competitors' confidence, like the famous occasion on which he had described Damon Hill as a 'number two driver' before their title showdown. With Villeneuve such tricks did not work. He is a very self-contained person and although he had lost his focus at certain points during the season, he was on form for the showdown.

The Williams team were also well used to being in this situation. Key figures like Patrick Head, Frank Williams, chief mechanic Carl Gaydon and team manager Dickie Stanford had all won multiple championships together in the previous ten years and they were remarkably relaxed throughout the weekend, an attitude which rubbed off on Villeneuve. For the Ferrari team this was the first time that many of them had ever been in a title decider, and it showed. Brawn, who had been there before of course, steadied the ship, making sure that a calm, methodical approach was observed at all times.

The race itself started well for Schumacher; he got past Villeneuve, who dropped to third behind Frentzen. Schumacher then opened up a four-second lead and, although Villeneuve passed Frentzen, he could not close the gap. The two drivers were pushing each other hard. They were so well matched that at one point they again recorded identical lap times, the kind of thing which happens once in a lifetime, not twice in two days.

There were so many subplots that day too, which all added to the high quality drama. At one point the leaders came up to lap the Sauber of Norberto Fontana. The Sauber team was a customer of Ferrari for engines. On the face of it, Fontana let Schumacher through and then held up Villeneuve for several corners, costing him 2.5 seconds. Nine years later, on hearing news of Schumacher's retirement, Fontana telephoned a newspaper in his native Argentina and spoke about that incident. It caused an uproar. He claims that he was sitting in the Sauber motorhome (Peter Sauber was not present at the time) when he received a visitor: 'Two or three hours before the race started,' recalled Fontana, 'Jean Todt entered and went straight to the point. "By strict order of Ferrari, Villeneuve must be held up if you come across him on the track. To whoever this applies." And this applied to me.'

Fontana said that he had decided to tell the story now because time had passed and because he felt the moment, with Schumacher retiring, was right. His motive for spilling the beans was simple. 'It harmed me. First, Schumacher never thanked me for it nor Todt, as they lost the championship, they left the motorhomes heated and I never spoke with him again. And, months later, that situation finished me.' Fontana's F1 career did not progress and he was soon back in domestic racing series.

Peter Sauber strenuously denies this version of events. He reacted immediately to the story by saying that in nine years of using Ferrari customer engines, 'Ferrari never expressed the desire that we should obstruct an opponent of Schumacher out on the track.'

But according to Villeneuve's engineer, Jock Clear, it was obvious that Fontana was doing a job for Ferrari. 'Is there anything in it? Of course, it's absolutely true,' says Jock. 'It was deliberate. I don't question it because surely they would have done that. We'd have done the same if there was another team with Renault engines who could help us like that. Nowadays it's against the regulations, but in those days it wasn't and people used to use others quite a lot in that way. You had mates and there was quite a lot of collusion going on. In the same vein we urged Frentzen, Jacques' team-mate, to get in Michael's way as often as possible.'

There was, however, a deal between Williams and McLaren. Ron Dennis and Frank Williams met before the race to discuss tactics. Team orders were allowed in the sport in those days, although collusion between two teams was not something which was often considered as rival teams are usually hell-bent on competing against each other. Williams and Dennis are from the same school in many ways; they have similar sporting values and ideals, but manage their teams in differ-ent ways. Both have been hugely successful, of course, and between them they had carved up most of the world champ-ionships between 1980 and 1996. They were also doubtless very suspicious of the Ferrari management under Jean Todt and the growing threat it posed to their grip on the sport.

The two McLarens had qualified fifth and sixth, with Mika Hakkinen ahead of David Coulthard. This would prove decisive later on as McLaren ordered Coulthard to let Hakkinen through to win the race.

Clearly Villeneuve would not want to be held up by the McLarens, should he find himself behind them following a pit stop. After his first stop Villeneuve did emerge behind Coulthard, who pitted a lap later allowing him through. Throughout the race the meetings continued. I was in the Williams garage for most of the race and watched Dennis come in and pass messages to Williams. The McLarens were effectively controlling the Ferrari of Eddie Irvine, who could not get past them. Villeneuve's team-mate, Frentzen, was also helping him, dropping his pace by two seconds per lap after Villeneuve's first pit stop to allow him to catch up quickly to the leading pack.

Schumacher, in contrast, was out on his own in front and isolated. Irvine was trapped behind the McLarens and for Schumacher it was just a case of drive to the finish. But after his second pit stop, a lap before Villeneuve's, he took it easy on the tyres to start with, not wanting to blister them with 26 laps still to go. Villeneuve did not follow suit. He was hammering his tyres in an attempt to catch Schumacher. The gap went from 2.6 seconds to nothing as Schumacher did not respond to Villeneuve's pressure. Schumacher was sticking to his own plan, as Ross Brawn explains:

> We had agreed earlier that we needed to take it easy on the tyres. Michael was doing a couple of easy laps to settle them in, because we had had some painful experiences that year with blistering tyres and we couldn't afford to let it happen in this race. We were being very conservative and judging by the way the tyres had been performing, we expected the attack from Villeneuve to come at the end of the stint, not the beginning.

Jock Clear was on the Williams pit wall, in contact with Villeneuve by radio and watching the race on the television monitor. He saw his driver tucked up behind the Ferrari through the long uphill right-hander which leads on to the back straight. He knew instantly that his driver was about to launch an attack. 'It was a bloody good race and Jacques outdrove him on the day. I knew he was going to overtake him, there was a low shot on the previous corner and I could see that Jacques had a real tow from Michael and that he was going to have a go. If Michael had seen in his mirrors what I saw on the television he would have moved a fraction to the right and blocked any path through for Jacques.'

Villeneuve used the element of surprise and it did for Schumacher. It is unusual in modern Formula 1 for drivers to take risks like Villeneuve did, especially when fighting for a world championship. So much is at stake that drivers tend to proceed with caution. But that was not Villeneuve's style. He made an instant decision to go for it and caught Schumacher out totally. Eddie Irvine looks back at this race now with the benefit of hindsight and thinks that after coming out of his pit stop ahead, Schumacher allowed complacency to creep in.

'Michael really screwed up because he got overconfident,' says Eddie. 'He did his final pit stop, he thought, "I'm there." So he backed off, partly also because he was scared of blistering his tyres, but he let Jacques get too close. If there is one driver you don't want to allow to get too close it's Jacques. Villeneuve lunged down the inside of Schumacher into Dry Sack corner, a right hander.

That move also for me deserved the world championship. There is not another driver on the grid who would have come from that far back to make the move. Because one thing Jacques did have was big balls. But he was actually going to make the corner as well. Michael, as always, his instinct is not great. For sure his instinct was saying that he couldn't have this. Throughout his career he has shown that where he had to act on instinct he made a bad decision.

I've taken people out, but I've probably done it a bit better than that. I'm not saying I'm whiter than white, I'll hold my hand up. Michael refuses to hold his hand up and that is the only issue I have with him – the hypocrisy. I have no issues with anything he has done, It's just the hypocrisy. And a big guy can't do that, because it exaggerates the issue.

Ironically Irvine himself had played a vital and hitherto unknown part in Villeneuve's bold move. In free practice two days earlier, Irvine had deliberately got in Villeneuve's way. Villeneuve stormed out of his car and went down the pit lane to confront him. Jock Clear says:

> Ferrari were probably sniggering to themselves that Jacques had lost it, that Eddie had got to him, but I really think it backfired. Because Jacques was strong enough to get angry and use it to his advantage, rather than get angry and get out of shape. I think the move Jacques made in the race came from the anger that had built up over the year and then Irvine, with the act [in practice], brought it to a head. Suddenly he put that little bit of extra into Jacques, who said, 'Right, now it's personal and I'm going to fucking have him.' And that is what undid Michael on the day.

Villeneuve came from a long way back, but as Irvine says, he managed to slow the car enough and get it on to a line where he would have made the corner. The on-board camera from Schumacher's car is the most damning. He is surprised by Villeneuve and makes a move with his hands on the wheel to turn outwards, away from the other car, to avoid a collision. That is the instinctive part. Then in a split second he changes his mind and turns into a certain collision with Villeneuve.

'Michael's initial reaction was to turn away because he didn't expect to see a front wheel there,' says Jock Clear. 'That was instinctive. His second reaction is not instinctive, it happened in a split second, but for him it took ages to calculate. He worked out that this was his only opportunity. It was wholly calculated.'

Suddenly subjected to a moment of unforeseen, intense

pressure, Schumacher had become incredibly myopic, reducing the whole championship, his career with Ferrari and his image as a sportsman to the immediate surroundings of himself, Villeneuve and a simple question; 'Shall I or shan't I?' He completely lost all perspective. He decided to go for it and live with the consequences. But he failed. Villeneuve drove on to become world champion, whilst Schumacher crashed out and was demonised.

Niki Lauda, one of Schumacher's most passionate cheerleaders, believes that the detailed television coverage of the incident played a vital role in the way it was perceived.

> He always tried to win and he was unfortunate that, because of television, he was caught doing things which to me are quite normal. But different generations have different standards so it's difficult to be too critical as all he is doing is seeking to press home his competitive advantage to the maximum. Fangio, Senna they did exactly the same. Schumacher was single-minded with all the positives and negatives of being the best in the world. His only handicap was that he did not immediately explain honestly why he did what he did.

And that is the nub of the problem with Schumacher and the reason why he remains such an enigma. In many ways the Jerez incident is similar to other moments in his history, where he was caught out acting in an unsporting way. He had no need to look back on Adelaide because he won the world title and no one made too much fuss about it. What makes Jerez stand out in his story, however, is the fact that he has since put his hands up and admitted he was wrong and expressed regret. At the time, and indeed for some time afterwards, he maintained his usual line of refusing to do so. Eventually he broke his own rules, largely because of advice from people close to him.

Schumacher's own analysis today of what happened at Jerez is simple.

> Within the rules of our sport you can move once to block. I should have done that. I should have gone much earlier to the inside and that would have been it. I shouldn't have given him any chance, but for me it was clear he was well enough behind me and would never try it. In a moment he was there. I reacted far too late to try to take my line and close the door. I have thought about it a lot since then and thought, how stupid I was to let that happen.
>
> It took me a long time to see what I'd done. I probably didn't want to admit it. At first I thought that Jacques wasn't in front of me and that I was right to defend my line.

After the incident Schumacher stood by the side of the track for a while, then made his way back to the paddock. He disappeared into the Ferrari motorhome, emerging only to visit the stewards to explain what had happened. The stewards decided that it was a 'racing incident' and no further action was necessary, which confirmed the driver's own feelings about it. At the time he felt that Villeneuve had not been ahead or even level with him and that he was right to defend his line. None of those close to him at that moment were telling him otherwise. Believing he had been exonerated, Schumacher returned to the motorhome, where he sat with Corinna, Ross Brawn, Jean Todt and Willi Weber.

They were all in denial. They had come close to winning a world title they hadn't expected to compete for and it hadn't worked out. End of story. Move on. Famously, Bernie

Ecclestone dropped by for a chat about skiing holidays. Schumacher had no idea of the mounting sense of outrage and indignation in the Jerez paddock and around the world.

Once the race had finished I was waiting with a crowd of other television reporters outside the Ferrari motorhome. When Schumacher emerged he looked disappointed but otherwise quite relaxed. When he was asked why he had done what he had done, he looked quite genuinely surprised at the question, admitting only that he had made 'a mistake', but not accepting in any way that he had deliberately tried to take Villeneuve out. He even said that given his time again he 'probably wouldn't have done anything different'.

I remember thinking at the time that this was a classic example of the great champion who always thinks he is in the right, just as we had seen countless times with Senna. Such men can construct an argument in their own minds where everything falls into place and makes perfect sense and has no negative bearing on themselves at all. It is a feature of the complete self-belief these rare men have which nothing can dent.

What made Jerez different from other Schumacher misdemeanours was that someone important in his life faced him down and told him he had been wrong. Luca di Montezemolo had flown from Bologna to southern Spain immediately after the race, both to console his team and to face up to Schumacher. The Italian media's instinctive reaction to Schumacher's move was that he had 'taken a beautiful jewel [Ferrari] and thrown it in the bin'. Clearly Montezemolo was thinking along the same lines. No one is whiter than white in Formula 1 but Schumacher had crossed the line of what was acceptable and that reflected badly on Ferrari.

The two men had spoken on the phone before Montezemolo's plane took off and he said that Schumacher had told him, 'I made a big stupid naïve mistake. I didn't expect Villeneuve to attack me there and yet I left him space to try. When he caught me out the anger at having made a mistake made me react instinctively, but it was too late.'

Montezemolo, who always had the capacity to challenge Schumacher, was the first to bring his driver down to earth and make him realise that his view of what had happened didn't wash. 'I was stunned when he said something along the lines of, "What have you done?" ' recalls Schumacher. 'And I thought, "I beg your pardon? How come I'm suddenly the idiot?" He was the first one to approach me about it and in the course of the next few weeks I came to recognise that I was wrong. If there is one thing I could do over again in F1 it would be that race in Jerez.'

Schumacher has since compared his action at Jerez to footballers who deliberately take a dive to win a penalty. 'They were regarded for a long time in Germany as being rather smart. Suddenly they were being slated for it. That's how I feel about Jerez.'

Much of the judgement of Schumacher stems from the fact that, to the outside world and particularly to the media who were the first on the scene, he appeared once again to be ducking the blame. Heiner Buchinger, who was Schumacher's assistant from 1995 to 1999, was surprised by the way Schumacher behaved after the race.

The problem was in those two hours after the race before he spoke to the media. I did not realise that he did not realise what was going on. In the past he had reacted well, like at Monaco in 1996 when he crashed in the race and the Italian press wanted an explanation. At the time Michael could easily have said that the car let him down but instead he said that it was all his own fault and that he was very sorry. I thought he would do this again, but of course he didn't.

Although Schumacher still believes that the Jerez incident was whipped up by the media and his jealous enemies in the paddock into something much bigger than it really was, the reaction of Montezemolo and others made him realise that he did have something for which to apologise. Over time, he has moved to a full acceptance of his guilt over Jerez, but Willi Weber still maintains that his driver is not fully to blame. 'If he had done it properly, if he had wanted to, then he would have really driven into the car and they would both have gone out,' he says. 'It was a simple, reflex action, definitely at the moment he did it and in that moment he was so very sorry.'

The explosion of outrage in the press the next day was astonishing. The German and Italian media went for the jugular, the Italians calling for 'public penitence', the Germans mourning the death of Schumacher's sporting reputation. 'It is the end of the image of the infallible driver,' was written in one newspaper.

Villeneuve stoked the fire. The day after his championship was won, he did a series of satellite television interviews from a studio at the circuit and he stuck the boot firmly into Schumacher's reputation.

I can understand what pushed him to try to drive me off the road. We were fighting for the title. I could have done the same thing to him at Suzuka and been champion there but it's not in my nature. It's a question of character. In a situation like that even if your brain tells you different, you follow your instincts. And Michael's instinct was to drive me off the road. My character is different. I would never feel good inside if I tried that. But he lost at his own game.

Ironically a few hours earlier Villeneuve and Schumacher had been partying together at their hotel. Returning home from dinner in the early hours of the morning, they had bumped into each other and persuaded the security man to open the bar. Schumacher even put on one of the blond wigs which the Williams mechanics had had made as a jokey tribute to Villeneuve and his peroxide-blond hair. The two rivals downed cocktails, got very drunk and enjoyed each other's company.

But a few days later the mood turned sour when photos of the scene appeared in a German magazine. It gave the impression that the pair were friends and that there were no hard feelings. It was a cynical attempt to play down what Schumacher had done. Villeneuve felt, 'It was a private party, suddenly photos are published. That's no way to carry on. You just don't do that kind of thing. And then Michael says that we are friends. I'm sick of it. He gets on my nerves. We are not friends and we never will be. What he did on the track isn't important to me, but what he's done here certainly is.'

* * *

Although the stewards in Jerez dismissed what had occurred as a racing incident, FIA president Max Mosley did not. He scanned the barrage of negative press and decided that the stewards' decision made the governing body look weak. Schumacher was summoned to appear before a special

PA PHOTOS

Above: A proud moment as Schumacher equals the great Juan Manuel Fangio's tally of five world titles in 2002

Right: His victory at the Belgian Grand Prix sealed his seventh world title in 2004

LAT PHOTOGRAPHIC

Left: One of the most important men in Schumacher's success. Benetton and Ferrari technical director Ross Brawn was the voice in his ear for 88 of his 91 Grand Prix wins

ACTIONIMAGES

Left: Former *Die Welt* journalist Sabine Kehm was Schumacher's assistant and press officer from 2000 until his retirement

ACTIONIMAGES

Left: Jean Todt brought Schumacher to Ferrari and, in Schumacher's words, often went 'way beyond the call of duty'. The pair became firm friends

ACTIONIMAGES

Right: Chief designer Rory Byrne was one of the unsung heroes of Ferrari's domination of F1. He formed an extraordinary partnership with Ross Brawn

PA PHOTOS

Schumacher won the six-car Grand Prix at Indianapolis 2005. Michelin couldn't race unless a chicane was built, but no solution was found

PA PHOTOS

Below: Schumacher's last race at Interlagos Brazil, October 2006.
After a series of setbacks including a burst tyre (rear right),
he put in one' of his best drives

PA PHOTOS

Opposite page, clockwise from top left: Schumacher with Mark
Webber *(right)* after the Australian finished fifth for Minardi on his debut
in Melbourne 2002; Schumacher always knew that one day someone
younger would come along and take his crown. That man was Fernando
Alonso *(left)*; Mr Twenty Per Cent. Manager Willi Weber was a hotelier
before he spotted Schumacher. Since then he has masterminded all
of Schumacher's multi-million pound deals; Schumacher showing his
unease at smart social functions. Here greeting his former Benetton boss,
Flavio Briatore, at a gala dinner in 2000; Bernie Ecclestone jokes with
Schumacher. Schumacher's career was generally good for F1's business
but his domination from 2000–2004 sent the TV audiences down in
many countries

GETTY IMAGES

ACTIONIMAGES

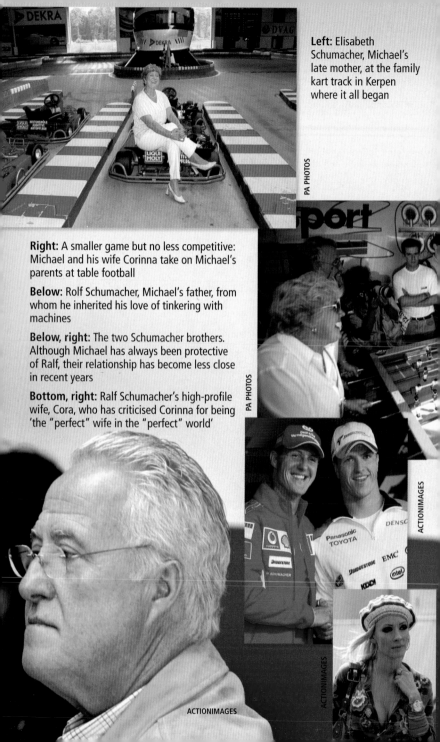

Left: Elisabeth Schumacher, Michael's late mother, at the family kart track in Kerpen where it all began

PA PHOTOS

Right: A smaller game but no less competitive: Michael and his wife Corinna take on Michael's parents at table football

Below: Rolf Schumacher, Michael's father, from whom he inherited his love of tinkering with machines

Below, right: The two Schumacher brothers. Although Michael has always been protective of Ralf, their relationship has become less close in recent years

Bottom, right: Ralf Schumacher's high-profile wife, Cora, who has criticised Corinna for being 'the "perfect" wife in the "perfect" world'

PA PHOTOS

ACTIONIMAGES

ACTIONIMAGES

ACTIONIMAGES

LAT PHOTOGRAPHIC

Above: Michael is hugely defensive of his family's privacy. Here, a rare photo of him at home in Switzerland with Corinna

Right: And one of Corinna and their daughter, Gina Maria, watching Michael play football, his other passion

PA PHOTOS

'He's fast… but not very good at heading' says his coach. Schumacher has a passion for football and continued playing after his retirement

PA PHOTOS

disciplinary hearing the following month. He had painful memories of 1994 and the bans he still felt were unfair. Clearly the FIA meant business again. Montezemolo reacted quickly and organised a press conference the following day at Maranello. He wanted a very Italian show of penitence. Knowing what lengths Schumacher was prepared to go to in avoiding showing any kind of regret or emotion in public, this press conference must have been one of the worst experiences of the German's life. He appeared in a dark suit, looking contrite, and said:

> I did not try to take him out, I just wanted to win the world championship. I committed an error of judgement and I will accept whatever the consequences may be. People do not expect me to make mistakes. But from what I have seen the reaction has been exaggerated. Worse things have happened in motor races than what happened last Sunday. As for the 1994 incident with Hill, that was a different thing and I wasn't driving for Ferrari then.
>
> I hope that if I do well in the future it will cancel out this episode. I will explain to the FIA exactly what I have told you today. I am keen to make myself understood. I'm sorry if it has taken me a while.

As the press filed out of the hall, Pino Allievi, one of the very best journalists in F1, spotted an old acquaintance in the crowd. It was the former motorcycle champion Umberto Massetti. 'Pino,' he said, 'the exact same thing happened to me as happened with Schumacher. Back at Spa in 1952 I was racing against a guy and he put out his leg and tried to make me fall off. At the end of the race he came to me, apologised and said he hadn't done it deliberately.' 'What did you do?' asked Allievi. 'I punched him,' said the old man.

Schumacher was hammered by the FIA at its disciplinary hearing. He was stripped of his second place in the championship, to this day the only time a driver has been disqualified from a championship for unsportsmanlike conduct. It was the clearest signal yet from the FIA that the culture had changed in Formula 1 under the Mosley regime and that deliberate collisions would no longer be tolerated. It hurt Schumacher, as once again he seemed to have been singled out and punished for something which had gone unpunished a few years earlier with Senna.

But many people still felt he had been let off lightly. Some even thought that the FIA should suspend him from some of the races in the 1998 world championship, but it was never going to do that. Schumacher was a big box office draw around the world. The FIA was accused of putting commercial considerations before sporting ones, but as Bernie Ecclestone pragmatically pointed out, 'I can take the heat. I've got promoters and television to think about. Michael was a silly boy but they want him at the races. People will forget about this soon enough.'

I went to visit Schumacher a few times during the winter following Jerez. He was testing at Ferrari's test track in Tuscany, Mugello. He had had a few months to reflect on his penalty and he seemed cheerful and accepting of what had happened to him. 'In the past that was the way you did it,' he said. 'If you wouldn't have done it you would have been criticised the other way around. Nevertheless we live in different times.'

He also said that the experience had hardened his view that the press always polarise everything. It is the job of the media to put a certain spin on things, but many elements of the media, especially the tabloids, go too far. Men like Mosley and Montezemolo are naturally sensitive to press headlines as they strive to protect the image of their sport or their brand and can be relied upon to respond with action when the headlines get really bad. Schumacher's natural reaction and even more so Jean Todt's, is to give nothing away and never to accept blame. They are less affected by the fickle attentions of the newspapermen.

There is no doubt, however, looking back on it now, that the public show of remorse which he had been forced to go through by Montezemolo hardened his resolve never to be put in that position again. He would go so far but no further in accepting blame for the Jerez incident, but once the new season started it would be old news and not something he wished to discuss any more. Thus Schumacher went into the 1998 season feeling optimistic that the public around the world would move on, as he had.

The real fans are the ones who stay with you whether you win or lose. I believe that most people do not reduce the season to one race. I'm aware that the season ended badly for me, but I have to look to the future. I made a mistake and I can't correct that wrong. All I want to do is win the world championship and repay the team.

I really messed up. That I am criticised for Jerez is okay, but you know I am not God and I am not an idiot. I always see things down the middle. I've certainly got something to put right, that's clear, but on the other hand there's never anything that one should totally regret. Look at the season as a whole, I had some good performances. It's not as if I messed up the whole season, it was just one race and no one would have turned a hair if it was for tenth place. What is special about Jerez is that the world championship was at stake and every racing driver in my place would have tried everything to win.

What was also special about Jerez was that it was the first time he had been caught red-handed doing something unsporting. Adelaide was different because he got away with it, while all the other bullyboy tactics on the track were debatable: he pushed the interpretation of the rule to the maximum, exploiting grey areas. But Jerez cemented his reputation.

CHAPTER FIFTEEN

The Renaissance man

When I was offered the job [at Ferrari], I spoke with lots of people who had worked there. Alain Prost was very clear, he said it was impossible to make the team successful. For me those words were a real stimulus to accept the challenge. At times I have to admit that I began to think Alain was right, but those moments did not last long!

Jean Todt

Schumacher's Ferrari career is divided into two distinct phases. There are the four fruitless years from 1996 to 1999, when he either lost the world title at the last round or was unable to compete for it, then the breakthrough in 2000 which led to five consecutive world titles and his unprecedented domination of the sport.

It was hard during the early phase to imagine that the Ferrari experience would turn out as successfully as it did, although all the tools were there. The old saying used to be, 'Stand outside Ferrari and you wonder why they don't win every race. Stand inside and you wonder how they manage to win any at all.' In other words, the buildings and obvious resources of the team, such as the test track adjacent to the factory, were always of the highest standard, but the disorganised shambles which greeted the visitor inside the factory fell a long way short of the professionalism of the leading British teams like Williams and McLaren.

Under the Jean Todt regime all that changed. Ferrari became a well-structured team with a clear direction, rigorous discipline and a clear sense of purpose. Todt's great achievement was to take the politics out of it, especially the way in which the team could be blown off course by the media. As a great manager, he took all the pressure on to his own shoulders, giving the team a sheltered environment in which to work.

Before Todt got a grip on media relations, the team leaked like a sieve, with stories and rumours filtering out to the Italian press about every area of team activity. This undermined confidence within the team and stymied its progress. Ferrari was like a reed in the wind of press criticism. Todt stood up to the press and put one of his most trusted lieutenants, Claudio Berro, in charge of the press office. Later Berro was replaced by Luca Colajanni, the son of a communist minister in the Italian government and a very skilled media manipulator.

With a stronger press office the team was able to prevent the media from driving a wedge between driver and team. Only once in 11 years did that happen, when Schumacher was injured in 1999 and there were conflicting stories about whether he would make a comeback in the final races of the season. The German press seemed several steps ahead of the

Italian press and their howls of indignation quickly reached Montezemolo's ears. Soon afterwards Schumacher fired his assistant, Heiner Buchinger. In general, the Todt/Schumacher years were characterised by an unbreakable bond between team principal and driver. The two men became far more than just colleagues, they were friends, which had a positive effect on the way the team was run.

In the early years Todt was engaged in repairing all that was wrong with the team and putting in place the building blocks of success. He described Ferrari as 'like a beautiful castle, but with leaks everywhere and repairs to do, otherwise it will fall down'. It took him a long time, because many areas needed work and the expertise was not always to be found in Italy. But once the essential blocks were in place, success soon followed, then success turned into domination and the team's mentality – pushing hard to maximise their competitive advantage in every area and never giving anything away – evolved and became ever more refined. Critics believe that their view became so narrow and so focused on themselves that they lost sight of the wider picture and of their responsibility to the sport.

The Todt era is the most successful by far in the history of Ferrari as a racing team. The key players were all locked in to what Ross Brawn calls a 'circle of fear', meaning that each was motivated as much by the desire not to let the others down as by the desire to succeed. They were constantly engaged in the search for an extra few per cent in every area, sometimes crossing the line in an interpretation of a rule to press home competitive advantage. When they were coming up, trying to reach the level of the established top teams, it made for great entertainment, but when they carried on in the same vein, despite having a dominant position, it became a less attractive spectacle.

The 1998 season began badly for Ferrari, as McLaren strolled to a one-two finish in the season-opening Australian Grand Prix at Melbourne. The result was bad, but what was truly painful was the margin McLaren had in hand. In the race they lapped the entire field and were almost two seconds per lap faster than the Ferraris, which seemed an unbridgeable gap. Mika Hakkinen thought as much prior to the Argentine Grand Prix, the third round of the championship, when he said, 'It will take a miracle for anyone to catch us.' And yet Ferrari were able to turn the situation around relatively quickly. Schumacher won in Argentina and at the next race in Imola. 'I guess the miracle happened!' he laughed. He took the title fight to the final race of the season in Suzuka, but lost out to Mika Hakkinen after he stalled his engine on the grid, perhaps feeling the pressure too much.

All season long there were insinuations from McLaren about devices on the Ferraris which were outside the rules, but nothing was ever proven. Traction control was still banned and once again Schumacher's success prompted dark mutterings about illegal systems being used on the cars. At the same time, McLaren were forced to take their revolutionary 'brake steer' system off the car which they had been using for ten races. The idea of the system was that the inside rear wheel was slowed in a corner to help the car to turn in more crisply and maintain grip. After McLaren's runaway success in Melbourne, Ferrari questioned its legality and the FIA decided that the system was indeed illegal and told McLaren to take it off the car. When a photographer was found in his garage, who admitted to being the brother-in-law of a Ferrari aerodynamicist, McLaren boss Ron Dennis was moved to say:

> People like a winner but no one likes a consistent winner. For years I have had to watch Frank Williams winning and I never complained, instead I got a feeling of admiration and a desire to win again. When we dominated in Australia and Brazil, Frank congratulated us, so in Formula 1 there can be a sense of loyalty and sportsmanship. But not everyone sees it that way.
>
> I had great respect for Enzo Ferrari. I liked his great dignity and the way he achieved his objectives. And my respect for him is what leads me to not want to comment on the Ferrari of today.

* * *

It was Bernie Ecclestone who had suggested Jean Todt's name to Luca di Montezemolo in 1992. He was looking for the right man to lead Ferrari out of the wilderness and Ecclestone had an interest in that too, as an underperforming Ferrari was bad for business. The timing was right all around. Todt was looking for a new challenge, having led Peugeot's sports department for 11 years. He had recently overseen Peugeot's victory in the Le Mans 24 Hours race when he went to Montezemolo's house in Bologna during the August holidays of 1992. Todt arrived at the house in a Mercedes, but Montezemolo soon forgave him for that. The Frenchman was disappointed that Peugeot had not taken up his idea of entering F1 as a constructor, instead deciding to come in solely as an engine supplier. As a result Todt felt entitled to leave them. Without him, Peugeot's F1 experience was a disaster and they skulked out of the sport after seven seasons without ever looking like winning a race.

Todt discovered motorsport in the 1960s. He was in the right place at the right time when one of France's leading rally drivers, Guy Chasseuil, found himself in urgent need of a co-driver for an event. Todt stood in and so began his career in motorsport. Initially his goal was to be a Formula 1 driver himself, but he quickly gave up on that dream when his co-driving career took off. His skills then drew him towards management; he organised events and took on the role of representing the drivers in discussions with the FIA. By the age of 35 he was in charge of Peugeot Sport.

One of the key moments which defined his attitude to sport and winning came in the 1989 Paris-Dakar rally. The Peugeot cars were showing a clear dominance of the event, so that Ari Vatanen and Jacky Ickx were actually racing against each other. In the dangerous desert conditions and with six days of the rally still to go, Todt did not want his two drivers to push each other into taking risks which might cause them to crash. He called a meeting in his tent and tossed a coin to decide who should win the event. Vatanen won the toss and with it the rally. Both drivers were told to take it easy and come home in first and second places. Todt had delivered Peugeot its dream result, but sport had been the loser.

Todt, the son of a doctor, describes himself as 'a hard man with a soft heart, someone who bears a grudge, is honest, loyal and ambitious. A passionate and dedicated hard worker, as capable of making compromises as of not making them, depending on the moment. I'm reliable, methodical, fussy and intolerant.' He is the kind of man who feels he needs to know what everyone is up to. He is very good at delegating, but he needs his information network to be feeding back to him what every area is working on and what is being said. In 2006 he was promoted to head the entire Ferrari operation, both road cars and racing team. He has two jobs effectively and although he has been able to delegate much of his responsibility for the race team to his number two, Stefano Domenicali, he still attends every race and all the critical meetings. His life is no longer all about winning races, it has broadened out. But he does not want the whole enterprise to sink back to where it was before he arrived, so he maintains his influence and dictates the culture.

The Frenchman puts in amazingly long hours at the factory. On a typical week when he is based in Maranello and not travelling, he will not leave his office until around 11pm from Monday to Thursday and then on Friday he flies to Paris for the weekend. He loves the social life of Paris, attends grand dinners and goes to nightclubs, is a man about town. Everyone needs a hobby, a distraction from their intense work lives and for Todt it is his social life.

He is an incredibly superstitious man. He feels the need to touch wood all the time and so had a small wooden box made which he carries with him in his pocket at all times. If you look closely at his hands, all ten of his fingers are bandaged because he is an inveterate nail-biter and he has to keep what is left of his nails covered up. 'I do not believe that I have ever relaxed one hundred per cent during my whole career,' he once said. 'Even when I am on the podium, when I'm celebrating a win, part of me is focused on the next race, on the dangers which lie ahead. I never switch off. I hold the record for longevity in this post but that does not mean that I am irreplaceable. One of the reasons why I have never fully settled in my house in Italy is based on this uncertainty. I have to be ready to leave suddenly. I came close a few times, but I held on.'

One of his more amazing skills is mental arithmetic; he can add up or subtract numbers instantly and claims never to need a calculator. He has a very ordered mind. Schumacher is in awe of his mental discipline:

> I'll give you an example. Once, at the start of the 2003 season, I had a list for him with many questions on it, really specific things on the development of the car and other precise areas. You know we work almost non-stop and you have to have an eye on everything, be across everything that is going on. I gave him the list of questions and very soon afterwards he came back to me with all the answers, one after another, bang, bang, bang. When he had finished he said, 'I'm getting old, but I can still answer your questions.' That guy is amazing. He can stop a storm and level everything out before it becomes a problem.

Unlike Schumacher, who does not really enjoy talking about himself, Todt is very self-referential. Perhaps that is a cultural thing: prominent French people throughout history have had a tendency to fashion their own narrative. Todt has been highly decorated by his native country, he holds the Legion d'Honneur and is much sought after for his views on successful management. One memorable self-portrait came in an interview with the prominent French journalist Stephane Samson:

> You should never have methods, only principles. Seeking perfection, humility and honesty are things which important to me. Formula 1 in general lacks principles. Far

too many people stare at their own navels. I ask a lot of my people, I don't tolerate the easy route. I think I'm a fair boss, I listen. I'm like a fireman; I put out fires at all hours and allow people to work in the best conditions possible. The door of my office is always open. I welcome new recruits personally. I put a lot of importance on paying attention to people. I'm lucky enough to have around me a group of people who have a lot of qualities in common with me, but who come from different worlds. This helps to keep the feet on the ground.

This is probably the real secret of why Ferrari was so successful under Jean Todt. He managed to assemble a group of individuals from very different backgrounds but who clicked when they worked together. A good manager can achieve a magical blend of characters where everyone knows their role and respects the job the others are doing. A successful team cannot tolerate trouble-makers who swim against the current.

The Ferrari team understood very clearly what Todt expected of them and how it would be achieved and bought into his vision because it was in line with their own. The core team at Ferrari was rather like the Beatles in the 1960s; men with significant talent who would have been relatively successful on their own, but when put together they became world-beaters. So it was with the five in the inner circle at Ferrari: Jean Todt overseeing the direction of the team and the commercial side, Ross Brawn and Rory Byrne building the fastest car and racing it cleverly, Paolo Martinelli building reliable, strong engines and Michael Schumacher taking the product out on to the race-track and delivering the results.

These key men bonded to an exceptional degree at Ferrari. Brawn and Byrne, who were together at both Benetton and Ferrari, are one of the great technical double acts of F1 history. Brawn is the front man, the organiser, the disciplinarian. His job was to oversee the technical department, to lay out the vision and direction and manage the process of getting the maximum performance and reliability out of the car at the race-track. A tall, owlish man with a wispy beard and thick, beer-bottle spectacles, he likes to talk about his work and loved the cut and thrust of the competition. Rory Byrne is a much more low key character. A South African by birth, he is quite a modest man, who does not seek the limelight and prefers to be based at the factory, making only one appearance a year at the Italian Grand Prix. Byrne has an intuitive feel for taking a car design to the limits. His cars were always aerodynamically efficient as well as beautiful and his astute management of the research and development department meant that the team kept up a relentless rate of progress.

As Formula 1 has become more sophisticated over the last 20 years, so the influence one man can have on a team has diminished. Critics liked to say that Schumacher ran the team, that he had control over everything, but that is a hopelessly naïve view. He was a vitally important cog and he probably did go further into the deeper layers of the team than any other driver had done before, but the true strength of Ferrari was that each person knew their role, stuck to it and had respect for the role the others were playing.

The sense of teamwork was always very impressive. As Ross Brawn said many times, the bad moments bonded them and the good moments gave them a taste of what they wanted to have all the time. If they had a bad season, they would learn from it quickly and be hungry to succeed again.

All Formula 1 teams are very hierarchical and the top men like Todt and Brawn were being paid millions of pounds every year, but what always impressed me was the way that they would travel out to races on the same plane as their team. Almost all the other bosses, and certainly the really successful ones, have their own private jets which no humble mechanic is ever allowed to board. At Ferrari, however, the top management would always be on the same Alitalia charter flight out of Bologna airport to whichever European destination they were visiting.

The sense of unity among the team came across loud and clear in public, too. At the circuit, Todt always wore the same shirt and trousers as the man who strips the gearboxes, whereas the McLaren-Mercedes bosses have their own separate uniform, completely different from the mechanics. It may seem a small thing, but it says a lot about the way team spirit is built. Certainly in the early days the Ferrari team contained many expatriates working away from home and they would tend to eat together in the evenings at the Montana restaurant, near the Fiorano test track. When he was there for a test session Schumacher would always join them as well. The family that eats together stays together.

Of course the team came in for a lot of criticism for the way in which they sometimes went about things, pushing the limits on legality with the car, overstretching the mark on gamesmanship and on track behaviour. Todt and Schumacher together set the tone for this within the team. If they were so obviously giving no quarter, then the rest of the group felt obliged to follow their lead. Todt denies however that he is the brutal, crafty wolf, whose motto is 'win ugly'.

> I'm the opposite. I am naïve. I have a tendency to give people my confidence spontaneously. And I'm often had over. However when that happens, my anger overtakes my naïvety. I have one quality, memory, and one defect, I bear a grudge.
>
> Ten years ago no one thought Ferrari would win again. We brought success and immediately people put the wins down to favourable circumstances, to luck or trickery. Many people wanted Ferrari to get back to the highest level, to be a real team with no scandals and no polemics. Now they just look for the faults.

Like all Formula 1 team bosses, Todt thinks first of his own team's interests when any decisions need to be taken regarding the sport as a whole. He believes that the destiny of F1 and that of Ferrari are interlinked; it is the only team to have survived from the very first season of Formula 1 racing in 1950. Many great names have disappeared since then, such as Lotus, Brabham and Tyrrell. Ferrari has always stayed close to the governing body, always voted with it on issues which have threatened to split the sport in half. To Todt, F1 without Ferrari would be merely a deluxe Formula 2. 'Ferrari is the capital on which F1's success is based and everyone benefits from it,' he says. 'If certain teams hadn't won their world championships by beating us then they would have passed almost unnoticed. People had got used to seeing Ferrari take part but not winning and that seemed to suit them. We woke them up.'

When Todt started at Ferrari in July 1993, the team was divided – literally, as we have seen, with John Barnard's department in England handling design, composites and suspension. There was no wind tunnel, (the team used a British Aerospace one) and there were 350 people in the team working on the chassis and engine side. In ten years that number had mushroomed to 700. All personnel now work on the same campus at Maranello, just across the road from the main road car factory, in a division of Ferrari which Todt christened *Gestione Sportiva* (sports management). The engine department, where approximately 200 people work on designing, developing and building F1 engines, is connected to the chassis department by a short corridor, so the communications between the two sides are as clear as they can possibly be. This is not the case with most teams, whose engines come from a different town, even a different country.

'When I was offered the job, I spoke with lots of people who had worked there,' recalls Todt. 'Alain Prost was very clear, he said it was impossible to make the team successful. For me those words were a real stimulus to accept the challenge. At times I have to admit that I began to think Alain was right, but those moments did not last long!'

Todt changed the mentality but not the culture of Ferrari, he maintains. Certain bad habits had become ingrained, like wine on the mechanics' table at lunch time. The effect that he, Brawn and Schumacher had on Ferrari has been described as 'like penicillin on a colony of bacteria'. They gave Ferrari its pride back and transformed its fortunes. Whereas before they had had to pay for the 35 sets of fireproof overalls the mechanics needed for pit stops, for example, by 1997 the manufacturers were fighting each other to buy the contract to supply the team.

The personal relationship between Todt and Schumacher

was very significant – the hugs and kisses after a race victory, the total solidarity through thick and thin. They suffered a lot together and they rejoiced a great deal together. When Schumacher broke his leg in 1999, Todt put everything to one side to make sure that nothing was overlooked which might improve Schumacher's situation. He went 'way beyond the call of duty' in Schumacher's words.

The two men share the same values when it comes to sporting competition and to what is and what is not acceptable in pursuit of victory. They are of different generations and come from very different backgrounds: Todt the middle class, well-educated son of a prominent doctor, Schumacher, the working class son of a bricklayer, who fought his way to the top. Todt's father was ambitious for him, encouraging his son to get on in the world and make the most of every opportunity. Schumacher's parents were not ambitious, yet he had the same outlook because it came from his own instincts.

Todt is a family friend, sharing weekends and holidays with Schumacher's family. Todt would usually stay at Schumacher's house in Norway over the New Year holiday, which would always spill over into a party for Schumacher's birthday on 3 January. It became a tradition for the men to go out into the wilderness for a few nights, staying in a cabin and cooking their food on an open fire, getting away from it all.

Todt also taught Schumacher to play backgammon and introduced him to modern art. In their professional field, there was nothing that Todt could teach Schumacher, but culturally the younger man was a blank canvas. Todt helped him to pick up the cultural references that a man of his wealth and status should know.

Todt is always quick to point out that although he was close to his driver, he did not allow that to blur his vision. 'We have shared good times and bad,' Todt says, 'but sooner or later you have to be able to separate friendship and business. I love working with him, but my top priority is always the team.'

CHAPTER SIXTEEN

Agony and ecstasy

Racing is life and life is a risk.

Michael Schumacher

A Formula 1 car is a prototype. It rarely stays the same from one race to the next and things are changed on it constantly in search of enhanced performance. For this reason it is an inherently dangerous place to sit. Before the advent of carbon fibre monocoques, safety cells which protect the driver even in the most savage impacts, it was very rare for a driver who always drove on the ragged edge to enjoy a 16-year career as Michael Schumacher did. He would more likely either have been killed, like Jim Clark, or too badly injured to continue, like Stirling Moss. Some made it through, like Juan Manuel Fangio who played Russian roulette for eight seasons, or Jackie Stewart for nine, before getting out. Damon Hill's father, Graham, was an exception – he had a career of similar length to Schumacher's, but he was only competitive for about half of it.

Schumacher had many serious accidents during his F1 career which would have killed him if he had suffered them 20 years earlier, but thanks to the safety of the cars he was only badly hurt on one occasion, at Silverstone in 1999. Ironically it was one of the lowest speed impacts of his career, but he was unlucky in the way the car broke up on impact. Coincidentally the accident occurred at what turned out to be more or less the halfway stage in his Formula 1 career and it was a turning point in many ways.

For one thing, it meant that the world championship was again beyond his reach as he sat out most of the second half of the season. It was another in a string of disappointments, but this one had a silver lining. It gave Schumacher the opportunity to step off the intense treadmill he had been on for eight years, to rest and to take stock of his situation. The Schumacher who returned triumphantly at the end of 1999 was a vastly improved version of the previous one. The months he spent sitting on the sidelines allowed him to recharge his batteries, to re-evaluate his career and the relative importance of things. When he came back he was fitter, stronger, even more focused and as a result his driving skill was at an even higher level than before. I have always believed that the recuperation period after the accident gave him the energy and the momentum to go on and dominate the sport in the 2000s. Without it he would probably have retired earlier than 2006.

It was a strange accident, in a sense eerily reminiscent of Senna's accident at Imola in that the driver was powerless to stop the car flying off the road and in the impact a piece of suspension broke off and caused the injury. But beyond that the conditions were vastly more favourable for Schumacher, who was travelling at a lower speed on impact and who hit a tyre barrier rather than a concrete wall.

Ironically the accident was quite unnecessary, as the race

had been stopped due to an incident at the start-line. The Ferrari team tried to tell their drivers via radio, but they did not hear. They were locked in a personal duel down the back straight at well over 190mph. Schumacher had been quite clear before the start that he needed to keep Hakkinen behind him in the opening laps, otherwise the McLaren driver would simply pull away from him, such was its superior pace. So after a poor start and having fallen behind his team-mate, Eddie Irvine, he was desperate to get past the Ulsterman and get at Hakkinen. Irvine made life difficult for Schumacher as they approached Stowe corner and then when Schumacher hit the brakes, they failed and the car careered headlong off the race-track, through the gravel trap and ploughed into the tyre barrier.

The story behind the accident though goes back a few weeks before the British Grand Prix. Eddie Irvine was in a delicate phase of his career. He was in discussions with Ford about leaving Ferrari to head up the new Jaguar Racing team, which would be built on the foundations of the Stewart team. Irvine was asking for big money and so had a lot to prove as the negotiations were ongoing with the Ford board. In the French Grand Prix just before Silverstone, Irvine had lost 35 seconds when the Ferrari team put the wrong tyres on his car. Carving his way back through the field, he came up behind Schumacher, who was in fifth place, nursing a gearbox problem, whilst just ahead of him was Ralf Schumacher who was also much slower than Irvine's Ferrari. Instead of finishing in sixth place, Irvine knew that fourth was there for the taking. But the team would not allow Irvine to overtake Schumacher, so he sat in the German's tracks to the finish. Little did he know it at the time, but those two extra points he could have had that day for fourth place would have made him world champion at the end of the season, Ferrari's first for 20 years. But that is not how the scripts were being written.

After the race, Irvine saw some quotes from Schumacher playing down the role of team orders at Ferrari, denying that Irvine was forced to play the role of number two driver, or had helped him much in races.

> He was saying, 'Eddie has only been told to move over for me once.' I thought, 'Well, I've only been told once, but I've moved over plenty of times before I got the call because I knew the call was coming.'
>
> So then I decided, 'Okay from now on I'll wait for the call.' I beat him off the start line, as I always did because he wasn't a very good starter because he's got a slow reaction time, which people don't realise. Anyway I gave him room and put him in a position where if he tried to brake later than me he wasn't going to make the corner. I did and he braked, then he locked up immediately because he'd braked far too late so he came off the pedal, then braked again and the rear nipple broke and he broke his leg. The impact was less than a hundred miles an hour so he should never have broken his leg in that shunt, but to be honest, that car had issues because on another occasion the front wing broke off when the car was lifted up so there was an issue there.
>
> Good for me that he did break a leg. Not a nice thing to say, I know, but it changed the path of my life in a way because I became the number one.

Schumacher recalls:

> When I put my foot on the brakes I realised that this would go wrong. There are nicer things in life than crashing into a

wall of tyres. I tried to get out of the car after the accident
but it didn't work. I couldn't get my legs out of the cockpit.
I was lying there listening to my own heartbeat and it got
quieter and quieter, like in slow motion and then suddenly
it was gone. All around me was darkness. I heard the
medics talking but it was all very quiet. I was really scared,
I really thought that's it.

Schumacher had broken his leg in two places. He was taken to
Northampton General Hospital where he was operated on.
Meanwhile the race continued and Irvine finished third
behind the McLarens of Coulthard and Hakkinen. In the press
conference afterwards he showed his true feelings. 'I was the
only Ferrari driver in the race and I drove in a different way
from normal. When I'm alone I feel stronger because when
Michael's there the whole team is concentrated on him. I felt
a new sense of responsibility.'

He was asked how he felt now that he was Ferrari's sole title
hope. 'I have a contract as a number two driver,' he said. 'If I
don't respect it I get fired. I will do whatever the team orders
me to do.'

It was a typical piece of crass Irvine mouthiness, but Ralf
Schumacher was less than impressed by the sentiments.
'Irvine should learn to keep quiet,' he said. 'In the last few
weeks he's done nothing except moan about Michael's
privileged status as if he didn't have the chance to show what
he's worth. Michael has always been the faster of the two. I
would like to say to Mr Irvine, stop complaining and show that
he is faster.'

Nevertheless Irvine had highlighted the rich irony of the
situation. Ferrari had put all its eggs in one basket. Now they
would have to get behind Irvine, who, for a fraction of the

money they had paid Schumacher, might bring the holy grail of the first world title for 20 years to Ferrari. He knew, like Schumacher, that he was sitting in the best Ferrari either of them had ever driven. Now it was up to Irvine to get the job done. But would Ferrari want that?

After Silverstone decisions were taken at Maranello. One of them was to stop developing the current car and instead put extra effort into the design of the 2000 car. Irvine was getting signals from the team that they supported his title bid, but only up to a point. Says Irvine:

> The level of support from the team was fine. The problem was that they took the car out of the wind tunnel to start work on the 2000 car. We had a car which wasn't going to beat the McLaren, we knew that, but as it turned out we could have beaten them if we'd left the 1999 car in the wind tunnel.
>
> They made the decision not to develop the car, they figured, 'We've got no chance' and I understand that, because we didn't have a chance really, but then we got a couple of good results, Mika had some problems and we were in the hunt.

As he sat in his hospital room, staring at the bunch of 35 red roses, one for each of his wins, sent to him by Montezemolo, Schumacher was despondent. Four years had elapsed since he had last won the title and now he would have to wait another year. No other champion in history had endured such a lean spell in the middle of his career. He said that he was 'focused on getting back into a Ferrari and racing before the end of the season'. Little did he realise at the time how contentious an issue that would become.

Schumacher thought a lot about the accident. He always

had to have a complete explanation of why an accident had happened so that he could put it out of his mind. Accidents for which he had no explanation were rare but they stayed in his mind and troubled him.

For example, one accident he had at Imola in 1995 – when he simply threw the car off the road on a partly wet track – was never fully explained. The car went light as he crested a rise and he lost control of it. No one else made the same mistake and it was entirely out of character for him to make one like it, especially on a tricky surface, where he normally excelled. I interviewed him for television immediately after he returned to the pits and you could see that he was troubled by it, couldn't say for sure that it was his mistake, but equally could see no other reason for it. Years later he was still referring to it as an example of an unexplained accident that lingered in his mind.

Though he had been fully briefed on why the rear brakes failed at Silverstone, the accident still niggled because it was unnecessary. The race had been stopped and he shouldn't really have been put in that position by Irvine. He kept thinking about the impact and what he had experienced immediately afterwards. He said a few years later, in a reflective mood:

> There are moments again and again when I think about that accident. And I think, well if it were to happen again, it really looks quite bad. But I don't catch myself driving slower while doing this. As a racing driver you try to find your limits. And to achieve that you always have to go slightly above them. But the dangers of motorsport are calculable – at least that's what I would claim. I believe I can estimate them quite well.

Irvine did not visit Schumacher in hospital, but spoke to him on the phone, joking about the time he had broken his leg skateboarding as a child. Eddie claimed it would be sheer hypocrisy for him to visit; after all, they both knew that Schumacher's misfortune was Irvine's big break.

To understand the level of despondency Schumacher felt it is necessary to recall the notion he had about owing a debt to the Ferrari team. He had been hired to win the world title for them and he had so far failed to deliver. As the years went by the anguish at his failure to do so made him increasingly tense. He always saw things in black and white. He focused everything on that goal and would not be able to forgive himself if he did not deliver. The Silverstone accident complicated his simple view, but as it turned out, it was probably the best thing that could have happened as it set him up for seven years of almost constant success.

In the meantime he had to contend with some unwelcome comments, not least from former Ferrari driver and *tifosi* favourite Clay Regazzoni, who slammed him in the Italian press, saying that Ferrari should drop him:

> If I was in the position of Montezemolo, I would use this time to review my contract with Schumacher. He has been overpaid in order to get the World Championship. That he has not achieved this in four years is a flop. Ferrari can afford to give up Schumacher; they should finally put their trust in Irvine, who can do the same job as Schumacher for less money. Schumacher will also come back with less motivation – he would even help Irvine. It's time for Schumacher and Todt to leave.

This was not a commonly held view by any means, but these were strong words from someone whose views were taken seriously in Italy and amongst certain factions within the Ferrari management. Of course Regazzoni was proved wrong on virtually every point. Irvine wasn't able to do the same job as Schumacher, who returned more motivated than ever, and did help Irvine when he finally came back at the end of the season.

The story of the comeback was a bit of a soap opera. It dragged on all summer and was played out in the press, especially in Italy and Germany. Things started to get tricky in August, a mere 40 days after the accident, when Schumacher visited doctors in Geneva to see whether he was fit to drive again. He still had a metal plate and two screws in his leg, but the doctors were satisfied with his progress and said it was up to him to decide when he should drive again. The following day, back behind the wheel of the Ferrari for a test session at Mugello, he completed 65 laps, with a best time which was faster than Irvine's. But the experience was not without pain. The next Grand Prix was due to take place at Spa the following weekend and Schumacher declined to drive, saying he needed more time. He was based in St Tropez that summer and was photographed extensively by the paparazzi riding a mountain bike in the hills above the coast. He decided to escape their attentions and retreated to his house in Norway.

His next appointment was at Monza for the traditional September test the week before the Italian Grand Prix. Schumacher was in pain straight away as the cars give the drivers a terrible pounding over the kerbs at Monza. Again the comeback was delayed. Then things got really complicated.

At the beginning of October, Schumacher went back to see

Professor Gerard Saillant, a close friend of Jean Todt's, who had been supervising the driver's recovery. There were two races left in the world championship and Ferrari had a good chance of winning both. In Schumacher's absence Irvine had taken a couple of wins, Hakkinen had had some retirements and it was wide open. Schumacher was in a difficult position. He might have expected that the drivers' championship would have been beyond Irvine by now. Heiner Buchinger (Schumacher's assistant at the time) let it be known before the examination that it was unlikely that the driver would be fit to return, citing some inflammation of the knee due to his intense training programme on the bicycle. Nevertheless a press statement put out by Ferrari said that Schumacher had been given the all clear.

Ferrari asked him to test again at Mugello on 4 October. This time he covered over 200 miles and despite going off the road and hitting a tyre barrier, was again very fast. But he insisted afterwards that he would not race in Malaysia and was also angry at the impression given by the Ferrari statement:

> It's not true that I am okay, I am not okay. The statement after the visit to Paris created a false impression. The doctors said that I was okay to pursue normal activities, like make bread or go to an office, but I am not okay to drive a Formula 1 car.
>
> The leg hasn't hurt me especially, but my neck is sore, I am very tired and when I drive my heartbeat seems abnormal. All of this from doing a few laps. It would be impossible in my current condition to do a full Grand Prix distance. I've tried everything to get fit for my return but I have not succeeded.

He was angry at suggestions that he was abandoning Ferrari in its moment of need, but said emphatically that he would not drive again until December at the earliest, long after the end of the world championship. It was well known that Montezemolo felt he should drive, even if winning the race was beyond him, at least to give Ferrari hope. The final race at Suzuka was a further three weeks away, by which time he would be even more ready, but Schumacher wasn't having it. What was significant was that Jean Todt, who had been with Schumacher every step of the way during his recovery, speaking to him at least once a day by telephone, was not present at the test. He appeared to be distancing himself from the situation, as it was now a battle of wills between Schumacher and Montezemolo.

A widely reported story at the time held that Montezemolo had phoned Schumacher at home only to be informed by his young daughter, Gina Maria, that her father was not available as he was putting on his football boots. The impression being given out covertly was that Schumacher was taking Ferrari for a ride, ducking his responsibilities.

In reality this was another situation in which correct judgement was critical. Schumacher probably did not relish being put in a situation where he had to help Irvine to win the world title for which he had been striving for four years and for which he was being paid perhaps five times Irvine's salary. It would jeopardise the whole Ferrari project in which he had invested so much for his team-mate to be the one to grab the glory. Rather than be put in that position some accused him of trying to stay well clear of the whole thing. Even if he had chosen this route, however, Irvine might still win the title if Hakkinen's car proved unreliable in the final races.

In the context of the sporting challenge, the all-important *sfida* as the Italians call it, the rumours that Schumacher would not try were incomprehensible. The Italian media felt that he owed it to them to make an effort and accept the challenge. McLaren led Ferrari in the constructors' championship by just 8 points with 32 still available. It could only be won if Ferrari had two strong drivers out there. The press coverage of Schumacher's refusal to compete was largely negative.

Four days later Schumacher drove again at Fiorano and had a meeting with Todt and Montezemolo over lunch. Immediately afterwards he announced that he had changed his mind. He would drive in the final two races and come to Ferrari's rescue. What changed his mind, what pressure was brought to bear on him? Schumacher admitted that Montezemolo had 'really insisted, from day to day, from hour to hour' on his return. 'Sometimes it is better to change your mind than to carry on making a mistake.'

Schumacher said that his reaction to the earlier statement from Ferrari that he was fit to race had been to protect himself, hence his announcement, but now he was apologising for having 'perhaps spoken a little too hastily'. As to the all-important question as to whether he was prepared to help Irvine become world champion, Schumacher was quite clear on the matter and one almost had to pinch oneself to believe what one was hearing. 'I'm coming back to help the team and yes, to help Irvine,' he said. 'I think that over the distance of the race I might have some problems, but it's very important to Ferrari that I am there. I hope to be able to help the team and Irvine, but I'm not promising miracles.'

During the test sessions Ferrari had been trying out some

new aerodynamic modifications, which had made the car significantly faster, hence the lap records which Schumacher was able to set. After the race in Malaysia attention focused on the deflectors behind the front wheels, colloquially known as 'barge boards', which were found to be the wrong size and as a result the two Ferraris were disqualified, a decision later reversed at an appeal hearing in Paris. But rival teams suggested that there were changes in the floor of the car too, which were far more likely to be responsible for the sudden improvement in performance. Schumacher ended up on pole, 1.2 seconds faster than the McLarens.

'I was relieved when he turned up,' says Irvine. 'We had made a big aerodynamic step for the last two races, whether it was legal or not I don't know, but anyway the car was faster and Michael comes back and everyone goes, "Michael's back, look at the difference." I thought, "For fuck's sake!" '

In the race itself, Schumacher did what no one would have believed he would ever do. Twice he let Irvine through into the lead, and then concentrated his attention on blocking Hakkinen in third place. It was brutal, not exactly sporting, but under the rules as they were written at the time it was entirely legal. Ferrari got the tactics spot-on and pressed home their advantage over McLaren. Even Hakkinen was forced to admit that his team had been second best. 'It was the hardest race of my life,' said Hakkinen. 'I was flat out all the way, but Ferrari had brilliant tactics and I don't really blame them. I spent most of the race behind Michael, but could not get past him. I didn't want to get caught out by his inconsistent driving patterns. He was lifting [off the throttle] in high speed corners and fluctuating his speed, so I had to be careful not to run into him.'

Irvine won the race, Schumacher finished second and Hakkinen was third, meaning that Irvine would go into the final round four points ahead of Hakkinen, with Ferrari a similar margin ahead of McLaren in the constructors' championship. Despite Schumacher's protestations of a lack of fitness, on the podium he was visibly the least tired of the three.

When the stewards' decision was announced disqualifying the Ferraris, initially Ross Brawn put up his hands up and admitted that the cars had been outside the regulations. There had been a small measuring error on the team's part which gave no performance benefit to the car, but it was outside the rules. I was present in the Ferrari team's office that evening as the light faded outside, while Brawn held up a barge board and used a ruler to illustrate the measuring problem. The team had used the same barge boards at the previous race in Germany, but as Irvine had finished seventh there, nothing had been done after the race.

On his return to Maranello, Todt offered his resignation to Montezemolo, who turned it down and told him to concentrate on turning the situation around. Incredibly, despite Brawn and Todt admitting after the race that the car had not conformed to the rules, the team was able to win the appeal. Measured in a certain way, the amount that the bargeboard was out was only five millimetres and that was within the acceptable general tolerances set out in the rules. Ferrari won the appeal and the points table stood going into the final race.

Despite his misgivings about returning to help the team, the final race worked out perfectly for Schumacher. Ferrari won the constructors' world championship, its first since

1983, which gave the team some payback for all their hard work, while the drivers' world title went to Hakkinen, thus leaving the way open for Schumacher still to become the first to win the drivers' title for the team.

Had he won the race, then that would have given Irvine the title, but starting from pole he never looked likely to beat Hakkinen, losing the lead to him and then shadowing him to the finish. Hakkinen won the race and with it the world championship, while Irvine trailed in over a minute behind Schumacher in third place. Schumacher was not obliged to let Irvine through for second, because even if the Ulsterman and the Finn finished level on points Hakkinen would have won on a countback of wins. Irvine's lack of pace at Suzuka that weekend, a track he knew intimately from his many years racing in Japanese F3000 and had always excelled at, was surprising. 'Basically I couldn't get into the corners as quick, I couldn't go through the corners as quick and I couldn't come out of the corners as quick as Michael. I almost got lapped in the race. And I qualified – what – 1.6 secs off him? The following year I was within seven tenths of him in a Jaguar. But I don't think it was Ferrari . . .'

Schumacher had enjoyed a successful return but he couldn't stop himself from becoming embroiled in an unseemly spat after the race with David Coulthard. He had come up to lap the McLaren driver and was held up for three corners, losing three seconds in the process. After the race, instead of celebrating Ferrari's world title (publicly) and Irvine's failure (privately), he lashed out verbally at Coulthard in the press conference, accusing the Scot of blocking. He also made a reference to the incident at Spa the previous year, 'I'm not sure now whether I should believe what happened at Spa last year wasn't done purposely, the way he behaved today. It cost me about ten seconds.'

This was not only totally inaccurate, it was also unnecessary and undignified. Coulthard was livid. 'If he doesn't apologise I'm going to sue him,' he said. 'I am very disappointed with his comments, especially questioning my integrity over Spa. I have never tried to endanger any driver on the track.'

McLaren team boss Ron Dennis accused Schumacher of hypocrisy: 'After what he put Mika through in Malaysia, I don't want to hear one word from Schumacher about being held up. He should look at some of his own races and some of the things he's done himself.'

Schumacher should have just walked away happy at the job he had done, but the bully in him had to give out some pain to restore what he saw as the natural order in the F1 paddock. Coulthard was always an easy target for him, because he often complained about Schumacher and because for the most part Schumacher had him easily covered on the race-track. Critics have always levelled a charge of hypocrisy at Schumacher and this was a prime example.

For Dennis there was a quiet satisfaction that despite having failed on two occasions to recruit Schumacher to his team, he had for the second year running seen his driver, Mika Hakkinen, win the world title, beating Schumacher and Ferrari in the process.

CHAPTER SEVENTEEN

Mission accomplished

I don't have to prove anything else to myself. I did what I really wanted to do in 2000 with my first world championship with Ferrari.

Michael Schumacher

In October 2000, after five years of failure, five seasons of joy mixed with agony and anguish, Schumacher fulfilled his destiny and became Ferrari's first world champion since Jody Scheckter in 1979. At a stroke he restored pride to a great institution, which had languished in the doldrums for 20 years. The confidence flowed through the whole team; they were riding a wave which would not drop them back down again for five years.

Winning that first world title for Ferrari was without doubt the greatest achievement of Schumacher's entire career and its major turning point. From then onwards he was able to cast aside the incredible burden of pressure he had placed on himself and race for pleasure. He had had tunnel vision until 2000, not allowing himself to be distracted by anything until he had fulfilled what he saw as his duty. Sabine Kehm says:

In 2000 he did what was expected of him. He didn't open up before that because he hadn't fulfilled his duty. He wouldn't have forgiven himself if he hadn't achieved it and maybe had the feeling that if he'd concentrated more he would have achieved it. From 2000 and with every title he felt more secure and he opened up inside the team and then he let all the emotions of Enzo Ferrari and all the Ferrari myth suck in. He dared to go out with them in the evenings, in the beginning he didn't dare because he hadn't delivered and he felt that it wasn't right to do that. Before he had to have everything a hundred per cent organised or he felt that it wouldn't work out, now he likes the Italian way as well, he's relaxed about it a lot. He loves spending time in Italy, but it's hard for him because if the people found out he was there they'd eat him up.

But unlike most of the championships that followed, winning the 2000 title was no picnic. The car was a match for the McLaren as the season started (Schumacher won the first three races) but by mid-summer a series of retirements and poor results again put the whole campaign in jeopardy. For a few critical months it looked as though the nightmare was going to continue for a fifth straight season. But then an incredible and emotional win at the Italian Grand Prix in Monza put the challenge back on track and Schumacher sealed it in Japan, with victory in one of the most tense races ever seen in Formula 1.

It was one of those classic seasons, which ebb and flow the whole way through. Formula 1 teams design and build their cars using different concepts, then add in variables like tyres, engines and drivers, yet they are within a few tenths of a second of each other over a 90-second lap, because the teams constantly push each other, drive each other on. When you are in front you try to consolidate, when you are behind you have to push. The 2000 season had all of these ingredients as Hakkinen and McLaren sought to make it three world titles in a row, while Schumacher put almost intolerable pressure on himself to deliver what he had promised to Ferrari.

He welcomed the arrival of a new team-mate, Rubens Barrichello, with the words, 'I reckon he's quite fast. You cannot make someone slower by contract. I don't think his situation is different from Eddie's last year. If he's faster he's faster. And whoever is faster is going to be the number one.' But there would be ample demonstrations over the years to come of the true pecking order at Ferrari. Barrichello says that he did take a different approach from his predecessor to partnering the world's fastest driver. 'I went there to be world champion,' he says today. 'I went there to have a competitive car. Obviously if you drive for Ferrari it is everybody's dream. I always felt that I had the talent to win and the fact that Michael was there made it even better because then I would be compared to the very best. I didn't accept, as Eddie did, that Michael was better and then just hope for a couple of wins.'

Barrichello knew when he signed that he was going up against not only the best driver in Formula 1, but also one who had well-established relationships with the key people. When he actually started working at Ferrari however, Barrichello quickly realised that he had underestimated just how close the relationship between Schumacher and Todt really was. 'I underestimated so many things,' he says. 'I could show you my contract and there is nothing in there that says that the spare car is Michael's, but when I got there it was the case. You don't know how big he is until you go there. Unfortunately I had six years of that. My first year was marvellous, though, I won a race, I out-qualified him a few times.'

Although the season was ultimately triumphant for Schumacher there were two races where he was well beaten and which form part of the folklore of his career for that reason. Schumacher once said, 'I never thought I was the best or unbeatable,' and these two events illustrate that. First came the French Grand Prix in Magny-Cours, where David Coulthard enjoyed a rare moment of superiority over Michael in the race and famously gave him 'the finger' after a close shave on the track. Then at the Belgian Grand Prix, at Spa, Mika Hakkinen beat him with one of the finest and bravest overtaking moves ever made.

At Magny-Cours, Coulthard was incensed by a move made by Schumacher off the start line, where he chopped across the front of the McLaren into the first corner, forcing the Scot to lift off the throttle. The code among drivers when it comes to overtaking is that the lead car is allowed to weave once across the path of the following car, but no more than that. (Some drivers believe that even this is wrong as it is effectively a licence to use the car as a weapon.) No one had ever considered that the rule might be applied to the start of a race, but Schumacher, ever the driver to look for the extra angle in pressing home an advantage, had decided to try this a few times off the start line. He upset many of the drivers, including his brother, with the tactic but was very intolerant of anyone, especially media commentators, who criticised him for it. The drivers would bring it up in the drivers' meeting which takes place every Friday of a Grand Prix weekend and challenge Schumacher, whom they felt, in his role as chairman of the Grand Prix Drivers Association, should be the one setting a positive, rather than negative, example.

At Magny-Cours, after some wheel banging which led Coulthard to make the abusive hand gesture, the Scot came back for another attack and passed Schumacher cleanly and fairly at the hairpin, taking the lead. 'It was a great moment in my career because I beat him in a battle. My anger and frustration at Magny-Cours came from the start where he tried to put me in the wall,' recalls Coulthard. 'We all agreed among the drivers that you can move only once.'

At Spa, Hakkinen was also the victim of a tough move by Schumacher, which inspired him to pass him on the next lap. Schumacher had set his car up with more downforce than Hakkinen, expecting wetter conditions. In the closing stage of the race, when the track was dry, this meant that, rather like Macau ten years earlier, he had a straight line speed disadvantage to Hakkinen. With four laps to go to the end of the race Hakkinen made a move as they drove down the long straight after Eau Rouge, but Schumacher chopped him, forcing him towards the grass. Hakkinen regrouped and then next time they exited Eau Rouge he went for it again.

In the middle of it all was Riccardo Zonta in the BAR. 'I looked in the mirrors and saw Schumacher coming up behind me like a rocket,' said Zonta. 'I was about to give him room, when I spotted the tip of the McLaren's nose just behind him. I held my line and held my breath. I don't like to think what might have happened if I had moved one inch either way. I knew that either side of me I had the two drivers who were fighting for the world title.'

Hakkinen's mother Aila and father Harri were spectators at Spa. Harri used to work in shipping radar but was told to retire on medical grounds as the stress was too much for his heart.

He chose this race as his first for many years to watch his son racing. It cannot have helped his heart much.

Hakkinen was in Schumacher's slipstream, but as he pulled out he realised that Zonta was in the middle of the road. Schumacher went left around Zonta, Hakkinen went right and even though his wheels were touching the grass, he kept his foot down hard and passed Schumacher for the win.

'Bravo, that was a fantastic move by Mika,' said Schumacher sportingly afterwards. 'He caught me completely by surprise, but he could have passed me on the right or the left, his car was stronger than mine. I would never have thought that he had enough room to squeeze past me. But he did have a car which was faster on the straights.'

After the race the two drivers could be seen in earnest conversation in the *parc fermé*. Hakkinen initiated the conversation as he wanted to talk about Schumacher's move on the lap before he had passed him. He was angry, but he refused to share the cause with the media, however much they tried to coax it out of him. 'I never criticised him in public or went to the press because it wasn't going to change anything,' says Hakkinen today. 'I have respect for Michael because I've been racing against him since I was a kid. We both reached our goals and got great results. It's great that he says that he respects me more than the other drivers.'

Following the time-honoured F1 tradition of giving some pain to the man you've just beaten, McLaren boss Ron Dennis had a dig at Schumacher after the race, when comparing him to the normally reserved Hakkinen. 'He's a great talker and thanks to that he's built a great name for himself, but I look at the facts and say, who makes the most mistakes and on the other hand who gets the results? I think that the answer is under everyone's eyes.'

Although it had been a famous win for Hakkinen, Ferrari knew that the hard work they had put into the car had paid off. Ross Brawn says:

Spa was the turning point, we got the car sorted out, it was working much better. We didn't win because Mika did that fantastic pass. But I thought we were back in the hunt again after a difficult summer. We rethought the approach on the car, the set-up. We sat down and objectively looked at the problem. We didn't get personal about it, just worked as a team. It was one of many such times, 2003 was similar, but 2000 was particularly critical. It's the way the business works. You are in front, then another team catches up and their impetus takes them past you. You respond.

* * *

The pressure on Schumacher prior to the Italian Grand Prix was intense. He was six points behind Hakkinen, with four races remaining. Ferrari desperately needed a turnaround in results. The press was in raptures over Hakkinen's stunning pass on him and as a result Schumacher was highly motivated to level the scores at Monza. He was very tense all weekend. There is something about Monza: it is a place steeped in the history of motorsport, dating right back to the 1930s, and it is loaded with deep resonances for Schumacher. Sabine Kehm recalls:

He was very tense all summer. There was a feeling of 'this cannot happen again', because it seemed to be slipping between our fingers. The fear was growing in him that this would not work out. Looking back now I do not know what would have happened if he had not won the title that year.

At Monza the pressure was extremely high. He really felt that if he didn't win there the title would be gone again.

On top of the race pressure other factors were weighing on his mind. On the morning of the race came news that his close friend Willi Bergmeister had suffered a major heart attack and was in a critical condition. Then on the opening lap of the race a collision at the second chicane led to a marshal being killed by debris, although it would only be later, after the race, that Schumacher heard of this.

In the end Schumacher held his nerve and, apart from four laps after his pit stop, he led the entire race, winning by four seconds from Hakkinen. The relief was immense and as the *tifosi* swept on to the track just as it had done so memorably in 1996, Schumacher got caught up in the moment, deeply moved by the passion of the enormous crowd.

He made his way from the podium straight into the television press conference, where the interviewer pointed out straight away that he had just equalled Senna's career total of 41 wins. Schumacher, who always kept such a tight leash on his emotions, aware that he had a line he did not wish to cross, beyond which he was liable to lose control, now wept like a baby. The cause was a combination of factors; the release of the pressure of the past weeks, his friend in intensive care and certainly the link to Senna, took him over the edge. He lowered his head, pinched the bridge of his nose and shook as the tears poured out. The hardest man in world sport was allowing himself to be seen in a totally new light.

Hakkinen, seated to his right, put an arm around his shoulder. Meanwhile his brother Ralf, who had finished third that day, sat immobile and embarrassed, unsure what to do but seeming not to sympathise with his brother's plight.

Afterwards Schumacher was angry with himself for lowering his guard. 'We left the press room and he was totally confused and hassled by his own reaction,' says Sabine Kehm. 'We walked down the stairs and I said to him, "You don't have to be ashamed", and he said, "Yes, but I am." The Senna part of it was a big deal for him.'

Predictably, because it was something he had steadfastly refused to allow before, his public show of emotion was greeted with almost universal sympathy around the world and actually did him a lot of good in many people's eyes. The German tabloid newspaper, *Bild*, ran a headline, 'Schumi we have seen your heart'. But despite all the favourable reaction he continued to feel embarrassed that he had lost his self-control. It was so important to him always to seem the hard man, to radiate the total confidence which kept his opponents in their place. Blubbing like a child did not fit in anywhere in that grand scheme. And being Schumacher he analysed the reaction more deeply than most and resented the fact that many people took such a superficial view of him. 'I take issue with people who only want to understand that I am a human being like everyone else when they get some kind of proof, like emotion or mistakes. I am very controlled because I'm very balanced.'

Luck was with him after Monza and he won again in Indianapolis while Hakkinen retired with engine failure. Thus he travelled to the penultimate race in Suzuka with the chance to clinch the world title. As an indication of just how committed he was to doing so, rather than continue west around the world to get to Japan, which would help to counteract jet lag, he had travelled from America back to Italy to test some new parts on the car – aerodynamics, details on the brakes, suspension geometry. It was a successful test but it came at a price. When Schumacher finally got to Japan his body clock was all over the place and as a result he slept badly all weekend, no more than a few hours each night. But thanks to the new parts, the car was working very well and had the edge over the McLaren so he went into the race feeling confident. If he won the race, regardless of what Hakkinen did, he would be champion.

I will never forget that race. I watched it from the McLaren and Ferrari garages, which were next door to each other on the sloping Suzuka pit lane. Although the whole race hinged on a pit stop call by Ross Brawn, what was so stunning about the contest was that the two main protagonists were totally in a class of their own, exhibiting the highest levels of skill I have ever seen in a Grand Prix.

It is a cliché for drivers to say that they drove every lap with the intensity of a qualifying lap; by definition that is impossible, the car and tyres would not take it, let alone the driver. But this was the closest thing to it. The ferocious intensity of the battle was breathtaking as for lap after lap the two drivers pushed their cars and themselves to the limit. It was a re-run of many great fights between them from Macau to the more recent Spa duel but this was the ultimate expression of the racer's art. It is arguably the most important race in the whole Schumacher story, as not only did it bring the first title for Ferrari but it is also Schumacher's fondest memory of what he calls 'pure racing'. It turned out to be their last great duel as the following year Hakkinen's motivation waned and he called it a day.

Schumacher got pole, but once again Hakkinen got the better start. Schumacher cut across the track at him, but Hakkinen held his nerve and took the lead. He led for a lot of the race. The moment of truth came halfway through it, when some light drizzle fell for a few minutes, enough to make the surface greasy for several laps. The change knocked Hakkinen off balance at just the wrong moment. He had pitted slightly earlier than Schumacher and this had allowed Ross Brawn to measure how much fuel he had taken on at his stop and to make sure that Schumacher had three laps more. Hakkinen knew that he had to push hard on his new tyres to make up for the extra fuel he was now carrying relative to Schumacher, who had yet to stop, but he lost five seconds on the lap out of the pits.

Schumacher was struggling too at times and had a close shave with a Benetton which had spun, but as he drove away from his pit box having made his second and final stop he could hear Brawn on the radio, assessing the gap to Hakkinen. Schumacher had to wait for what seemed like an eternity before he could release the pit lane speed limiter button and all the time Hakkinen was at full speed approaching the start/finish line.

'It's looking good,' said Brawn, 'it's looking good, it's looking bloody good!' Schumacher flashed out onto the race-track and scythed across to the left to take the racing line into the corner. Hakkinen was behind him.

'That was the happiest moment of my racing career,' says Schumacher. He steered the car home and when he crossed the line, he became the first Ferrari driver since Enzo Ferrari's death in 1988 to win a world title. Five years after his last world title and the move to Maranello, he had fulfilled his destiny. Describing the emotions of that moment to Sabine Kehm a few years later he said, 'I suddenly felt trapped in the car, as if I was about to burst. I felt so happy. I had finally done it after so many years of disappointments. I was overcome with tears and it was as if I was standing next to myself, looking in on the moment. It was almost as if I were someone else.'

A five-year investment in him by Ferrari and its main partner, Philip Morris, amounting to close on £100 million, had finally paid dividends. The team members, who had had to endure failures at the final hurdle for three consecutive years, were ecstatic. Suddenly 'made in Italy' was a badge of pride again. Eight years after Bernie Ecclestone had whispered Jean Todt's name into Montezemolo's ear, the project for the renaissance of Ferrari had finally borne fruit.

McLaren demonstrated its great sporting values with two nice gestures at the end of the race. First Hakkinen graciously accepted defeat, refusing to make any criticism of Schumacher's driving tactics. 'Compliments to Michael, he has been great. Ferrari has done a great job and we were not capable of matching them. I have been a happy world champion and now I will try to be a good loser. Life is like this.' It was a real lesson in style. Shortly afterwards, some mechanics from the McLaren team went to the next door garage with the number one sticker off Hakkinen's car and put it on the nose of Schumacher's Ferrari. The Ferrari mechanics accepted it graciously and the new world champion had himself photographed sitting in his number one car.

'I feel even stronger emotions than I did in Monza, but don't expect any tears,' Schumacher joked to interviewers. And he paid tribute to Hakkinen, 'Mika should not consider himself the loser. We have battled all season, shoulder to shoulder and always fairly. He is a great man and a great driver.'

As darkness fell around Suzuka, thousands of Japanese fans still sat silently in the grandstands, soaking up every last drop of atmosphere. In the paddock, behind the garages, a makeshift banqueting table was set up. Not wanting to tempt fate by booking a restaurant for a celebration, the team had decided instead to have a dinner among the packing cases and freight boxes out at the back. On a day already heavy with symbolism, it seemed entirely right that the team which had put so much work into getting back into the title race and then getting the job done should celebrate in a working environment. Schumacher and his wife, Corinna, sat down with Todt among the mechanics, there was a lot of toasting, many cries of '*Campioni!*' and '*Forza Ferrari!*' Amid the high spirits, one of the cooks, Salvatore Belgiovine, got carried away and fell off a wall, breaking his arm, but even that did not dampen his, or anyone else's, spirits. Schumacher wanted to soak up the atmosphere too and unlike two years before where he had got drunk to forget the disappointment of losing, as the victor he drank only a single beer.

Such had been their focus on this race that Michael and Corinna had made no plans about what to do with the ten days before the final race in Malaysia. As the dinner went on they kept changing their minds about where to go: 'Africa? But what about the children? Australia?' Having fulfilled his duty, as he saw it, Schumacher was now free to go wherever he wished. The pressure was finally off. This was a tremendously significant moment in his life and career, the fulfilment of his ambition, from this point on anything else was a bonus, as he articulated a few years later. 'I don't have to prove anything else to myself. I did what I really wanted to do in 2000 with my first world championship with Ferrari. We worked hard for it. We all did. And we fought hard for it.'

It was left to Gianni Agnelli, the Fiat boss who had bought a controlling interest in the Ferrari company to bail out Enzo Ferrari in difficult times, to put into context what this championship meant to Ferrari and to Italy as a whole:

> There is no comparison to this world title for Ferrari. Italy has been waiting for this for twenty-one years. It is an achievement of great value in every respect. A great driver, impeccable technology, the team, the tradition, the strength of the opposition.
>
> I will always be a fan of the German, who seems so unsympathetic because he does not speak our language, but who has exceptional qualities. So many people were moved when they saw him crying at Monza. I say, he let fall the mask, he broke down. It's very important for the country. Ferrari sends out a message to the world that Italy is a very advanced country, it is loved everywhere. I'd say that Ferrari is very important to Italy.

Schumacher was always admired by the *tifosi*, but never loved. When he arrived at Maranello he was perhaps unaware of the importance of the history of the team and the significance of driving for them. He was also quite dismissive of the level of Ferrari's expertise at the time, comparing the engine department to his friend's go-kart workshop in Kerpen. This did not endear him to the Italians to start with, and later, although he won races for them, they found it hard to forgive him for Jerez. As the years passed, though, he became steadily more aware of what Ferrari really meant to the Italians and the passionate displays of joy beneath the Monza podium clearly hastened that process.

* * *

Ferrari is not just about cars and a racing team, it is part of the fabric and culture of Italy. It transcends sport. As a brand it is one of the most potent international symbols of Italian style and quality. Within Italy the enthusiasm for Ferrari is like a thread between generations, like a passion for a football club. But whereas there are lots of clubs in Italy, there is only one Ferrari and that is why its fans, the *tifosi*, are so numerous and so passionate. They are kept informed by four daily sports newspapers, of which the best is the *Gazzetta dello Sport*. The others are more gossipy. It is often the pressure to come up with news and content for these papers which leads to some of the more fanciful rumours in Formula 1.

The historical dimension is fascinating too. Motorsport played a vital role in the rebuilding of Italy after the devastation of World War II. The Mille Miglia, a 1000-mile road race around Italy, first run in 1927, had been a popular event before the war and the organisers were anxious to put it on again soon afterwards. Bridges which had been destroyed all over Italy were rebuilt so that the race could be run. The bridge over the River Po, symbolically the link between the two halves of Italy, was down, meaning that Italy remained a divided nation. That bridge too was rebuilt so that the race could go ahead and it symbolically reunited Italy. Ferrari was an important part of that story.

Enzo Ferrari had started his own racing team in the 1920s using Alfa Romeo cars. He took as his logo the *cavallino* or prancing horse, a black stallion on a yellow shield, which had been the emblem of a fighter pilot called Count Barracca. Throughout the 1930s the Italian Grand Prix at Monza pulled in crowds of over 200,000 people, far more than today. Enzo Ferrari became an icon in Italy because he lived through such different eras of Italian history and played a role in many of them. In the 1930s the dictator Mussolini, like Hitler in Germany, used motorsport as a propaganda tool, trading on its popularity and its image of power and glory, which chimed well with Fascist ideology. Ferrari lived through this and outlasted Mussolini.

In Britain, Enzo Ferrari is sometimes referred to as the *commendatore*, which is the Italian equivalent of the British knighthood, but in fact he was more commonly known in Italy as 'Il Drake', a nickname given to him by the Americans, who compared him to the legendary Offenhauser engine-tuner John Drake. Ferrari hated the nickname because he was a constructor, not a mere tuner, but in Italy the nickname stuck and still does to this day.

Ferrari carefully promoted the myth of his cars and his brand, and his name eventually became associated with passion, speed, triumph and tragedy. It was a unique privilege for Schumacher to be allowed to stay in Enzo Ferrari's office at Fiorano, something which, when it first happened, was almost considered a sacrilege. It is a large, square, white building in stone with five windows on the first floor and four on the ground floor. The front door is large and arched with a number plaque on the wall. Although there are no other houses nearby this house is number 27, Gilles

Villeneuve's race number when he was at Ferrari. There
is a large photo of Villeneuve in a characteristically full-
blooded slide among many others in the building. The walls
exude Ferrari history, including a marvellous picture of the
Drake at the wheel of a car from his own early racing days in
the 1920s. Schumacher remembers vividly the first night he
spent there. 'I went in there rather timidly and was spell-
bound by his desk above which there is a silver frame with
his photograph in it. I always tried to move about in there
with respect, not to upset anything. For a driver to occupy
Ferrari's house is like a musician being able to stay in
Mozart's house.'

It is perhaps too trite to say that a bit of Schumacher's
discipline rubbed off on the Italians and that in return they
got him to open up a bit, but he does admit that the Italians
changed him for the better as a person. 'The Italian spirit has
certainly changed my way of speaking, of seeing things, of
behaving. The Italians are very warm people, which makes life
much more pleasant. There are friends in Maranello, which I
consider the centre of Italy for obvious reasons, who are like
family. I'm talking about Mama Rosella. She is very important
to me.'

Rosella is the lady who owns the Montana restaurant. She is
in her fifties, very friendly, very normal, her food is simple but
excellent, the welcome is always warm. In short, she is a
typical Italian restaurateur. Yet she formed a unique bond
with Schumacher, one of the most famous people in the
world. Her home, which she shares with her husband
Maurizio and their son, is above the restaurant and it became
his refuge. If the restaurant was very busy, he would simply eat
upstairs in Rosella's living room, surrounded by ornaments

and pictures of her family. For him it provided sanctuary and a reminder of his own home.

He is entirely genuine when he speaks of his affection for Rosella and it is clear that she became like a mother to him. He certainly saw her far more frequently than his own mother and her love for him was real and unconditional. When he was testing at the track next door she would deliver him his lunch and when he was staying overnight in Ferrari's house, he would go to Montana for his dinner.

Rosella is not a sophisticated woman of the world, she is entirely down to earth, and not part of the feline, duplicitous Formula 1 paddock. Yet she is surrounded by Ferrari, its intrigues and its heritage. Rosella likes Schumacher for who he is, not what he is. She believes that the Michael Schumacher she knows is the true character, not the one portrayed by the media.

The Montana restaurant is to the side of a road bridge, which passes right alongside Ferrari's test track at Fiorano. You drive along the Abetone Road, leaving the road car factory behind you and in less than a kilometre you pass over the bridge and spot the Montana down to your left. It is a wooden building, with a small terrace outside and seating inside for 80 people. On the walls of the restaurant are helmets, race suits, signed photos of all the great drivers of the last 30 years, men like Gilles Villeneuve, Niki Lauda, Mario Andretti. All of the photos are inscribed to Rosella, who has fed most of the world's best known drivers since she was a young woman. At the back of the restaurant, next to the bar, is a sliding door and behind it is a wood-panelled room, which is where the top people from the Ferrari team go when they want to eat and talk in privacy. If they are not in, anyone can eat there. On the walls are newspaper and magazine cuttings about Ferrari, including a feature from *Paris Match* where Schumacher wears an apron while Rosella teaches him how to roll out fresh pasta. The kitchen is down some steps, a level below.

Rosella dresses like all Italian working women of a certain age, her long black hair is flecked with grey around the temples, her big round eyes are dark and smiling. She has just returned from the end-of-season Ferrari Day celebration at Monza, where Schumacher was overwhelmed with the reaction he received from the 30,000 fans who came along to thank him for 11 years of service. Where else in the world would the lady who runs the local restaurant be invited by a Formula 1 team to be part of such a day? In Italian, her speech eloquent, flowing and pacy, Rosella says:

> He always said he felt at home here. After eleven years together it was like having another son, we don't see him all the time but when he comes we know what he wants, what he'd like to eat. His favourite is spaghetti with garlic and chilli, he also likes tagliatelle ragu, he loves the classic Italian pasta dishes.
>
> One year just before Christmas he came and there was no table so he went upstairs to my house to eat. At that point he understood that he was at home when he came here. From that moment on he had a new respect. From then on he often ate up there if he wanted some privacy or if he was alone. He would take a look at how many cars there were in the car park and would come in through the front door of the house rather than the restaurant, as if he were in his own house.

Rosella and Schumacher struck up an almost immediate rapport, but she acknowledges that he has definitely opened up more with the Italians, particularly in recent years.

> I saw a real difference in him from the first time he walked in to now. I can assure you that he has improved a lot because he is above all a shy person and sometimes that shyness makes him seem closed and sometimes helpless. However now you can see what kind of man he is and the things he has done; he has lifted the spirit of the team, he's apologised for some of the things he's done.
>
> Everyone thought Michael was one thing and they came to see that he was something else. I always saw what he was, always thought he was a wonderful person and always defended him. People didn't see that, but when people saw him here at the restaurant they came to me and said 'Rosella you're right, he's just as you said he was, he isn't the way the newspapers say he is.'
>
> Michael is one of the best men ever, of all the men I've had the pleasure of working with and knowing, he's unique. Michael is very reserved, he has a lot of respect in everything he does and for all the people around him. He's not the kind of guy to make a fuss about what he does, quite the opposite. And this is in spite of all the success he's had. Let's not forget that he's managed, along with Todt and Montezemolo, to bring all the right people here to Maranello, people like Ross Brawn and Rory Byrne. They created a winning team and let's not forget Ferrari hadn't won the championship for twenty-one years. Michael gave them so much and gave so much to Italy. A few years ago if you said Ferrari anywhere in the world people would think of Enzo with his dark glasses. Now they will think of five people; Enzo, Michael, Todt, Montezemolo and Ross. They brought Ferrari back to the top.
>
> He's like a son to me, I hug him, I kiss him. He comes to

see me, there is a feeling we have. Here he feels like he is with his family. I've never profited from the situation and he understood that. I've never asked him for anything but he's given me a lot.

Yesterday was my son's birthday and today a present arrived for him from Michael. Every year he sends me something for my birthday – it's extraordinary. No other driver has ever done that.

He's very misunderstood, but here at the Montana he's understood. When he walked through my door for the first time on 14 February 1996, it was the best present anyone ever gave me. To have known Michael has been a great honour.

CHAPTER EIGHTEEN

The private Schumacher

He's fast and has exceptional all-round vision, but he's not very good at heading.

Roland Chaer, coach of Schumacher's local soccer team, FC Echicens

Michael Schumacher has always valued his privacy above all else. There can be few people in the world as famous as him who eschew celebrity to the same extent. He has never done a photo shoot at his home, never attends balls and glamorous society occasions. He maintained his dignity and his clean-cut image throughout his career, never having an affair nor becoming involved in scandal of any kind. Unlike Kimi Raikkonen, his replacement at Ferrari, who is a well-known party-goer and often finds himself the subject of lurid reports in the newspapers, Schumacher lives a low-key life, beneath the radar. But he still takes care over his image; indeed since the debacles of 1994 with Benetton he has employed an experienced full-time assistant to liaise with the media on his behalf.

He has taken great care to ring-fence his family and his private life from his public life. He always accepted that the nature of his job meant that he would be in the spotlight from the moment he arrived at a Grand Prix venue on a Thursday until the moment he left on a Sunday night. But he and Corinna were determined to keep the media out of their home life and they succeeded. He says:

> You still have to watch what you do, of course. If I were to be photographed at the track making meaningless small talk with some hostess, probably the next day it would appear in the papers that my marriage was in crisis. This is where my ability for self-protection comes into play. I avoid all possible scenes and situations and don't get myself into that position in the first place. I'm often accused of arrogance because of this.

With a fortune in excess of £500 million, the massive house and the private jet, perhaps Schumacher's greatest challenge will be raising his children to be normal. It is a project which will take all of his legendary attention to detail and force of will to achieve.

The world his children inhabit is a world away from the childhood he knew in the gravel beds of Kerpen kart-track. But he and Corinna are determined to try to keep the children's feet on the ground. They attend an international school in Switzerland and take part in all the activities. They have a lot of love from their parents, but Schumacher has taken great care not to let them feel that they are anything special in the eyes of the wider community. He has never brought them to the race-track, although they often come along on the trips abroad and stay in houses or the hotel while their father works. Schumacher was struck by what happened at Monaco in 2001 when Mika Hakkinen brought his baby son Hugo to

the paddock. They were surrounded in seconds by photographers and camera crews, flashbulbs popping, the noisy
crowd all around them completely overwhelming poor Hugo.
Schumacher often uses that incident to explain why he has
kept his own children out of the spotlight:

> How can a little boy understand all the hubbub, the
> crowds, the flashes? I think it damages children. They will
> find it hard to lead a normal life. My children ought to be
> able to grow up just as Gina Maria and Mick without the
> pressure of being Michael Schumacher's children. Our
> daily family life is like that of an ordinary family; we eat
> together, take the children to school.
>
> My children know my job, they watch the television and
> know a bit about it. Since they were about two years old
> they recognised the red car and know that is Daddy's car.
> I'm very open with them, answer all their questions.

Schumacher has tried very hard to give his children as normal
an upbringing as possible. This is part of the reason why he
left Monaco and moved to a green, leafy and very private area
of Switzerland in the summer of 1996, as soon as he learned
that Corinna was pregnant with Gina Maria. But he admits it
is very hard to know whether he is getting it right or not.

> To be honest I often ask myself, 'Are you doing the right
> thing here?' I've often talked to my father about it, and to
> other parents too, but it seems there is no patent recipe. I
> believe you have to be yourself, by which I mean be as
> genuine as possible. Everyone conveys the life experiences
> and principles that are important to him. In my case that
> means fairness and being straight with people. I can't
> praise Mick and Gina for something today and then punish
> them for the same thing tomorrow. And if they injure

themselves doing something in spite of my warning, then that doesn't mean I start shouting at them. I give them a hug, comfort them and then explain everything quite calmly.

From them I have learned a thousand little things; their freedom, their lack of inhibition, their curiosity, their courage, their many astonishing, amusing comments. All sorts of things.

Schumacher always paints a picture of a perfect family life and it is an image he is careful to cultivate. He wants to be seen as grounded and normal and he must genuinely be both of those things to have survived for so long at the high pressure end of Formula 1. With a less stable life, full of distractions away from the track sapping energy out of him, he would not have made it so far.

Yet there are many challenges ahead. There is a phenomenon, which has been the subject of research in recent years, whereby the children of very wealthy and successful parents often suffer from depression in their teenage years as they contemplate their life ahead. Perhaps they realise that they have a lack of ambition or motivation because nothing they can do will ever match up to the level of life that they have enjoyed to that point. Of course the challenge for all parents is to give their children some ambition. Some do this by handing over the keys to the family business and letting the children get on with it, while others are more reluctant to let go and frustrate their children by refusing to allow them to grow. Schumacher has made his money and is one of the world's most famous faces. He has said that he 'wants to become anonymous as soon as possible' and he will probably succeed up to a point, but he will still be worth a fortune and his children will have to deal with that. As he says:

> They have to learn that wealth is not to be taken for granted. They get pocket money like other children, two euros a week, they can save it or buy things with it. When it comes to giving them presents for birthdays or Christmas we certainly try to be as normal as possible. But you cannot expect the presents to be the same as if we were in a family with an average income. It's the case that we earn more money and why shouldn't we give our children enjoyment with it?

Little is known publicly about his children, Gina Maria and Mick. According to family friends, Mick is a very sweet little boy, always sunny, always laughing. Gina Maria is a mummy's girl, as committed to horses as Corinna and always spending her free time with her mother at the stables, much as her father did with karts and the local track in the 1970s. Ross Brawn told me once that he has seen young Mick drive a kart and that he appears to have a great deal of skill, but there are no plans currently for him to compete.

Schumacher's children accepted that he needed to go away from them to do his job but he always went to great lengths to maximise the time he spent with them, claiming that it probably added up to more time than most working fathers spend with their children. Ferrari were very good in accepting this. In the late 1990s he was away from home around 200 days a year, with racing, testing and promotional activities, but he subsequently scaled that right down.

> I'm often at home for a whole day and can plan my training and my whole day around them. That's a privileged

position to be in. Other fathers work all day and when they come home the children are already in bed. They see their children less often than I do. I take my sport very seriously, but I told my manager after Gina was born that I wanted more time for my family, there had to be fewer appointments with sponsors and they had to be organised differently.

His children keep his feet on the ground, ensuring that he didn't get too carried away by success or failure. But they did have one way of supporting their father, which he did allow to spill out into the public domain. Sometimes they would give him a lucky charm to take with him, as Gina Maria once did famously with a hairbrush. He kept it in his pocket whenever he raced. Another time she gave him a locket for good luck and he dropped it in the paddock. A photographer found it and gave it back to him and the photographer reported that Schumacher seemed very relieved. The image of the caring daddy has often helped to soften the tougher side of his image.

Living in Switzerland has proved to be ideal for providing peace and anonymity – exactly what Schumacher was looking for. He tells a story of meeting a neighbour while out on a bike ride one day and after a long chat the neighbour asked him his business. 'I drive racing cars,' Schumacher told him, 'What kind?' asked the man. 'Ferraris,' replied Schumacher. Although Monaco was for many years the headquarters for Grand Prix drivers seeking a tax-free lifestyle, in more recent times Switzerland has proved a major lure because, in addition to the tax breaks and the easy access to the world from Geneva and Zurich airports, the Swiss allow their residents complete privacy. Jackie Stewart went there in the 1970s, but Alain Prost was the first of the modern Grand Prix stars to choose Switzerland, followed by Jean Alesi. In Schumacher's wake have come Alonso, Raikkonen, Nick Heidfeld and Jarno Trulli.

Schumacher lived for 11 years in a 17th century castle at Vufflens le Chateau, a village some three kilometres above Lake Geneva. More recently he has built himself a palace on the shoreline which had been a sideline project for several years and which features all imaginable creature comforts, including underground parking for 25 cars.

* * *

It was no coincidence that before the start of his final Grand Prix in Brazil in 2006, the footballer Pele was chosen to present Schumacher with his leaving present from the Formula 1 community. Football is a very important part of the private life of Michael Schumacher. It is a key part of keeping a balance. Interestingly, the man who existed only to win in Formula 1, who had exceptional talent and yet worked tirelessly to improve on it, who sought perfection every time he sat in a car, is perfectly able to go out on a football field and get great pleasure from doing something he isn't very good at. He says:

> With football there is this attraction that I'm not that good at it. When I went on to the pitch in a game, for instance, I was sometimes more nervous than when I got into my Formula 1 car. I also had to concentrate harder if I wanted to control a ball well than when I was approaching a corner, even if I was going very quickly. It's funny: in Formula 1 I always had spare capacity in my head. When I play football I think I hardly have any freedom to look at what's around me, take it in and build a move well.

When he played football, he didn't have to be obsessive about the details or worry that he might have left something out of his preparation. It allowed him to compete but to enjoy the sport for its own sake. It is astonishing that in his day job as an F1 driver he managed to maintain his motivation for so long, especially as he had so much success that it must have been virtually impossible to set fresh goals and targets in the last five years. But in football he was able to compete for pleasure – win, lose or draw. No one had any expectations of him and he could fail without any great personal penalty, without letting down hundreds of work colleagues and millions of fans. It was sport with no pressure. But being Schumacher he was not content merely to take part, there was always an edge to his desire.

> I expect to get the best out of myself and to beat the competition. That's the point of sport and it is quite prominent in me. Just taking part, like in the purely Olympic sense, is not my motto. I am just attracted by challenge, measuring myself, and it doesn't matter if it's on the track or on the football pitch.

Nevertheless, analysing his own performances as a footballer he would always laugh at himself and be self-deprecating, something he would never do in F1. 'I'm no great genius on the pitch,' he would often say. He will laugh as he talks about tying himself in knots when trying to perfect Ronaldo's elaborate step-over technique and it makes him seem more human. Being beaten to the ball by an electrician from a different canton of Switzerland allows him to know what it feels like to be a back-marker in F1, a mere mortal competing against others and being totally outclassed, something which could never happen to him on a race-track. Football undoubtedly made him a more rounded character than he is often portrayed. The coach at his club in Switzerland (FC Echicens), Roland Chaer, said of him, 'He's fast and has exceptional all-round vision but he's not very good at heading.' Schumacher is always happy to talk about football and is far less guarded than when discussing racing, where he wants to give nothing away.

Football isn't a vanity exercise for Schumacher, though, it is not just a badge he likes to wear. He has a genuine commitment to it and he was an extremely active player during even the most intense periods of his F1 career. Getting out on a pitch, running around and clattering into a few other men is a great way of letting off steam and forgetting about everything for a while. Schumacher played around 30 competitive matches a year, even in his golden period in F1 from 2000–2006. That is roughly half the number that a top international professional will play in a season, as long as he stays injury-free. But it is still a huge number for someone who has such a demanding day job. But being Schumacher he made things work for himself by ensuring that there were competitive games around Grand Prix weekends that he could play in.

He was also very prominent in charity games, which he would play up to ten times a season. These would typically take place on the Wednesday before a Grand Prix, raising money for UNESCO and other charities. His team was called the Nazionale Piloti, with chequered flag shirts, sponsored by Grissini, the Italian breadstick makers. Some of the other drivers, like Giancarlo Fisichella and Tonio Liuzzi, would turn out with him, alongside motorbike hero Max Biaggi and others. They would play against teams of pop stars with a sprinkling of ex-professional footballers on both sides from Italy, Spain and Germany. One of the more high profile matches is the pre-Monaco Grand Prix event, which is played in the Monaco stadium at Fontvieille. Schumacher says:

> I'm a midfielder with a slight attacking instinct but I like to track back relatively often because I simply like running. I try to coordinate the play in the game. In the Nazionale Piloti team I'm one of those who take it into their own hands and move off. Fisichella is a great team-mate. He's fast, good on the ball. You can involve him easily.

Another aspect of football which appealed to Schumacher was its function as a team-bonding exercise. In the last few years of his F1 career he played on Thursdays at Grand Prix meetings with mechanics and engineers from the Ferrari team. 'We have a chance to spend time together aside from the motor racing,' he says. 'That's always very difficult otherwise, due to our timetable. We get to know one another even better in doing so. In football you recognise the characters, learn how to get along with them. You just don't realise that otherwise in work.'

Schumacher has always followed the professional game closely. He has admitted that at school he used to lie that German goalkeeper Harald 'Toni' Schumacher was his uncle, to impress his classmates! Ironically Toni committed one of the worst fouls in World Cup history when he flattened a French forward during the 1982 semi-final, outside the penalty area, putting him into a coma.

Schumacher's passion for playing the game was ignited in 1996 when his local team in Switzerland, Aubonne, invited him to come down for a training session. He started playing regularly and really enjoyed it. He then moved on to Swiss third division side Echicens, where he usually played in the reserves. He couldn't take part in many of the weekend matches during the F1 season, but managed to attend training sessions three times a week when he was at home. On his private plane, no matter where he's flying to, there is always a football.

His status meant that he had the opportunity to play with some of the greats of the game and he was invited to play in the testimonial matches of three of them: Figo, Ronaldo and Zidane. He raves about their skill.

> It's fantastic to receive the ball right to your feet. When I play with champions everything seems easy. The ball comes at the right moment, in the right place on a pitch as smooth as carpet and suddenly everything works for me, I become a much better player than I am. But then I am sadly brought back down to earth because when I go back to my team in Switzerland, I'm decidedly less good than I was.

He has also been invited to train with Manchester United, Juventus and Bologna as well as the national teams of Germany and Argentina. He found that although he was left for dead on ball control and skills, he could easily keep up with them on fitness.

> I was surprised, the training was quite lax. I asked myself, 'Is that it?' I've only just got warmed up. But the proper preparation in the winter is far above what I'm used to doing. I cannot imagine being a professional cyclist or footballer. My bones wouldn't hold out.

The idea of Grand Prix drivers taking part in football matches was not always popular with team bosses. I played in one match on the eve of the 1991 Spanish Grand Prix in which Nigel Mansell turned an ankle and ended the day with an ice pack. His team boss, Frank Williams, had palpitations and banned Mansell from playing in any more games. It is easy to imagine a driver rupturing a knee ligament or snapping an Achilles tendon and being out of action for months: a whole season of F1 (and with it the investment of hundreds of millions of pounds, not to mention the effort of 700 people at the factory) could be jeopardised by a fun game of football. Schumacher had the most to lose and yet he put himself out there 30 times a year. I never played in a match with him but I watched a few and, although he might not have been Roy Keane, he certainly got stuck in. He says that he balanced the risks and insisted to Jean Todt that he be allowed to pursue his hobby without restrictions. As his friend as well as his team boss, Todt acceded to his wishes.

> You can't have a life without risk. You have to be balanced and rational. Jean knows that's how I am. I want to live my life. That is why I am motivated to do what I do on the race circuit because privately I live my life and the team let me do this. I think you have to judge on how much risk you can take. I believe it's fine as I'm doing it, I know what it takes though there can always be the unlucky day. But I believe in fate and fate will not be changeable.
>
> I've felt the famous elbow a few times. But admittedly as a rule I'm treated very fairly. And probably I have a certain bonus. In a dodgy situation the referee does get involved to calm things down. That's also a reason why I've never had a yellow card. I don't jump in like a madman. I don't want to injure myself or my fellow players.

He most certainly got the equivalent of a few yellow cards as a racing driver, maybe a few reds as well, but his footballing hobby required a different mentality.

CHAPTER NINETEEN

The dominant years

I hate saying it because I am such a big Ferrari fan,
but they remind me so much of America the way
it has behaved under Bush and Cheney. 'It's our
way or no way.' I understand that sometimes they
are right, but because they are the big guy they
have to be beyond white.

Eddie Irvine

By winning Ferrari's first world title for 21 years Schumacher
may have fulfilled his main ambition in life, but that did not
mean that he was about to rest on his laurels. When he
emerged from his long winter rest after the 2000 season, he
spoke of his fresh challenge for the years to come as being to
create 'a Ferrari era'. In this, as with most things in his
extraordinary life, he succeeded.

The five seasons from 2000 to 2004 saw an unprecedented
period of success for one team and one driver. He won 48 of
the 85 races and five consecutive world titles. The spell was
broken in 2005 by Fernando Alonso, the driver most like him
in many ways. At 24 years of age, driving for Renault (the latest
incarnation of Schumacher's old Benetton team), Alonso took

his crown, prompting the great man to retire at the end of 2006 at the age of 37.

There are two sides to the story of Ferrari's success during those years. On the one hand there is the glory, the glamour and the sheer joy, which it brought to millions of fans around the world. The grandstands at the race-tracks of Europe, Asia and America were seas of red Ferrari flags and caps as the world celebrated the rebirth of one of sport's greatest brands. The team had acquired the winning habit and even when the rules were changed in 2003 to try to give another team and driver a chance, still Ferrari managed to win the championship! Schumacher was an irresistible force, at times able to drive well within himself as the car was so far ahead of the opposition. At other times, for example in 2003, he had to fight like a dog to win the title. He showed that despite all of the success he still had the stomach for a fight. Some of his performances were sublime and he never gave up, no matter how unpromising a position he found himself in during a race weekend.

But the dark side of these years was that the team did not appear to know when to stop when pressing home their competitive advantage. The collective mentality of never giving anything away was fine when they were up against it, fighting hard to get to the top. But having fought so hard and lost out so many times on the way up there, once they had achieved the dominant position, they felt compelled to fight even harder to keep it. At times their critics felt that they lost a sense of perspective of their responsibilities to the Ferrari brand and to the sport in general. There were several incidents which highlighted this very graphically and these coincided with a drop in television audiences around the world. The world grew tired of seeing Schumacher dominate and when he and the team were seen to be laughing at the opposition as well, it had the effect of alienating a large section of the audience. Schumacher had been so successful, was he now killing the sport?

Mark Webber's comments in Chapter Seven illustrate some of the ways in which he believes Ferrari and Schumacher put up 'constant little hurdles' in front of the opposition, which he considered constituted an abuse of their dominant position. Flavio Briatore talks of racing against Ferrari as being 'like handicap racing', referring to some of the setbacks his Renault team suffered in 2006, whilst another team boss has called it 'racing against the Town Hall'.

Some key tactical decisions taken by the inner sanctum of the Ferrari management undoubtedly showed the team in a bad light, the worst of which was during the Austrian Grand Prix of 2002. Team orders were employed early in the season and Rubens Barrichello was ordered to hand an undeserved victory to Schumacher as they crossed the finish line.

The background to the decision was straightforward enough; team orders are nothing new in Formula 1. The dominant Mercedes team of the 1950s had choreographed everything between its drivers, leaving an innocent public none the wiser. In more recent times, McLaren had twice asked David Coulthard to let Mika Hakkinen past to win, but in both cases this was because Hakkinen had lost his place to Coulthard through a 'team error'. Giving away a victory is never easy to take, either for an audience or for a driver. As he crossed the line in second place for the second time, in Melbourne in 1998, Coulthard is alleged to have said over the radio to his team, 'There, now I've finished doing fucking charity work.'

Ferrari had previously asked Irvine to move out of Schumacher's way a few times where a few extra points were to be gained and no one could argue with that, as often in the early Ferrari years the title was decided by just a couple of points. Also in Austria in 2001 there had been mild controversy when the team had asked Barrichello to let Schumacher through to finish second behind David Coulthard. Alain Prost commented after the race that if he had been in Schumacher's position he would not have accepted the place from Barrichello because the Brazilian had been the faster driver all weekend. In fact Austria was something of a bogey track for Schumacher. He never really got on with the place and struggled to match Barrichello there every year. Barrichello could have won the race but for a poor start and a less perfect strategy than Coulthard's. He was not happy at the decision. 'I obeyed the order but I wasn't happy,' said Barrichello at the time. 'What surprised me was that the team took a decision like this so early in the season – it was only the sixth race. The year before I knew I had to work for Michael, but I thought that, having done so, this year would be different.'

At the time in 2001 Schumacher was only four points ahead of the Scotsman in the world championship and although the McLaren challenge faded later in the year and Schumacher wrapped up the title at the Hungarian Grand Prix in August, it seemed at the time of the Austrian Grand Prix that perhaps the battle could be tighter. Schumacher had been battling with Montoya early in the race and went off the track losing position to Barrichello, so although Barrichello took it badly, there were grounds for asking him to make way.

But what happened at the same event the following year was quite different. Schumacher had started the 2002 season with four wins from five races, beating his nearest challenger, Montoya, by over half a minute in the Spanish Grand Prix. The Ferrari F2002 was a rocket ship, easily the fastest car in the field. In Barcelona, Schumacher's fastest race lap had been a second and a half faster than the next car. Going to Austria he led the championship by 21 points from Montoya. It was obvious that he would be champion by August at the latest. But in the closing stages of the race, with the Ferraris running one-two and the next car almost 20 seconds behind, Jean Todt gave the order once again for Barrichello to pull over and let Schumacher win. Barrichello had been the faster man in both qualifying and the race and totally deserved to win. However he had just signed a new contract keeping him at the team for a further two years for significantly more money and he felt constrained by that. Although he struggled with the order (clearly it had an overall demotivating effect on him for the remainder of his time at Ferrari), he obeyed once again. He left it until the final few metres so as to make his point, then stamped on the brakes and allowed Schumacher through.

I was in the ITV commentary box above the grandstands and the moment the cars crossed the line you could hear the boos coming from the crowd below and feel the stamping of feet coming through the floor. It threatened to turn ugly. When the drivers climbed from their cars in *parc fermé* the boos grew in volume. On the podium the Austrian Chancellor, Dr Wolfgang Schussell, was deeply embarrassed when Schumacher pushed Barrichello on to the winner's top step and the poor man did not know who should be presented with the winner's trophy. The crowd was chanting Barrichello's name. He was the moral victor, the people's champion.

The incident threw into question the sporting values of Formula 1, undermined Schumacher and made millions around the world question why they bothered to watch such a sport. The FIA had to be seen to act because the damage to the sport looked so severe, such was the ferocity of the reaction from the public and the media. There was little the FIA could do about the team orders because they were legal at the time, but a new rule was brought in as a result of this affair banning team orders altogether.

Ferrari could only be punished directly for violating the podium protocol. A meeting of the FIA world council decided to impose a fine of $1 million on the team and the drivers and issued a statement saying that although there was no sanction available to them on the team orders side, they 'deplored' the cynical way the team had applied orders in the race.

Many people new to the sport were confused by what happened in Austria, while even the most seasoned F1 insiders were appalled. Williams's Patrick Head called it 'the worst thing I have seen in 25 years of racing', while Flavio Briatore summed up most people's feelings when he said, 'F1 is much bigger than Ferrari and they should remember it.' And this was the crucial point. The incident was a watershed moment, which undermined so much of what Ferrari achieved in the 2000s. Perhaps because they were so locked into the siege mentality which had served them so well as they fought their way to the top, the inner group at Ferrari had lost sight of their responsibilities to the sport as a whole. They acted as if there was no context for their actions.

Immediately after the race Todt was defiant. 'I'm not

bothered. It was a difficult decision but the most important thing is that the team wins. The clouds will pass,' he said.

Schumacher, though, was in damage limitation mode. First, distinctly uncomfortable at being booed by the crowd, he made the awkward gesture on the podium to 'promote' Barrichello, then speaking after the race he appeared to distance himself from the team decision. 'Last year I was sort of involved in the situation because I felt that the championship was much more tight than this year. This year I didn't even think about it and before the race I was asked and I said, "I don't believe there is going to be a team strategy decision involved." Then suddenly they told me that he would move over and yeah, I'm not very pleased about it either.'

Barrichello disputes this version of events. 'I have a transcript of the radio conversation and although he doesn't talk a lot he was very aware of what was going on,' he says. 'So it's not true that he had nothing to do with it. I was surprised when it happened because Todt told me the year before that if the fight was for first place that would never happen.'

Sabine Kehm says that Michael backed the decision.

He may not have wanted to do it that way, but he supported them. I'm not sure if it was out of loyalty to Ross and Jean. The year turned out to be brilliant for us but at that time we were still not sure about our performance. It seemed to be a logical thing to do. The way it was done was terrible, I can understand that from Rubens' side.

After the podium there was a very strange press conference. Then when they came back to the motor-home, Michael and Rubens sat down with Jean. When you talk with Michael now he would say that it was not nice, but you have to do it for the team. In the Tour de France it's

exactly the same, you have to see who is the one who is
going for the championship and then back them.

Todt began to express some regret at the next race in Monaco,
where Schumacher was roundly booed every time he took to
the race-track. Ferrari had been inundated with complaints
from its fans around the world and Todt had finally got the
message. 'The opinions of our fans are very important because
they are the heart of Ferrari's history. I accept the opinion of
the *tifosi*, but not the people in this paddock because they will
never be sincere.'

Todt's view was always that Ferrari's success was the most
important thing. Yet at the same time the team is very protective of its image and comes down hard on anyone,
especially in the Italian media, who damages it. Years later
Todt looked back on the 2001 incident and admitted he had
made a mistake. 'Calumny is a totally bearable evil, which I
expect. That said I was surprised by the reaction to Austria.
Clearly this was an error of judgement on any part. But I have
my own opinion on it. I cannot say that Austria was the best
managed situation ever, but the reaction was totally out of
proportion.'

The episode set a negative tone to what was otherwise a
hugely impressive demonstration by Ferrari and Schumacher
over five straight years of utter supremacy. If the ultimate goal
of a racing team and a driver is the quest for perfection then
they achieved that for an unprecedented period. Given the
circumstances and the nature of the characters involved it is
unlikely that the feat will ever be repeated. But the team did
not know when to stop.

Eddie Irvine, Schumacher's team-mate during his first,

relatively unsuccessful, phase at Ferrari, believes that what happened over the ten-year period during which Schumacher was there was a natural cycle, but wishes they had reined themselves in a bit when the team started to dominate.

I hate saying it because I am such a big Ferrari fan, but they remind me so much of America the way it has behaved under Bush and Cheney. 'It's our way or no way.' I understand that sometimes they are right, but because they are the big guy they have to be beyond white.

I think that when you are at the very top it does matter if you are unsporting. When you are coming up, when you are poor you have got to get rich however you can and then when you are rich you've got to get clean. That's the way of the world. It's the same with Ferrari. We did everything, not particularly nice things, to get up there and beat Hakkinen [and McLaren in 1998 and 1999]. We had to. We had a car that was a second and a half slower, how the fuck are we going to win a world championship? And you know what? Everyone kind of let us get away with it because we were doing everything we could to compete. That's fair enough.

But when you have a much faster car and then you start . . . [trails off] it's like, 'Now you are taking the piss out of us.' And that is where they overstepped the line. We see it so often though, in countries, in businesses, where the pursuit of excellence overshadows all other factors.

The feeling that Ferrari were mocking their rivals and acting as though they were bigger than the sport was exacerbated later in the 2002 season when Schumacher slowed on the finish line of the US Grand Prix at Indianapolis, allowing Barrichello to win the race. This was not his intention, it emerged privately after the race, as he had apparently merely been slowing down for a formation finish for the cameras, but his legendary attention to detail let him down for once. He had forgotten that the finish line at Indianapolis is some 400 metres further down the track from the start line and so Barrichello, who was as confused by Schumacher's behaviour as the public, sailed past him to take the win. But even today Barrichello is unsure of exactly what Schumacher thought he was doing:

> In the back of his mind I think he wanted to get away from Austria. But we never talked about it. I would always rather pay for something. If someone gives you something you've always got to wonder what is coming next because maybe they ask you for something in future. So, honestly when I saw him back off, I backed off. Then he accelerated again, so I accelerated. I didn't know what was going on, whether he was backing off to let me by or what. But then when I accelerated again he backed off again and you saw the rest. I never understood it. I went on the podium and took the trophy.

After the race Schumacher insisted publicly that he had intended to gift the race to Rubens and tried to laugh it off, but the Americans did not see the funny side. In a highly competitive and sports-mad nation, top athletes don't give victories away, especially when all the rhetoric handed out by the F1 people in the build-up to the event was about how tough it is to win in the world's premier motorsport category.

In Schumacher's mind, looking back on that incident now, he puts it down to a need to redress the balance after Austria, a need to put things right. It is an interesting insight into the way his mind works and harks back to the old mentality from his penniless karting days of owing a debt which needs to be cleared. 'In my heart I sort of got even with what happened in Austria,' he said. 'I felt I had to do something and it wasn't discussed beforehand and I didn't feel arrogant enough to discuss something like that beforehand anyway because Rubens was very fast and then as it happened that I was in front, in the end of the race I thought it was the right opportunity.'

* * *

During this early period of his domination, Schumacher passed some key milestones. When he won the Belgian Grand Prix in 2001, he passed Alain Prost's record of 51 Grand Prix wins, and was now officially the most successful driver in the history of the sport. The following summer he added his fifth world title, to equal Fangio's record which had stood for 50 years and which no one believed would ever be beaten. Weekend after weekend, race after race, came joy unbridled as the red machine crushed all opposition, racking up points, victories and championships. There were moments of high emotion, like the podium at Monza in 2002, which swung out over the top of the crowd on the track and gave the amazing spectacle of Ferrari being literally on top of the world. Schumacher ended the 2002 season with 11 victories, a feat he surpassed two seasons later in 2004 with 13 wins from 18 races.

I spoke to him at length at the end of 2002 and reminded him of what he had said in 1998 about it being more fun to win against a dominant car rather than drive one yourself. Had his attitude changed now that he was sitting in a rocket ship? He said:

When you beat the dominant car then it's an extra effort you have to put in and it's an extra pleasure. But being able to develop something with the team which then becomes dominant is another kind of challenge which I enjoy as well. To do what I'm doing I still put the effort in as when I have maybe not been in the best car. So for me it hasn't really changed except that we have the opportunity to be up the front all the time.

It had been a tough year for Barrichello, despite four wins, including the enormous honour of victory at Monza. He had come out of the Austria debacle with a lot of sympathy from the press and public, but it had highlighted the true nature of Ferrari's racing philosophy and showed that it was virtually impossible for the Brazilian to take Schumacher on from the inside. Barrichello says:

It made me so much a better person, because to beat Michael I had to do double what I would have done to beat someone else. I had to find different set-ups, drive differently, find a new way with traction control, create things, develop things. I had to wear the brakes and tyres less than him. People don't know that. They say 'You'll never be world champion', but by now I could have been world champion twice. You ask the Honda guys, they say 'After fifteen years, how the hell have you got so many ideas?' Well, it was because I had to keep trying to beat Michael and I had to keep on going. I never drove for Ferrari for the money, I always had the passion that I could beat him.

Obviously I had a lot of pleasure racing with him, it wasn't all bad. But people have no idea how I had to work. If I left for another team I would not have the best car. Seeing that, I said that I will stay and work with the car and the people. But for me it was always sincere, not going around behind people's backs. I've always been sincere and I've always slept well at night.

The most impressive thing that Michael did was to make the car work for him. He was very good at that. It was probably the area where I learned the most from him, because I would quite often be faster than him on Friday, but not always faster on Saturday.

The difference between Michael and Ayrton was that Ayrton was more passion-driven, he would say, 'I know I can find another two tenths in myself,' whereas Michael would find another two tenths in the car. He would work the whole package so that he could take a certain corner flat, whereas Ayrton would go flat, whatever it takes, even if he risked a big shunt.

So why did Michael spin a lot and go off the race-track? Because he only knew how to drive the car on the limit. Which is a good and a bad thing, because you need to look after the car as well. Michael didn't know how to go slowly.

In 2003, after two seasons of domination, came a challenging year in which Schumacher clinched the title by a mere two points after a season-long battle with Kimi Raikkonen, the man who ultimately would replace him at Ferrari. Ferrari were hit by a raft of new regulations from the FIA, announced not long before the start of the season. It left them wrong-footed with a car which had been designed for the old rules. It meant that they struggled to be as competitive in race tactics as they had been. Also the tyres which Michelin were supplying to their main rivals, Williams and McLaren, were now clearly superior to the Bridgestones that Ferrari were using.

The turning point of the 2003 season was another controversial incident in its closing stages, when the FIA decided to ban the Michelin front tyres used by Ferrari's main competitors on the grounds that they were designed to wear down at the front and provide a wider contact patch with the ground than was allowed in the rules. Williams and McLaren argued that this was a new interpretation of the rules and that the tyres had been perfectly legal for the whole season, but the ban took the stuffing out of their challenge for the title. Having been in a strong position before the Italian Grand Prix in September, the race at which the tyres were banned, they could only watch as Schumacher won in Monza and at Indianapolis to give himself a great chance of clinching the title in Suzuka. Raikkonen needed to win with Schumacher not scoring a point, for the result to be different.

Schumacher did win the title, becoming the first ever six times world champion, but it was a far from convincing performance as he finished eighth in the race, having collided with another car during it. Afterwards he seemed totally deflated. 'It's been a difficult season,' he said. 'I was very nervous today and the race was stressful, one of the toughest of my career. I'm completely emptied, completely exhausted and I feel nothing. I rounded off all my other titles with a victory, today I was eighth, it's a bizarre feeling.'

CHAPTER TWENTY

The last lap

Lap after lap I said goodbye to my life as a racing driver. This was the first time in my career that I asked myself, 'Why am I doing this? Why am I investing so much time into work if I'd rather be at home with my family?'

Michael Schumacher

Schumacher's career is remarkable for so many reasons – for its extraordinary success, for the sheer effort he expended and for the level to which he elevated the art of the Grand Prix driver. He changed everything.

No longer was it acceptable for a driver merely to drive the car; he had to work on every aspect of his game, to be an athlete, to be seen to improve himself technically year by year. The young drivers following in Schumacher's wake are more rounded, more technically proficient than those who preceded him because he raised the bar so high in terms of what a team can expect from a driver. Compare a Fernando Alonso or a Lewis Hamilton with the raw youth Schumacher was when he began in F1 in 1991. The difference between them illustrates the revolution which he inspired.

It is astonishing that Schumacher was able to sustain the effort for so long and I firmly believe that had he not broken his leg in 1999 and rested for half the season, he would have burned out before 2006. As it was he suffered a year of failure and disappointment at the mid-point of his career which gave him pause for reflection and then, when Ferrari moved to secure his long-term replacement, Kimi Raikkonen, he was forced to ask himself whether he had the energy and the hunger to beat the first team-mate of his own level or whether to call it a day. The rise of Alonso, a driver who appeared to have all of Schumacher's strengths and none of his weaknesses, also preyed on his mind. He knew that there was nothing to choose between them in performance and that Alonso was cut from the same cloth, just as ruthless and just as determined to win as he was. But Alonso was 12 years younger and buoyed with the confidence of winning the world title at a young age, as Schumacher had been.

Schumacher knew that Alonso was to him what he had been to Senna. I remember asking him way back in 2002 who the next big threat was, thinking he would say Montoya or Raikkonen but he said Alonso, who was at the time a mere test driver for Renault. But in test sessions alongside him, he had seen the quality of the driver. That conviction had grown in their duels on the track during the years which followed and some close to Schumacher even believe that he came to realise that Alonso was actually better than him. The writing was truly on the wall. Could he bring himself to train extra hard, to put in all the extra work which would be needed to keep one step ahead of the young pretender?

The 2005 season was a strange one for Schumacher and he ended it angry with himself for not doing a good enough job.

On the face of it there was little more he could have done: his car and more specifically his tyres were the handicap. The FIA brought in a new rule which obliged the drivers to use the same set of tyres throughout qualifying and the race. Bridgestone were not able to make a tyre which could perform at its optimum level over a single qualifying lap and then maintain a high level of performance for the 200 miles of the race. The result was a season in which Schumacher was rarely a contender. There were occasions, such as Imola, where his car would suddenly come alive as the tyres reached their peak and his lap times would be mesmerising as he fought to get himself a good result, but he was forced to spend large parts of the races as an also-ran, unable to compete or to get involved.

Michael was not programmed to accept uncompetitiveness and its bedfellow failure, but perhaps it was an indication of how close the team was both in success and adversity that they never argued or soured their relationship during this period. Schumacher found it hard to exist in a competitive environment without the pressure which comes from challenging for the title. He was still risking his life every time he stepped into the car, still competing for every inch because that was the way he was built. Most sportsmen in his situation would have felt their motivation seep away, especially in their 14th season in the sport. To those of us who study the drivers closely on a weekly basis, Schumacher did not seem to be anything less than totally committed throughout the season, but he was very hard on himself when looking back on the year for not having given 100 per cent effort during the season:

Clearly I made mistakes in 2005, which I should never have allowed myself to make. After all the success, mistakes start to creep in, you allow routine to take over. I could have done more for my fitness – then perhaps got a tenth of a second per lap more out of the car. At any rate we were so far behind that would have made little difference to the results. There were races like Monza, for example, where perhaps with a little more application I could have finished eighth rather than tenth. However when you are spoilt by success and set yourself such high standards as I do, then it's damned hard to still find the motivation for so small a step. That applies to me as well as the team.

In fact he had already begun to notice problems with his neck and shoulders, the weak link in the racing driver's anatomy and the most heavily stressed by high g forces in cornering and braking. Throughout 2005 he suffered intense pain in this area, which also meant that he could not train as effectively as in the past, something which was one of the cornerstones of his approach to racing. Sabine Kehm says:

Preparation is extremely important to him. Getting into the car and driving was just the last step. He needed to have the feeling that he did everything he could have done in order to compete. Not to step out of the car and have the feeling that there was something else he could have done differently and then exploit it better in the race. He needs to have that feeling in order to make him calm. To make him able to really concentrate fully.

In 2005 he was angry with himself because he was not on his best level. He said, 'You don't see it in the driving', he was still giving a hundred per cent, 'but if I had come into the situation where I had needed to give more I'm not

sure that I would have been able to give the extra. Given
the physical preparation I had at the time.'

At Imola he put on a thrilling display, chasing down Alonso
and battling for the lead with him for the last 15 laps. But the
Spaniard proved stubborn and more than able to soak up the
pressure. Then at Monaco Schumacher showed his true
fighting spirit with a bold and uncompromising overtaking
move for seventh place at the chicane in the final laps, on his
own team-mate Barrichello, who was furious with him
afterwards and handed out some very public criticism. 'A
world champion should not drive like that,' said Barrichello,
echoing Schumacher's words about Senna in Brazil 13 years
earlier. 'The risk was really too great. I've told him to his face
that I would never have tried such a risky move.'

Barrichello's own relationship with Ferrari was coming to
an end. He and Schumacher had been quite friendly for most
of their time together, but by 2005 Rubens had begun to
complain more about his treatment at Ferrari, and Monaco
was the most extreme example of his complaints about
Schumacher. He told me that the breaking-point came at
Indianapolis, but for the moment the detail of what they fell
out over must remain a secret as neither man is telling.

By mid-summer the Brazilian had negotiated an early exit
from his contract in order to join the Honda team, whose
sporting director, Gil de Ferran, was an old friend. Barrichello
could see that his dream of becoming team leader at Ferrari
was not likely to be fulfilled. His position in the team was
becoming complicated by the moves being made by di
Montezemolo and Todt to hedge against Schumacher retiring
in the near future. Felipe Massa was very close to the Todts and

was on standby, while it soon emerged that Kimi Raikkonen was the driver Montezemolo in particular wanted to lead the team forward and had been signed. Despite the fact that Barrichello had shown himself to be the closest team-mate Schumacher had had on pace, it was clear that the team did not see him as a future number one. It was time to move on.

Schumacher's only win of the season came at the controversial US Grand Prix at Indianapolis, the notorious race where only six cars took the start after all the cars using Michelin tyres withdrew at the end of the formation lap.

Although the main responsibility for the problem at Indianapolis lay with Michelin, which had failed to bring safe tyres to the event, Schumacher's stubbornness in dealing with his adversaries and his refusal to make any concessions played a role in the outcome, according to his critics. The drivers were infuriated with him when he refused even to consider ways in which an embarrassing shambles for F1 might be avoided.

Ferrari and Bridgestone had the upper hand that weekend, as Michelin had brought tyres which could not handle the cornering forces through the banked Turn 13. Perhaps Schumacher's attitude was hardened by the fact that it had been a miserable year for the Scuderia as Bridgestone had thus far been outclassed by Michelin and he therefore wanted to give the opposition some pain.

Perhaps also it was because his own brother, Ralf, had suffered the accident due to a Michelin tyre failure in practice which triggered the crisis. As it became clear that it would not be possible for the Michelin teams to take part in the race under normal circumstances, one solution put forward was to build a chicane before Turn 13, to slow the cars down and thereby reduce the cornering speed to within Michelin's tolerances. Naturally it was proposed by the Michelin teams that this would be done solely to 'put on a show' for the public in Indianapolis and those watching around the world on television. They proposed that Ferrari should be allowed to take the maximum points from the weekend, with the Michelin teams scoring no points, just so that a show could be put on for arguably F1's most important market.

The talks continued until a few hours before the start of the race without agreement and although it was not Schumacher and Ferrari's responsibility to decide what should happen, their attitude contributed greatly to the FIA's decision to refuse a chicane. Additionally the FIA had already stated that it wanted to move to a single tyre supplier in Formula 1 for 2008 and Michelin's embarrassment provided a great political opportunity. Ferrari and Jean Todt in particular were more than willing to help the FIA by holding an uncompromising line.

So only the six Bridgestone cars took the start, while the Michelin cars all pulled into the pit lane after the formation lap. The public was treated to the spectacle of Formula 1 scoring a major own goal and the debacle went down very badly both in the USA and around the world. Once again Schumacher found himself at the centre of a scandal which damaged the sport. Once again he felt that it was not his fault and of course it wasn't of his making. He was part of a greater political process and his loyalties were to his team, not to the other drivers, despite the fact that they all wanted to put on a show for the public.

Intriguingly a chicane was actually under construction at one point on the Saturday night before the race, but orders came from FIA race director Charlie Whiting to stop work and return the track to its original configuration. As one of his fellow directors of the GPDA at the time, David Coulthard was angered by Schumacher's attitude.

> Michael's actions at Indy were disappointing to me and to most of the other drivers. I genuinely believe that most of us were coming from the point of view that, 'Look we're going to look like a bunch of cocks here if Formula 1 can't put on a race. So sort out the points between Bernie, Max and the teams, they can steamroller rules through, so surely they can do something here?'
>
> A little bit of support from Michael would have made all the difference. But he was adamant, 'My brother's had a serious accident, you've brought the wrong tyres, it's a dangerous corner,' and so on. On the one hand I could see his position, but on the other hand, he was going to win the race whatever. We weren't trying to take away the advantage he and Bridgestone had created. We just wanted to start twenty-two cars and even if we the drivers all knew the race would be a bit of a farce, it wouldn't be the first time something was manufactured.

Mark Webber is another driver who had worked closely with Schumacher on the GPDA, who was disappointed that on this occasion, where the drivers' safety was clearly an issue, the man who had championed the drivers' cause for so long was prepared to abandon them:

> It wasn't a question of 'if' we were going to hit the walls it was a question of 'when'. Michael could have been in the pack and been part of that accident. From the drivers' point of view, just the position he's in, a seven times world champion, we just wanted him to give us a bit more support. He didn't even want to examine the question,

'What can we do to come to a solution?' He said that it was not a safety issue, but a technical one. It *absolutely* was a safety issue as we would have raced otherwise.

Obviously it wasn't Michael's fault that Michelin brought the wrong tyres. But there was just no compromise. He stood by Ferrari. He never saw it from our side, wanting F1 to put on a show. Afterwards he saw as we all did, what the outcome was, a totally embarrassing day for F1. Ferrari was going to get a one-two finish anyway and they would have done it with a lot less egg on face.

I was disappointed, he's so powerful, he carries so much weight and it can swing things, no question. You expect a top sportsman to give nothing away but sometimes there are situations, like Indy, where you expect them to give two per cent. But not him.

Ross Brawn is quick to defend his driver against the accusation that he was hypocritical about safety. He sees a consistency to Schumacher's argument:

You can separate these things. As an engineer I work hard at raising the compulsory safety standards so everyone has to meet them. But once we've defined what we want for safety, I'll then take the car to that limit. I won't build a safer car than I need to because it'll compromise performance. So you never get in a situation where you've got a car which is fast but unsafe, or you are forced to build a safe car which is not fast.

That's where Michael stands; he works hard to raise the safety standards then he drives in a very aggressive and competitive way. So then if anything happens the safety standards he has worked towards will help to prevent an accident. And you can separate the two. If you are a racing driver you race against the other guys and there is some risk, but you can reduce the level of risk overall. So it doesn't mean to say I'm working hard to have safe circuits so I'm going to drive safely and make sure I don't get near to anyone. The two things are totally compatible.

After Indy the drivers got a lot of criticism and there was a tidal wave of political wrangling. The GPDA wrote a letter to Max Mosley saying that they weren't happy with the way things were done in Indy. Schumacher was the only driver who wouldn't sign it. He refused because he felt that there was a lot going on between the teams and the FIA in the aftermath of Indy and that it was not the right time. David Coulthard says:

He's always had this thing his whole career, he doesn't give anything away. He is hard to define because he's not intimidating and hard, he's not Ron Dennis giving you the stare or Bernie with that presence. It's an awkward, traffic-warden-like, stand-your-ground thing with him. You end up saying 'Oh for fuck's sake Michael, come on!' It's easy for us British to stereotype the intransigent German behaviour, but . . .

It's hard for me because I've seen him privately, socially as well, I've been welcomed to some events with his family and I've seen Michael, with the kids, in a small group of people and I'm feeling slightly uncomfortable because they're all looking at me thinking, 'That's the bloke who gave Michael the finger at Magny-Cours and crashed into him at Spa.' But by the end of the night I felt comfortable and welcomed.

So I've seen the soft side of Michael and I don't see him as a Nigel Mansell type where you aren't sure if he's about to throw a punch at you. Senna had that aggression too at times, but not Michael.

It may well be the case that other drivers spent so much time complaining about Schumacher because it was one of the few areas in which they could compete with him and give him some pain. On the track he was always at the front and in his relationships with the team and with the FIA he made himself hard to compete with. But by complaining to the press about his behaviour, his competitors were able to cut him down to size; it was the only avenue open to them and they knew that in the media they always had a willing audience.

Schumacher knew exactly what would happen after Indianapolis: the drivers would rally around under the umbrella of the GPDA and complain that he did not care about their safety. The process actually culminated in an emotional drivers' meeting in Turkey the following year, where all the drivers ganged up on him. Then there was an embarrassing scene at his final drivers' briefing in Brazil where, instead of a rousing send-off, he was given a slow handclap.

In Schumacher's eyes, Indianapolis 2005 was simple: the other teams had brought the wrong equipment. He compared them to downhill skiers turning up with slalom skis by mistake. During the press conference after the race, when asked if nothing could have been done to prevent the farce which followed, he said:

I tell you one story from not so long ago. [He was thinking about the Italian Grand Prix of 2001.] In Monza we had the death of a marshal [the previous year] and all of us drivers agreed we would want yellow flags for the first two chicanes, and there were two or three team owners that told their drivers, 'You will not respect the yellow flag, just ignore what you have said. We want you to race and we force you to race' and it is the same people who have been on the other side today. So, Formula 1 is a tough business; we are working very hard. We had a tyre that was quicker but we didn't use it here because we knew what was going to face us. I am not saying the others purposefully chose something wrong, but whatever it is, it is their problem, not our problem. I don't think you can ask the people who are not responsible for it to take the responsibility.

Clearly he is referring here to Renault boss Flavio Briatore in particular. Schumacher, who shared the intransigent stance of Jean Todt, did not see why he should give away his advantage, but afterwards he felt he was blamed by the drivers for something which he couldn't do anything about. And then when he went up on the podium and the crowd booed him, he switched into that behaviour pattern we would see again in Monaco 2006, where his father's 'you bully me I'll bully you back' attitude led him to feel that he did not care, that this was F1's problem, not his. The organisers had totally failed to keep the public informed of what was happening and as far as he was concerned their reaction was born out of a feeling of having been kept in the dark.

Around Easter 2005 a significant milestone occurred in Schumacher's Ferrari career, but one with which he had no direct involvement. Kimi Raikkonen had signed a deal to race for the team in 2007. Mindful of the fact that Schumacher was now 36, Luca di Montezemolo in particular was anxious to secure the services of Raikkonen to ensure that Ferrari had a top driver for the future. The Finn had received an offer from Ferrari in 2001, but on that occasion he had not wanted to be Schumacher's number two and made much of the fact that he preferred the system at McLaren where both drivers are treated equally. But four seasons of frustration at McLaren, above all with poor reliability, had led him to look around again for a team which could make him world champion.

Before the 2005 season Ferrari had asked Schumacher for a firm commitment for 2007 and beyond but he was unable to give it. Ferrari then knew that they had to act quickly. Montezemolo was more anxious for Raikkonen to join the team in 2007 than Todt, who understood that the Finn's arrival would place his close friend Schumacher in a difficult position. And so it proved. Schumacher would almost certainly have raced for another season if the move had not been made so decisively by Montezemolo. As it was, the signing of Raikkonen left him with little room for manoeuvre.

Raikkonen and Ferrari both knew that he would be in demand; many teams wanted him. Ferrari had to secure his services and they began serious discussions at the start of the 2005 season. Schumacher was kept aware of these discussions and he knew when they were concluded.

Raikkonen was always Ferrari's first choice as a long-term replacement for Schumacher despite the fact that Fernando Alonso seemed a more complete driver and certainly had better results. This distaste for Alonso dates back to failed negotiations between Alonso and Jean Todt in 2001, which meant that the Spaniard was very much persona non grata at Ferrari. 'It was all done, he was to have become our test driver,' Todt recalled. 'We were writing up the contract. Then I found out that he had signed with someone else [Flavio Briatore]. I thought that we had finalised every detail with his manager, Adrian Campos, in the garden of my house.'

Schumacher was well aware of Raikkonen's imminent arrival at the team. He knew that he would have to make a decision about his own future. For 2006 Ferrari planned to replace Barrichello with Felipe Massa, who was under contract to the team while at Sauber and who was managed by Todt's son, Nicolas. So they were covered if Schumacher decided to retire at the end of his contract in December 2006; if he chose to continue they would put Massa on hold until Schumacher did eventually finish racing.

Jean Todt told Schumacher to keep an open mind, but both knew that Raikkonen's arrival would not fit in with Schumacher's way of working. He was used to his number one status within the team and it was important to him mentally to know that he had the full support of the team around him. He had asserted himself over team-mates in the past by being faster and getting better results, but always in his mind was the psychological boost of knowing the team was there primarily for him. With Raikkonen alongside, capable of driving faster than him, he would lose the comfort zone on which he had relied.

According to Sabine Kehm, Schumacher had no thoughts of retirement at the end of 2005 and even spoke privately to her and to those close to him about the challenge of having Raikkonen as a team-mate.

Michael didn't leave because he wanted to avoid Raikkonen. He was joking about it and saying 'It's going to be very interesting, if I still have it. I know he's going to be very fast, but I'm faster compared to Felipe than I expected to be.' If he was planning to avoid a strong team-mate he would not have been talking like that. He couldn't imagine raising that amount of effort again as they had at the start of the season. To make an effort like Ferrari did over winter 2005–06, you cannot do it very often. It took a lot of energy out of everyone.

In an interview with the German *Der Spiegel* magazine in February 2006 Schumacher outlined his thoughts about the future: 'Quite clearly the car must be competitive. If I don't even have the chance to win races and fight for the title then I don't think that I will feel a great desire to continue my career.'

Behind the scenes a lot was going on. Schumacher was aware that Ross Brawn was planning to take a year off at the end of 2006. The man most closely associated with his success felt that at the age of 51 and after ten years at Ferrari it was time to take a year out and enjoy some time away from the relentless pressure. Brawn was not finished with racing, indeed he harboured the desire to become a team principal, and a year out would allow him to plan his next move.

Jean Todt has since revealed that he, too, wished to step away from the cut and thrust of Formula 1, because his new role as CEO of the entire Ferrari business meant that he did not have the time to devote to racing that he had had before. Todt's job on the F1 team was offered to Gerhard Berger but he turned it down because he had already agreed a deal with the Red Bull company to run his own team, Toro Rosso, based on the old Minardi outfit. Perhaps this influenced Brawn's decision to go, but Berger's refusal obliged Todt to stay on for at least another year to ensure continuity. Asked by *Spiegel* if it was important to him that Brawn and Todt stay on board, Schumacher said:

> That would be nice. Admittedly, everyone is replaceable, me included. I wouldn't like to talk about individual personalities either. That's because at the moment it's not a question of who goes or who is moved but who is brought in new, who can make us stronger. And that what we have identified as

weaknesses really does change. If we want to make progress, then we need additional people. In F1 you cannot afford to stand still. I want to know, where is Ferrari's journey heading?

Schumacher put in a huge effort over the winter along with the team to develop the car for 2006 and the early tests indicated that it was competitive. The rules had been changed again, this time working out in Ferrari's favour, as the one-race tyre was dropped and in its place came a return to a more normal allowance of tyres for qualifying and the race. Bridgestone were back in business and Ferrari looked strong as the teams headed to the first race in Bahrain.

Schumacher had indicated in media interviews before the 2006 season that he would make his decision, about whether to retire or continue into 2007, by the middle of the year – but in fact when he started racing again, he found that the decision made itself.

Writing in German in a book published with Sabine Kehm after the season, called simply *Schumacher*, he explained how his decision had been made:

It was already clear to me before this season that we were competitive again. Therefore it was also clear that there wasn't much more to come after that, that there was little more to be accomplished, that you have to start thinking about stopping. I'm not the youngest any more. It wasn't that I needed the success to reach my decision. But I wanted to find a good time to do it, and so it all came together perfectly.

The first notion I had for stopping was at the first race in Bahrain, on the Saturday shortly after qualifying. Because something happened there that I had never consciously thought about. I equalled Ayrton Senna's record: 65 pole positions. That was like a release. It's not like this was a goal of mine in the sense that 'I will carry on driving until I've cracked these 65 pole positions.' But then when it happened and I knew we were going to have a good season, I just had a feeling that this would be a good time to stop. And after that this feeling hardened more and more. I became more and more certain of my decision.

After Bahrain Schumacher repeatedly discussed his retirement with his wife, with Willi Weber and with Jean Todt, who told him to hold fire before making any firm decisions. But Schumacher was conscious that his team-mate, Felipe Massa, needed to know what his future would be and so at Indianapolis at the beginning of July, he confirmed to Todt that he would retire at the end of the year. 'My feeling was that I had done everything I could do, I had accomplished more than I had ever dreamed of, and there's a young guy with bags of talent, who's really nice – why should I stand in his way?'

Clearly it was important to the Todt family that Massa's future was not compromised and Schumacher understood that implicitly. Since winning the 2000 title for Ferrari he had been racing for pleasure anyway, with nothing to prove and no debt owed to anyone. He had enjoyed the cut and thrust of racing, the working with a disparate group of people to achieve a difficult goal and he enjoyed the sheer thrill of driving the fastest cars in the world. Having developed a car which in 2004 had won 15 of the 18 races, he and the team had come as close to perfection as it is possible to come in modern Formula 1. 'I know this sounds trivial but driving in Formula 1 was just pure fun for me, a childhood dream come true; four wheels, a steering wheel, the duels on the track. Formula 1 was the realisation of a fascination that is deeply rooted in my childhood.'

Schumacher never lost the direct connection between the pleasure he got from driving go-karts around his father's track at Kerpen and driving Ferraris around the toughest race-tracks in the world. The negatives of a life at the top in Formula 1 were many – the media intrusion, the unwelcome and inescapable fame, the jealousy and bitterness of rivals in the paddock. He had had to develop a shell to protect himself from the vitriol. But it is not the case that he stopped because the negatives outweighed the positives. He simply ran out of energy and desire to do what he had done at the level he wanted to do it.

Schumacher desperately wanted to sign off by winning the championship; he saw it as his gift to the Ferrari team. He was very anxious that nothing should distract the team from its job and to that end he wanted any announcement about his retirement to be kept until the end of the season. But that wish was not granted by Luca di Montezemolo, who stepped in and created chaos by saying that Ferrari would announce its driver line-up for 2007 at the Italian Grand Prix in Monza. This had the exact effect that Schumacher had feared, as the media went into a frenzy of speculation through the summer as to what would be announced. Schumacher could not sit down in a press conference without the question of Monza and possible retirement coming up and doubt must have filtered through to the team. Only the key people at the top knew for certain that Schumacher was retiring and it would be impossible to keep that information private if it were shared among the wider team.

Schumacher's own performances suffered from the distraction too. In the two races preceding Monza, at Budapest and Istanbul, he drove erratically and made mistakes, losing crucial ground to Alonso in the championship. At Budapest in particular an opportunity was missed as Alonso had retired from the race and Schumacher looked set to score some points, but in the closing stages of the race, with his car really struggling for grip on old tyres, he tried too hard to defend his second position from Heidfeld and then third from Pedro De La Rosa. He should have accepted losing a podium, but still taken five points for fourth place off Alonso, instead of which he damaged his car in the fight and retired with no points. Ross Brawn regrets that he wasn't stronger with his driver that day. 'Hungary was a blip and an unfortunate one. I wish I'd said to Michael, "Hang on, we should just get the points we can." But he's a racer, it's in his DNA, and I am as well. If I think that there is a chance that we can do a bit better than we should then we try. Everyone wants to do a bit more. It's the nature of the business. We thought there was an opportunity but it didn't work out.'

Schumacher enraged his fellow drivers with the way he drove in the closing stages of the race in Budapest, particularly Pedro De La Rosa, breaking the rules regarding blocking and cutting chicanes which they felt had been agreed by all parties. He had simply ignored the rules when it suited him. At the following race in Istanbul the drivers' briefing was a highly charged affair characterised by a simmering discontent which had been building up ever since Indianapolis the year before.

De La Rosa wanted some answers from Schumacher about

his conduct towards him in Budapest. He felt he had him bang to rights and he wasn't going to let it go. The other drivers ganged up on Schumacher too, asking him why he was unable to accept that he was wrong when all of them agreed with De La Rosa. Schumacher was furious and felt bullied. Jarno Trulli made a strong point but Schumacher was in no mood to listen. Noticeably staying out of it were Raikkonen and Alonso.

And so the long road led to Monza, the scene of so many of the most dramatic moments of Schumacher's career. Sabine Kehm takes up the story:

Michael would have preferred to announce it [his retirement] at the end of the season. At Istanbul I spoke with him and he wanted to announce it at the end of the season. But Willi Weber had already spoken to *Bild* newspaper, which wasn't very helpful.

Then before Monza, we had a test and I travelled in the car to the track with Michael and he changed his mind. He said to me, 'I know I thought it would be better to wait until the end of the season. But if Jean speaks to you about this, tell him I don't have any problem with doing it at Monza. Then it's behind us and it's all done and I don't care about it, because I've known about it for a long time, what do you think?'

I said that we should do it at the end of the season because if you announce that you retire then the last three races will be terrible for you and you're fighting for the championship. I spoke to Todt, who wanted to do it at Monza. I said to him, 'If you don't announce it on Thursday then everyone is going to know he's stopping. Let's put it on Thursday,' but Todt said, 'No, we have a race to do and I don't want it distracting us.' It was one of those situations where whatever you do it's wrong.

It was an intensely dramatic weekend. When Alonso was penalised ten places on the grid by the stewards for allegedly impeding Massa during qualifying, the penalty prompted outrage amongst many in the paddock who felt that Alonso had been appallingly treated. Alonso called a press conference on the Sunday morning at which he showed television footage of the incident with Massa and then came out with the damning verdict, 'I love the sport, I love the fans coming here, a lot of them from Spain, but I don't consider F1 any more a sport.'

Alonso followed that up with an interview on Spanish radio the week after Monza in which he said, 'Michael is the driver with the most sanctions and the most unsporting driver in the history of Formula 1. No one is going to believe the penalty I was given for a long time.'

Unlike Schumacher, Alonso is a driver who is not afraid to speak his mind. Schumacher has improved himself in many areas and was always willing to learn, but in his dealings with the press he never learned the best method. He did not enjoy the game and was always too concerned about steering a safe middle ground, rather than speaking out as a strong champion, as Senna used to and as Alonso does now.

After winning at Monza, Schumacher was only two points behind Alonso in the drivers' world championship, with three races to go. As he returned to the *parc fermé* after the race many people noticed his lukewarm body language towards Montezemolo, who rushed to embrace him. Schumacher clearly felt that the Ferrari president had not helped the team's cause by forcing them to make the announcement at Monza and he was unhappy at the unnecessary distraction.

He felt very calm as he made his announcement in the press

conference after the race and even though most people had suspected it for a long time, it still seemed somehow a shock, that the greatest career the sport had ever seen was coming to an end. He said:

> This is going to be my last Monza race that I'm going to do. At the end of this year, I've decided with the team, I'm going to retire from racing. It has been an exceptional, really exceptional time that motorsport has given me in more than thirty years. I've really loved every single moment of the good and bad times. Those ones make life so special.

Schumacher won in China with Alonso second so they were tied on points as they headed to Japan. At Suzuka, scene of so much triumph and despair over the years, he was leading the Spaniard in the race, with only 16 laps to go, when the engine exploded. It was such a freak occurrence for Ferrari, the first time it had happened in a race for five years – and what a time for it to happen! As the white smoke curled up from the stricken car, with it went Schumacher's dream of signing off with an eighth world title.

Schumacher took it very well. He was not so much disappointed for himself, but more for the team; he had wanted desperately to give them another championship as a signing-off present. He was very philosophical about it and everyone was deeply impressed by his actions on returning to the pits, where he shook hands with every single member of the team. There were no hard feelings at all. All that was left was to travel to the final race and hope that he and Massa could clinch the constructors' championship as a parting gift to the Ferrari team instead.

But luck, which had usually seemed to be on his side throughout his career, deserted him in the leaving of it. First came the engine failure in Japan and then in Brazil he suffered a fuel pressure problem during qualifying, which meant he started only tenth on the grid. He was fighting his way through the field when he suffered a puncture, which dropped him to 20th place. The drive he put on from there to the finish was one of the most inspired of his career. He took risks despite being just 90 minutes away from never having to risk his life again, embodying the spirit of the adventurer, described by Fangio when discussing the youthful Schumacher of the early 1990s. This was Michael at his absolute best. He set fastest lap after fastest lap as he carved his way through the field. Max Mosley says:

> His final race was very impressive, when things went wrong. He had no chance to win the championship and he could have just cruised around to a happy retirement, but of course it wasn't in him to do that. I said to him afterwards, 'I could tell what you were thinking, that you had just to race.' And he said, 'Yes, but when I came across a battle between Heidfeld and another driver I thought to myself, This is bloody dangerous, but I couldn't help myself, I had to pass them.' And that's it really, he's an out-and-out racer and you have to admire it.

In the closing stages of the race, chasing a podium, he fought Raikkonen, the man who was to replace him at Ferrari. The Finn thought he had done enough to block him, but he left a tiny gap into turn one and Schumacher filled it instantly, forcing his way through and sending out the strongest possible signal that in his last race, he still easily had the measure of the young Finn. He finished fourth, but even with Massa winning the race, it wasn't enough to clinch the constructors' championship for Ferrari. Ross Brawn says:

> He had such a wonderful career and to me it was great that he went out with a drive like Brazil, I don't think you could have a better finish to a career. I gave him my opinion that I hoped that he would stop while at the top of his trade, still the reference point for everybody. Because personally I wanted my memories to be of someone who was still exceptional.
>
> But it wasn't a simple decision to reach, it was very complex. He had lots of conflicts because he loves driving and he loved the team but one day he was going to have to stop.
>
> I would have also respected it if he had chosen to keep going until he couldn't do it any more. Because he does love racing cars and driving them. How eventually he would balance his competitiveness against his love of driving nobody knows. There is a risk in the sport and he's had one serious injury and that's been it. You cannot ignore the risk, there is always that percentage there and the longer you go on . . .

Schumacher's father Rolf was there, having been persuaded to make the first long-haul flight of his life, along with his partner. Some of Schumacher's oldest friends from Kerpen were there too.

After the race he walked out of the paddock for the last time, taking with him his seven world titles and 91 Grand Prix victories. The greatest achiever in the sport's history became a civilian again once he stepped through the security gate and

drove away from the circuit. His life as a Formula 1 driver was
over.

But he hadn't driven an F1 car for the last time. A week later
he was at Monza for the traditional end of season 'Ferrari day'
celebrations at which customers race in the various Ferrari
production car series and the F1 team does a demonstration.
But this year it was different; the event was given over to an
emotional send-off for Schumacher. The whole Ferrari
hierarchy was there, Montezemolo, Todt, Brawn and the
drivers. Montezemolo paid tribute to Schumacher:

> Today we are here to say thanks to Michael for what he has
> done and for the way he's done it. To bow out like a
> champion with a race that will remain in everyone's mind,
> like Interlagos, was the best thing.
>
> He is the most extraordinary driver in Ferrari's history
> and that is saying something given that we have a long
> history of competitions so we have had some of the
> greatest drivers. He was always a team man and always
> willing to help others. With Michael we have always been
> united and strong.

A crowd of more than 30,000 people turned out to say thank
you to the man who had transformed the fortunes of Italy's
favourite team. Schumacher was totally overwhelmed. 'The
Italian people celebrated him so massively, we didn't expect
it,' says Sabine Kehm. 'I'm sure in Germany he would not have
been celebrated like that. In Italy they understood in the last
few years that he is not the person they thought he was. I
think it was because he didn't open himself up to the people.
But he was crying hard in Monza that day.'

Schumacher made it clear that once he had retired from

the sport, he wished to become anonymous as soon as possible. Those close to him believe that he will be true to his word, but since stepping out of the limelight in Brazil, he has returned to the F1 paddock several times as a consultant to Ferrari and continued to use his profile to publicise some worthy causes in which he believes and which help those people in racing who helped and befriended him.

He accepted the invitation of FIA president Max Mosley to be a spokesman for the Make Roads Safe campaign. He made a speech at the launch of the United Nations' Global Road Safety Week in April 2007, as the FIA lobbied the UN to organise a conference on the subject. He has continued to make public appearances to highlight the fact that every 30 seconds someone aged between 10 and 25 dies on the roads and that we must look for some solutions. He also took part in fundraising activities for the Institute for Cerebral and Medullar Disorders, the pet project of Jean Todt and Professor Gerard Saillant, who took care of Schumacher's treatment for his broken leg in 1999. Says Max Mosley:

> There is absolutely no reason for him to do this for us except goodwill. We don't pay him to do it, it's absolutely voluntary. Whereas in the old days a cynic might say, 'He wants to keep in with the governing body' he doesn't need to keep in with anyone now. He does it because he believes in it and he minds about it. He's very, very good. His answers to difficult questions are far better than most politicians.

The cynics might however argue that with each year that passes memories of the darker side of his sporting ethos will recede and he will be remembered in history as a great champion, an iconic figure, a man of towering achievements. As one of his rivals put it to me bitterly, 'history will airbrush out the bad things he did'.

Schumacher's role with Ferrari is intriguing. He continued to work with the team throughout 2007, appearing at the Spanish, Monaco, Canadian and German Grands Prix, and maintaining constant contact behind the scenes. I suspect that Jean Todt realised that in Raikkonen and Massa he had no natural leader in the team and he wanted Schumacher to cast his experienced eye over the restructured team to make sure that nothing had been overlooked. There is no doubt that the chief beneficiary of Schumacher's wisdom was Massa, who changed and matured greatly as the season went on. He acknowledged that Schumacher had helped him to focus on the race as a whole, rather than turning a few fast laps. Raikkonen meanwhile seemed oblivious to Schumacher's presence and even said that he preferred to work on his own with his engineers, rather than listen to the former world champion. However he proved his method was sound by winning the 2007 world championship, in his first season with Ferrari.

By mid-summer Schumacher had drifted into the background at Ferrari and openly admitted that he was unsure what his role at the team might be. For a man whose every day had been filled with an ambitious 'to do' list, he suddenly found himself adrift. Close friends in the F1 paddock expressed surprise at this. One change in his behaviour which was immediately obvious was his uninhibited enjoyment of evenings out during Grand Prix weekends, something which would have been inconceivable to Schumacher the driver.

Shortly after he announced his retirement in September

2006, I sat with Ross Brawn discussing what use Ferrari might make of him and Ross claimed that driving the car in a test would certainly not be on his agenda. He would not want to maintain that level of fitness and there would be nothing to prove.

So it was a surprise to many in November 2007 when Schumacher was drafted in to test the car at Barcelona. Rule changes for 2008 called for the introduction of a standard electronic control unit and the removal of traction control. Schumacher's opinion was sought on the new system and the best way forward for development. Despite being out of the cockpit for a year he was very fast straightaway, edging out Ferrari test driver Luca Badoer by two-tenths of a second.

'I was a bit nervous. I was probably a bit like a little kid, I felt like I did when I was 18 again. It took me a bit of time, maybe two laps and then I was back into the groove. I have to say I surprised myself that I was so quickly on it again,' he said afterwards.

It served to underline a feeling that many in F1 had throughout the 2007 season, that if he had carried on racing in 2007 he would almost certainly have beaten Raikkonen and won an eighth world championship. The Finn struggled in the first half of the season to adapt to Bridgestone tyres after many years on Michelins. The car also proved unreliable on a couple of occasions. And he made a series of unforced errors, through lapses of concentration, which cost him dearly. His collision with a barrier in the early stages of qualifying at Monaco was a prime example. And yet he had won the title, despite being 17 points behind Lewis Hamilton with two races to go. Raikkonen gave too much away; Schumacher would have got the job done more clinically.

He showed that he still had the fire in his belly too, by returning to the cockpit competitively in November, winning Felipe Massa's charity kart race in Brazil and in December 2007 appearing at the Race of Champions at Wembley, a made-up stadium event for charity involving rally and saloon cars. He won that too, beating top names from the world of rally, F1 and touring cars.

Early in 2008 Schumacher's role at Ferrari was more clearly defined; he was put in charge of developing cars for Ferrari's Gestione Sportiva, the F1 racing division. 'I'm a restless person,' he said. 'I still do training, play football often and do as much as I can. I can't just sit on the sofa and grow love handles.'

*   *   *

There are few people who understand what it takes to win in Formula 1. But everyone knows the value of that success. In many countries F1 is seen as a symbol for ultimate success; the best of the best.

To win at all in F1 is something which is granted to the very few and to sustain a winning habit over many years had always seemed impossible. Death or serious injury could cut short the adventure at any moment, while uncompetitive machinery was a less lethal, but still ever present, threat to a career. And if those evils didn't get you then the clock was always ticking on your motivation. Schumacher rose above all of these imposters.

He sustained a challenge at the highest level of the sport for 16 years, a totally unprecedented achievement. He did so not by taking it easy, but by constantly running on the very edge. He worked hard behind the scenes on many levels, using his influence within his own team, with other drivers and with the governing body, to make his life easier and to smooth his path to further success, because he understood that a winner in Formula 1 is not just the man who can drive the fastest.

Schumacher had the clearest and most thorough understanding of what it takes to win of any driver, and possibly any sportsman, in history. He pushed the rules to the limit in pursuit of his goals and sometimes he went over the limit, which is why he is such a controversial figure. But fundamentally he was an out-and-out racer and it is for this gift that he should be celebrated. He brought pleasure to millions with his competitive spirit. He was an extraordinary competitor, who lived life on the edge. And he got away with it.

Career statistics

Michael Schumacher born: 3 January 1969
Kerpen, Germany

F1 Career Summary

Grand Prix starts: 248 (present at 250)
Jordan – 1 start (Belgium 1991)
Benetton – 68 starts (Italy 1991 to Australia 1995)
Ferrari – 179 starts (Australia 1996 to Brazil 2006)
Wins: 91
First win: Belgium 1992
Final win: China 2006
Podiums: 154
Pole positions: 68
Championship titles: 7
First title: 1994
Final title: 2004
Championship points awarded: 1369
Fastest laps: 76

No	Year	Grand Prix	Venue	Car/engine	Grid	Result	Comments
1	1991	Belgium	Spa Francorchamps	Jordan 191/Ford	7	Retired	Clutch
2		Italy	Monza	Benetton B191/Ford	7	5th	First points
3		Portugal	Estoril	Benetton B191/Ford	10	6th	
4		Spain	Barcelona	Benetton B191/Ford	5	6th	
5		Japan	Suzuka	Benetton B191/Ford	9	Retired	Engine
6		Australia	Adelaide	Benetton B191/Ford	6	Retired	Collision

Championship: 14th (4 points)

No	Year	Grand Prix	Venue	Car/engine	Grid	Result	Comments
7	1992	South Africa	Kyalami	Benetton B191B/Ford	6	4th	
8		Mexico	Mexico City	Benetton B191B/Ford	3	3rd	First podium
9		Brazil	Interlagos	Benetton B191B/Ford	3	3rd	
10		Spain	Barcelona	Benetton B192/Ford	2	2nd	
11		San Marino	Imola	Benetton B192/Ford	5	Retired	Spun off
12		Monaco	Monte Carlo	Benetton B192/Ford	6	4th	
13		Canada	Montreal	Benetton B192/Ford	5	2nd	
14		France	Magny-Cours	Benetton B192/Ford	5	Retired	Collision
15		Great Britain	Silverstone	Benetton B192/Ford	4	4th	
16		Germany	Hockenheim	Benetton B192/Ford	6	3rd	
17		Hungary	Hungaroring	Benetton B192/Ford	4	Retired	Broken wing

#	Year	Country	Circuit	Car	Grid	Result	Notes
18		Belgium	Spa Francorchamps	Benetton B192/Ford	3	1st*	First win
19		Italy	Monza	Benetton B192/Ford	6	3rd	
20		Portugal	Estoril	Benetton B192/Ford	5	7th	
21		Japan	Suzuka	Benetton B192/Ford	5	Retired	Gearbox
22		Australia	Adelaide	Benetton B192/Ford	5	2nd*	

Championship: 3rd (54 points)

#	Year	Country	Circuit	Car	Grid	Result	Notes
23	1993	South Africa	Kyalami	Benetton B193A/Ford	3	Retired	Spun off
24		Brazil	Interlagos	Benetton B193A/Ford	4	3rd*	
25		Europe	Donington Park (UK)	Benetton B193B/Ford	3	Retired	Spun off
26		San Marino	Imola	Benetton B193B/Ford	3	2nd	
27		Spain	Barcelona	Benetton B193B/Ford	4	3rd*	
28		Monaco	Monte Carlo	Benetton B193B/Ford	2	Retired	Hydraulics
29		Canada	Montreal	Benetton B193B/Ford	3	2nd*	
30		France	Magny-Cours	Benetton B193B/Ford	7	3rd*	
31		Great Britain	Silverstone	Benetton B193B/Ford	3	2nd	
32		Germany	Hockenheim	Benetton B193B/Ford	3	2nd*	
33		Hungary	Hungaroring	Benetton B193B/Ford	3	Retired	Fuel pump
34		Belgium	Spa Francorchamps	Benetton B193B/Ford	3	2nd	
35		Italy	Monza	Benetton B193B/Ford	5	Retired	Engine
36		Portugal	Estoril	Benetton B193B/Ford	6	1st	

No	Year	Grand Prix	Venue	Car/engine	Grid	Result	Comments
37		Japan	Suzuka	Benetton B193B/Ford	4	Retired	Collision
38		Australia	Adelaide	Benetton B193B/Ford	4	Retired	Engine

Championship: 4th (52 points)

No	Year	Grand Prix	Venue	Car/engine	Grid	Result	Comments
39	1994	Brazil	Interlagos	Benetton B194/Ford	2	1st*	
40		Pacific	Aida (J)	Benetton B194/Ford	2	1st*	
41		San Marino	Imola	Benetton B194/Ford	2	1st	
42		Monaco	Monte Carlo	Benetton B194/Ford	1	1st*	First pole
43		Spain	Barcelona	Benetton B194/Ford	1	2nd*	
44		Canada	Montreal	Benetton B194/Ford	1	1st*	
45		France	Magny-Cours	Benetton B194/Ford	3	1st	
46		Great Britain	Silverstone	Benetton B194/Ford	2	Disqualified	
47		Germany	Hockenheim	Benetton B194/Ford	4	Retired	Engine
48		Hungary	Hungaroring	Benetton B194/Ford	1	1st*	
49		Belgium	Spa Francorchamps	Benetton B194/Ford	2	Disqualified	
50		Europe	Jerez (E)	Benetton B194/Ford	1	1st*	
51		Japan	Suzuka	Benetton B194/Ford	1	2nd	
52		Australia	Adelaide	Benetton B194/Ford	2	Retired	Collision

Championship: 1st (92 points)

53	1995	Brazil	Interlagos	Benetton B195/Renault	2	1st*	
54		Argentina	Buenos Aires	Benetton B195/Renault	3	3rd*	
55		San Marino	Imola	Benetton B195/Renault	1	Retired	Spun off
56		Spain	Barcelona	Benetton B195/Renault	1	1st	
57		Monaco	Monte Carlo	Benetton B195/Renault	2	1st	
58		Canada	Montreal	Benetton B195/Renault	1	5th*	
59		France	Magny-Cours	Benetton B195/Renault	2	1st*	
60		Great Britain	Silverstone	Benetton B195/Renault	2	Retired	Collision
61		Germany	Hockenheim	Benetton B195/Renault	2	1st*	
62		Hungary	Hungaroring	Benetton B195/Renault	3	11th	Fuel pump
63		Belgium	Spa Francorchamps	Benetton B195/Renault	16	1st	
64		Italy	Monza	Benetton B195/Renault	2	Retired	Collision
65		Portugal	Estoril	Benetton B195/Renault	3	2nd	
66		Europe	Nurburgring (D)	Benetton B195/Renault	3	1st*	
67		Pacific	Aida (J)	Benetton B195/Renault	3	1st*	
68		Japan	Suzuka	Benetton B195/Renault	1	1st*	
69		Australia	Adelaide	Benetton B195/Renault	3	Retired	Collision

Championship: 1st (102 points)

70	1996	Australia	Melbourne	Ferrari F310	4	Retired	Brakes
71		Brazil	Interlagos	Ferrari F310	4	3rd	
72		Argentina	Buenos Aires	Ferrari F310	2	Retired	Broken wing

383

No	Year	Grand Prix	Venue	Car/engine	Grid	Result	Comments
73		Europe	Nurburgring (D)	Ferrari F310	3	2nd	
74		San Marino	Imola	Ferrari F310	1	2nd	First Ferrari Pole
75		Monaco	Monte Carlo	Ferrari F310	1	Retired	Spun off
76		Spain	Barcelona	Ferrari F310	3	1st*	First Ferrari win
77		Canada	Montreal	Ferrari F310	3	Retired	Halfshaft
–		France	Magny-Cours	Ferrari F310	1	Did not start	
78		Great Britain	Silverstone	Ferrari F310	3	Retired	Hydraulics
79		Germany	Hockenheim	Ferrari F310	3	4th	
80		Hungary	Hungaroring	Ferrari F310	1	Retired	Throttle
81		Belgium	Spa Francorchamps	Ferrari F310	3	1st	
82		Italy	Monza	Ferrari F310	3	1st*	
83		Portugal	Estoril	Ferrari F310	4	3rd	
84		Japan	Suzuka	Ferrari F310	3	2nd	

Championship 3rd (59 points)

No	Year	Grand Prix	Venue	Car/engine	Grid	Result	Comments
85	1997	Australia	Melbourne	Ferrari F310B	3	2nd	
86		Brazil	Interlagos	Ferrari F310B	2	5th	
87		Argentina	Buenos Aires	Ferrari F310B	4	Retired	Collision

No.	Country	Circuit	Car	Grid	Result	Reason
88	San Marino	Imola	Ferrari F310B	3	2nd	
89	Monaco	Monte Carlo	Ferrari F310B	2	1st*	
90	Spain	Barcelona	Ferrari F310B	7	4th	
91	Canada	Montreal	Ferrari F310B	1	1st	
92	France	Magny-Cours	Ferrari F310B	1	1st	
93	Great Britain	Silverstone	Ferrari F310B	4	Retired*	Wheel bearing
94	Germany	Hockenheim	Ferrari F310B	4	2nd	
95	Hungary	Hungaroring	Ferrari F310B	1	4th	
96	Belgium	Spa Francorchamps	Ferrari F310B	3	1st	
97	Italy	Monza	Ferrari F310B	9	6th	
98	Austria	Spielberg	Ferrari F310B	9	6th	
99	Luxembourg	Nurburgring(D)	Ferrari F310B	5	Retired	Suspension
100	Japan	Suzuka	Ferrari F310B	2	1st	
101	Europe	Jerez (E)	Ferrari F310B	2	Retired	Collision

Championship: Disqualified from 2nd (78 points)

No.	Year	Country	Circuit	Car	Grid	Result	Reason
102	1998	Australia	Melbourne	Ferrari F300	3	Retired	Engine
103		Brazil	Interlagos	Ferrari F300	4	3rd	
104		Argentina	Buenos Aires	Ferrari F300	2	1st	
105		San Marino	Imola	Ferrari F300	3	2nd*	
106		Spain	Barcelona	Ferrari F300	3	3rd	

No	Year	Grand Prix	Venue	Car/engine	Grid	Result	Comments
107		Monaco	Monte Carlo	Ferrari F300	4	10th	
108		Canada	Montreal	Ferrari F300	3	1st*	
109		France	Magny-Cours	Ferrari F300	2	1st	
110		Great Britain	Silverstone	Ferrari F300	2	1st*	
111		Austria	Spielberg	Ferrari F300	4	3rd	
112		Germany	Hockenheim	Ferrari F300	9	5th	
113		Hungary	Hungaroring	Ferrari F300	3	1st*	
114		Belgium	Spa Francorchamps	Ferrari F300	4	Retired*	Collision
115		Italy	Monza	Ferrari F300	1	1st	
116		Luxembourg	Nurburgring (D)	Ferrari F300	1	2nd	
117		Japan	Suzuka	Ferrari F300	1	Retired*	Tyre

Championship: 2nd (86 points)

No	Year	Grand Prix	Venue	Car/engine	Grid	Result	Comments
118	1999	Australia	Melbourne	Ferrari F399	3	8th*	
119		Brazil	Interlagos	Ferrari F399	4	2nd	
120		San Marino	Imola	Ferrari F399	3	1st*	
121		Monaco	Monte Carlo	Ferrari F399	2	1st	
122		Spain	Barcelona	Ferrari F399	4	3rd*	
123		Canada	Montreal	Ferrari F399	1	Retired	Spun off

No.	Year	Country	Circuit	Car	Grid	Result	Reason
124		France	Magny-Cours	Ferrari F399	6	5th	
–		Great Britain	Silverstone	Ferrari F399	2	Did not start	
125		Malaysia	Sepang	Ferrari F399	1	2nd*	
126		Japan	Suzuka	Ferrari F399	1	2nd*	

Championship: 5th (44 points)

No.	Year	Country	Circuit	Car	Grid	Result	Reason
127	2000	Australia	Melbourne	Ferrari F1-2000	3	1st	
128		Brazil	Interlagos	Ferrari F1-2000	3	1st*	
129		San Marino	Imola	Ferrari F1-2000	2	1st	
130		Great Britain	Silverstone	Ferrari F1-2000	5	3rd	
131		Spain	Barcelona	Ferrari F1-2000	1	5th	
132		Europe	Nurburgring (D)	Ferrari F1-2000	2	1st*	
133		Monaco	Monte Carlo	Ferrari F1-2000	1	Retired	Suspension
134		Canada	Montreal	Ferrari F1-2000	1	1st	
135		France	Magny-Cours	Ferrari F1-2000	1	Retired	Engine
136		Austria	Spielberg	Ferrari F1-2000	4	Retired	Collision
137		Germany	Hockenheim	Ferrari F1-2000	2	Retired	Collision
138		Hungary	Hungaroring	Ferrari F1-2000	1	2nd	
139		Belgium	Spa Francorchamps	Ferrari F1-2000	4	2nd	
140		Italy	Monza	Ferrari F1-2000	1	1st	
141		USA	Indianapolis	Ferrari F1-2000	1	1st	

No	Year	Grand Prix	Venue	Car/engine	Grid	Result	Comments
142	2001	Japan	Suzuka	Ferrari F1-2000	1	1st	
143		Malaysia	Sepang	Ferrari F1-2000	1	1st	
Championship: 1st (108 points)							
144	2001	Australia	Melbourne	Ferrari F2001	1	1st*	
145		Malaysia	Sepang	Ferrari F2001	1	1st	
146		Brazil	Interlagos	Ferrari F2001	1	2nd	
147		San Marino	Imola	Ferrari F2001	4	Retired	Suspension
148		Spain	Barcelona	Ferrari F2001	1	1st*	
149		Austria	Spielberg	Ferrari F2001	1	2nd	
150		Monaco	Monte Carlo	Ferrari F2001	2	1st	
151		Canada	Montreal	Ferrari F2001	1	2nd	
152		Europe	Nurburgring (D)	Ferrari F2001	1	1st	
153		France	Magny-Cours	Ferrari F2001	2	1st	
154		Great Britain	Silverstone	Ferrari F2001	1	2nd	
155		Germany	Hockenheim	Ferrari F2001	4	Retired	Fuel pressure
156		Hungary	Hungaroring	Ferrari F2001	1	1st	
157		Belgium	Spa Francorchamps	Ferrari F2001	3	1st*	
158		Italy	Monza	Ferrari F2001	3	4th	

| 159 | | USA | Indianapolis | Ferrari F2001 | 1 | 2nd |
| 160 | | Japan | Suzuka | Ferrari F2001 | 1 | 1st |

Championship: 1st (123 points)

161	2002	Australia	Melbourne	Ferrari F2001	2	1st
162		Malaysia	Sepang	Ferrari F2001	1	3rd
163		Brazil	Interlagos	Ferrari F2002	2	1st
164		San Marino	Imola	Ferrari F2002	1	1st
165		Spain	Barcelona	Ferrari F2002	1	1st*
166		Austria	Spielberg	Ferrari F2002	3	1st*
167		Monaco	Monte Carlo	Ferrari F2002	3	2nd
168		Canada	Montreal	Ferrari F2002	2	1st
169		Europe	Nurburgring (D)	Ferrari F2002	3	2nd*
170		Great Britain	Silverstone	Ferrari F2002	3	1st
171		France	Magny-Cours	Ferrari F2002	2	1st
172		Germany	Hockenheim	Ferrari F2002	1	1st*
173		Hungary	Hungaroring	Ferrari F2002	2	2nd*
174		Belgium	Spa Francorchamps	Ferrari F2002	1	1st*
175		Italy	Monza	Ferrari F2002	2	2nd
176		USA	Indianapolis	Ferrari F2002	1	2nd
177		Japan	Suzuka	Ferrari F2002	1	1st*

Championship: 1st (144 points)

No	Year	Grand Prix	Venue	Car/engine	Grid	Result	Comments
178	2003	Australia	Melbourne	Ferrari F2002	1	4th	
179		Malaysia	Sepang	Ferrari F2002	3	6th*	
180		Brazil	Interlagos	Ferrari F2002	7	Retired	Spun off
181		San Marino	Imola	Ferrari F2002	1	1st*	
182		Spain	Barcelona	Ferrari F2003 - GA	1	1st	
183		Austria	Spielberg	Ferrari F2003 - GA	1	1st*	
184		Monaco	Monte Carlo	Ferrari F2003 - GA	5	3rd	
185		Canada	Montreal	Ferrari F2003 - GA	3	1st	
186		Europe	Nurburgring (D)	Ferrari F2003 - GA	2	5th	
187		France	Magny-Cours	Ferrari F2003 - GA	3	3rd	
188		Great Britain	Silverstone	Ferrari F2003 - GA	5	4th	
189		Germany	Hockenheim	Ferrari F2003 - GA	6	7th	
190		Hungary	Hungaroring	Ferrari F2003 - GA	8	8th	
191		Italy	Monza	Ferrari F2003 - GA	1	1st*	
192		USA	Indianapolis	Ferrari F2003 - GA	7	1st*	
193		Japan	Suzuka	Ferrari F2003 - GA	14	8th	

Championship: 1st (93 points)

No	Year	Grand Prix	Venue	Car/engine	Grid	Result	Comments
194	2004	Australia	Melbourne	Ferrari F2004	1	1st*	
195		Malaysia	Sepang	Ferrari F2004	1	1st	

No.	Year	Grand Prix	Circuit	Car	Grid	Result	Notes
196		Bahrain	Sakhir	Ferrari F2004	1	1st*	
197		San Marino	Imola	Ferrari F2004	2	1st*	
198		Spain	Barcelona	Ferrari F2004	1	1st*	
199		Monaco	Monte Carlo	Ferrari F2004	4	Retired*	Collision
200		Europe	Nurburgring (D)	Ferrari F2004	1	1st*	
201		Canada	Montreal	Ferrari F2004	6	1st	
202		USA	Indianapolis	Ferrari F2004	2	1st	
203		France	Magny-Cours	Ferrari F2004	2	1st*	
204		Great Britain	Silverstone	Ferrari F2004	4	1st*	
205		Germany	Hockenheim	Ferrari F2004	1	1st	
206		Hungary	Hungaroring	Ferrari F2004	1	1st*	
207		Belgium	Spa Francorchamps	Ferrari F2004	2	2nd	
208		Italy	Monza	Ferrari F2004	3	2nd	
209		China	Shanghai	Ferrari F2004	20	12th*	
210		Japan	Suzuka	Ferrari F2004	1	1st	
211		Brazil	Interlagos	Ferrari F2004	18	7th	

Championship: 1st (148 points)

No.	Year	Grand Prix	Circuit	Car	Grid	Result	Notes
212	2005	Australia	Melbourne	Ferrari F2004 M	19	Retired	Collision
213		Malaysia	Sepang	Ferrari F2004 M	13	7th	
214		Bahrain	Sakhir	Ferrari F2005	2	Retired	Hydraulics
215		San Marino	Imola	Ferrari F2005	13	2nd*	

No	Year	Grand Prix	Venue	Car/engine	Grid	Result	Comments
216		Spain	Barcelona	Ferrari F2005	8	Retired	Puncture
217		Monaco	Monte Carlo	Ferrari F2005	8	7th*	
218		Europe	Nurburgring (D)	Ferrari F2005	10	5th	
219		Canada	Montreal	Ferrari F2005	2	2nd	
220		USA	Indianapolis	Ferrari F2005	5	1st*	
221		France	Magny-Cours	Ferrari F2005	3	3rd	
222		Great Britain	Silverstone	Ferrari F2005	9	6th	
223		Germany	Hockenheim	Ferrari F2005	5	5th	
224		Hungary	Hungaroring	Ferrari F2005	1	2nd	
225		Turkey	Istanbul	Ferrari F2005	19	Retired	Crash
226		Italy	Monza	Ferrari F2005	6	10th	
227		Belgium	Spa Francorchamps	Ferrari F2005	6	Retired	Collision
228		Brazil	Interlagos	Ferrari F2005	7	4th	
229		Japan	Suzuka	Ferrari F2005	14	7th	
230		China	Shanghai	Ferrari F2005	7	Retired	Spun off

Championship: 3rd (62 points)

No	Year	Grand Prix	Venue	Car/engine	Grid	Result	Comments
231	2006	Bahrain	Sakhir	Ferrari 248 F1	1	2nd	
232		Malaysia	Sepang	Ferrari 248 F1	14	6th	
233		Australia	Melbourne	Ferrari 248 F1	10	Retired	Spun off

No	Year	Grand Prix	Venue	Car/engine	Grid	Result	Comments
234		San Marino	Imola	Ferrari 248 F1	1	1st	
235		Europe	Nurburgring (D)	Ferrari 248 F1	2	1st*	
236		Spain	Barcelona	Ferrari 248 F1	3	2nd	
237		Monaco	Monte Carlo	Ferrari 248 F1	22	5th*	
238		Great Britain	Silverstone	Ferrari 248 F1	3	2nd	
239		Canada	Montreal	Ferrari 248 F1	5	2nd	
240		USA	Indianapolis	Ferrari 248 F1	1	1st*	
241		France	Magny-Cours	Ferrari 248 F1	1	1st*	Final pole
242		Germany	Hockenheim	Ferrari 248 F1	2	1st*	
243		Hungary	Hungaroring	Ferrari 248 F1	11	Retired	Spun off
244		Turkey	Istanbul	Ferrari 248 F1	2	3rd*	
245		Italy	Monza	Ferrari 248 F1	2	1st	
246		China	Shanghai	Ferrari 248 F1	6	1st	Final win
247		Japan	Suzuka	Ferrari 248 F1	2	Retired	Engine
248		Brazil	Interlagos	Ferrari 248 F1	10	4th*	

Championship: 2nd (121 points)

* Denotes fastest lap of the race

Trivia

- He won all his 'landmark' Grands Prix. He won his 50th, 100th, 150th and 200th Grand Prix starts.

- The only events that he failed to win in his F1 career were the South African, Mexican and Turkish Grands Prix. He won all other events he competed in on at least one occasion.

- Schumacher won the French Grand Prix 8 times, a record for any event on the current or past F1 Championship calendar.

- He won 91 Grands Prix, the most by any driver in F1 history. His total is only one win short of the combined total of wins by the second and third winning drivers, Alain Prost (51) and Ayrton Senna (41).

- He won more Grands Prix, he won more championship titles, he scored more championship points, he appeared on the podium more times, he took more pole positions and set more fastest laps of the race than any other driver in F1 history.

- Schumacher finished an astonishing 76.6% of all his Grand Prix starts in the championship points.

- He led 56.9% of all Grands Prix he started.

- He holds the all-time record of the most Grand Prix wins in a row from pole position (6).

- Schumacher finished all 17 Grands Prix of the 2002 F1 season on the podium. He had finished the final 2 races of the 2001 season on the podium too. His achievement of 19 consecutive F1 podium appearances is an all-time record.

Stats provided by Mike Sheppard – with thanks.

Index

Note: 'MS' stands for Michael Schumacher, 'GP' for Grand Prix. Subheadings are in chronological order. Page numbers in *italic* indicate entries in the Career Statistics section.